THE PROFESSOR

AT THE

BREAKFAST-TABLE.

THE PROFESSOR

AT THE

BREAKFAST-TABLE;

WITH THE

STORY OF IRIS.

By OLIVER WENDELL HOLMES,
AUTHOR OF "THE AUTOCRAT OF THE BREAKFAST-TABLE."

BOSTON:
JAMES R. OSGOOD AND COMPANY,
LATE TICKNOR & FIELDS, AND FIELDS, OSGOOD, & Co.
1872.

THE PROFESSOR AT THE BREAKFAST-TABLE.

What he said, what he heard, and what he saw.

I.

I INTENDED to have signalized my first appearance by a certain large statement, which I flatter myself is the nearest approach to a universal formula of life yet promulgated at this breakfast-table. It would have had a grand effect. For this purpose I fixed my eyes on a certain divinity-student, with the intention of exchanging a few phrases, and then forcing my court-card, namely, *The great end of being.*—I will thank you for the sugar,—I said.—Man is a dependent creature.

It is a small favor to ask,—said the divinity-student,—and passed the sugar to me.

—— Life is a great bundle of little things,—I said.

The divinity-student smiled, as if that was the concluding epigram of the sugar question.

You smile,—I said.—Perhaps life seems to you a little bundle of great things?

The divinity-student started a laugh, but suddenly reined it back with a pull, as one throws a horse on his haunches. — Life is a great bundle of great things, — he said.

(*Now, then!*) The great end of being, after all, is —— -

Hold on! — said my neighbor, a young fellow whose name seems to be John, and nothing else, — for that is what they all call him, — hold on! the Sculpin is go'n' to say somethin'.

Now the Sculpin (*Cottus Virginianus*) is a little water-beast which pretends to consider itself a fish, and, under that pretext, hangs about the piles upon which West-Boston Bridge is built, swallowing the bait and hook intended for flounders. On being drawn from the water, it exposes an immense head, a diminutive bony carcass, and a surface so full of spines, ridges, ruffles, and frills, that the naturalists have not been able to count them without quarrelling about the number, and that the colored youth, whose sport they spoil, do not like to touch them, and especially to tread on them, unless they happen to have shoes on, to cover the thick white soles of their broad black feet.

When, therefore, I heard the young fellow's exclamation, I looked round the table with curiosity to see what it meant. At the further end of it I saw a head, and a small portion of a little deformed body, mounted on a high chair, which brought the occupant up to a fair level enough for him to get at his food. His whole appearance was so grotesque, I felt for a minute as if there was a showman behind him who would pull him down presently and put up Judy, or the hangman, or the Devil, or some other wooden personage of the famous spectacle. I contrived to lose the first part of his sentence, but what I heard began so: —

—— by the Frog-Pond, when there were frogs in it, and the folks used to come down from the tents on 'Lection and Independence days with their pails to get water to make egg-pop with. Born in Boston; went to school in Boston as long as the boys would let me. — The little man groaned, turned, as if to look round, and went on. — Ran away from school one day to see Phillips hung for killing Denegri with a loggerhead. That was in flip days, when there were always two or three loggerheads in the fire. I'm a Boston boy, I tell you, — born at North End, and mean to be buried on Copps' Hill, with the good old underground people, — the Worthylakes, and the rest of 'em. Yes, Sir, — up on the old hill, where they buried Captain Daniel Malcolm in a stone grave, ten feet deep, to keep him safe from the red-coats, in those old times when the world was frozen up tight and there wasn't but one spot open, and that was right over Faneuil Hall, — and black enough it looked, I tell you! There's where my bones shall lie, Sir, and rattle away when the big guns go off at the Navy Yard opposite! You can't make me ashamed of the old place! Full of crooked little streets;—I was born and used to run round in one of 'em——

——I should think so,—said that young man whom I hear them call "John,"—softly, not meaning to be heard, nor to be cruel, but thinking in a half-whisper, evidently.—I should think so; and got kinked up, turnin' so many corners.—The little man did not hear what was said, but went on,—

——full of crooked little streets;—but I tell you Boston has opened, and kept open, more turnpikes that lead straight to free thought and free speech and free deeds than any other city of live men or dead men,—I don't care how broad their streets are, nor how high their steeples!

——How high is Bosting meet'n'-house?—said a person with black whiskers and imperial, a velvet waistcoat, a guard-chain rather *too* massive, and a diamond pin so *very* large that the most trusting nature might confess an inward *suggestion*,—of course, nothing amounting to a suspicion. For this is a gentleman from a great city, and sits next to the landlady's daughter, who evidently believes in him, and is the object of his especial attention.

How high?—said the little man.—As high as the first step of the stairs that lead to the New Jerusalem. Isn't that high enough?

It is,—I said.—The great end of being is to harmonize man with the order of things; and the church has been a good pitch-pipe, and may be so still. But who shall tune the pitch-pipe? *Quis cus*——(On the whole, as this quotation was not entirely new, and, being in a foreign language, might not be familiar to all the boarders, I thought I would not finish it.)

——Go to the Bible!—said a sharp voice from a sharp-faced, sharp-eyed, sharp-elbowed, strenuous-looking woman in a black dress, appearing as if it began as a piece of mourning and perpetuated itself as a bit of economy.

You speak well, Madam,—I said;—yet there is room for a gloss or commentary on what you say. "He who would bring back the wealth of the Indies must carry out the wealth of the Indies." What you bring away from the Bible depends to some extent on what you carry to it.—Benjamin Franklin! Be so good as to step up to my chamber and bring me down the small uncovered pamphlet of twenty pages which you will find lying under the "Cruden's Concordance." [The boy took a large bite, which left a very perfect crescent in the slice of bread-and-butter he held, and departed on his errand, with the portable fraction of his breakfast to sustain him on the way.]

Here it is. " Go to the Bible. A Dissertation, etc., etc. By J. J. Flournoy. Athens, Georgia. 1858."

Mr. Flournoy, Madam, has obeyed the precept which you have judiciously delivered. You may be interested, Madam, to know what are the conclusions at which Mr. J. J. Flournoy of Athens, Georgia, has arrived. You shall hear, Madam. He has gone to the Bible, and he has come back from the Bible, bringing a remedy for existing social evils, which, if it is the real specific, as it professes to be, is of great interest to humanity, and to the female part of humanity in particular. It is what he calls *trigamy*, Madam, or the marrying of three wives, so that "good old men" may be solaced at once by the companionship of the wisdom of maturity, and of those less perfected but hardly less engaging qualities which are found at an earlier period of life. He has followed your precept, Madam; I hope you accept his conclusions.

The female boarder in black attire looked so puzzled, and, in fact, "all abroad," after the delivery of this "counter" of mine, that I left her to recover her wits, and went on with the conversation, which I was beginning to get pretty well in hand.

But in the mean time I kept my eye on the

female boarder to see what effect I had produced. First, she was a little stunned at having her argument knocked over. Secondly, she was a little shocked at the tremendous character of the triple matrimonial suggestion. Thirdly. —— I don't like to say what I thought. Something seemed to have pleased her fancy. Whether it was, that, if trigamy should come into fashion, there would be three times as many chances to enjoy the luxury of saying, "No!" is more than I can tell you. I may as well mention that B. F. came to me after breakfast to borrow the pamphlet for "a lady," — one of the boarders, he said, — looking as if he had a secret he wished to be relieved of.

—— I continued. — If a human soul is necessarily to be trained up in the faith of those from whom it inherits its body, why, there is the end of all reason. If, sooner or later, every soul is to look for truth with its own eyes, the first thing is to recognize that no presumption in favor of any particular belief arises from the fact of our inheriting it. Otherwise you would not give the Mahometan a fair chance to become a convert to a better religion.

The second thing would be to depolarize every fixed religious idea in the mind by changing the word which stands for it.

—— I don't know what you mean by "depolarizing" an idea, — said the divinity-student.

I will tell you, — I said. — When a given symbol which represents a thought has lain for a certain length of time in the mind, it undergoes a change like that which rest in a certain position gives to iron. It becomes magnetic in its relations, — it is traversed by strange forces which did not belong to it. The word, and consequently the idea it represents, is *polarized.*

The religious currency of mankind, in thought, in speech, and in print, consists entirely of polarized words. Borrow one of these from another language and religion, and you will find it leaves all its magnetism behind it. Take that famous word, O'm, of the Hindoo mythology. Even a priest cannot pronounce it without sin; and a holy Pundit would shut his ears and run away from you in horror, if you should say it aloud. What do you care for O'm? If you wanted to get the Pundit to look at his religion fairly, you must first depolarize this and all similar words for him. The argument for and against new translations of the Bible really turns on this. Skepticism is afraid to trust its truths in depolarized words, and so cries out against a new translation. I think, myself, if every idea our Book contains could be shelled out of its old symbol and put into a new, clean, unmagnetic word, we should have some chance of reading it as philosophers, or wisdom-lovers, ought to read it, — which we do not and cannot now any more than a Hindoo can read the "Gayatri" as a fair man and lover of truth should do. When society has once fairly dissolved the New Testament, which it never has done yet, it will perhaps crystallize it over again in new forms of language.

—— I didn't know you was a settled minister over this parish, — said the young fellow near me.

A sermon by a lay-preacher may be worth listening to, — I replied, calmly. — It gives the *parallax* of thought and feeling as they appear to the observers from two very different points of view. If you wish to get the distance of a heavenly body, you know that you must take two observations from remote points of the earth's orbit, — in midsummer and midwinter, for instance. To get the parallax of heavenly truths, you must take an observation from the position of the laity as well as of the clergy. Teachers and students of theology get a certain look, certain conventional tones of voice, a clerical gait, a professional neckcloth, and habits of mind as professional as their externals. They are scholarly men and read Bacon, and know well enough what the "idols of the tribe" are. Of course they have their false gods, as all men that follow one exclusive calling are prone to do. — The clergy have played the part of the fly-wheel in our modern civilization. They have never suffered it to stop. They have often carried on its movement, when other moving powers failed, by the momentum stored in their vast body Sometimes, too, they have kept it back by their *vis inertiæ*, when its wheels were like to grind the bones of some old canonized error into fertilizers for the soil that yields the bread of life. But the mainspring of the world's onward religious movement is not in them, nor in any one body of men, let me tell you. It is the people that makes the clergy, and not the clergy that makes the people. Of course, the profession reacts on its source with variable energy.—But there never was a guild of dealers or a company of craftsmen that did not need sharp looking after.

Our old friend, Dr. Holyoke, whom we gave the dinner to some time since, must have known many people that saw the great bonfire in Harvard College yard.

——Bonfire?—shrieked the little man.—The bonfire when Robert Calef's book was burned?

The same,—I said,—when Robert Calef the Boston merchant's book was burned in the yard of Harvard College, by order of Increase Mather President of the College and Minister of the Gospel. You remember the old witchcraft revival of '92, and how stout Master Robert Calef, trader, of Boston, had the pluck to tell the ministers and judges what a set of fools and worse than fools they were——

Remember it?—said the little man.—I don't think I shall forget it, as long as I can stretch this forefinger to point with, and see what it wears.—There was a ring on it.

May I look at it?—I said.

Where it is,—said the little man;—it will never come off, till it falls off from the bone in the darkness and in the dust.

He pushed the high chair on which he sat slightly back from the table, and dropped himself, standing, to the floor,—his head being only a little above the level of the table, as he stood. With pain and labor, lifting one foot over the other, as a drummer handles his sticks, he took a few steps from his place,—his motions and the dead beat of the misshapen boots announcing to my practised eye and ear the malformation which is called in learned language *talipes varus*, or inverted club-foot.

Stop! stop!—I said,—let me come to you.

The little man hobbled back, and lifted himself by the left arm, with an ease approaching to grace which surprised me, into his high chair. I walked to his side, and he stretched out the forefinger of his right hand, with the ring upon it. The ring had been put on long ago, and could not pass the misshapen joint. It was one of those funeral rings which used to be given to relatives and friends after the decease of persons of any note or importance. Beneath a round bit of glass was a death's head. Engraved on one side of this, "L. B. Æt. 22,"—on the other, "Ob. 1692."

My grandmother's grandmother,—said the little man.—Hanged for a witch. It doesn't seem a great while ago. I knew my grandmother, and loved her. Her mother was daughter to the witch that Chief Justice Sewall hanged and Cotton Mather delivered over to the Devil.—That was Salem, though, and not Boston. No, not Boston. Robert Calef, the Boston merchant, it was that blew them all to——

Never mind where he blew them to,—I said;—for the little man was getting red in the face, and I didn't know what might come next.

This episode broke me up, as the jockeys say, out of my square conversational trot; but I settled down to it again.

——A man that knows men, in the street, at their work, human nature in its shirt-sleeves,—who makes bargains with deacons, instead of talking over texts with them,—a man who has found out that there are plenty of praying rogues and swearing saints in the world,—above all, who has found out, by living into the pith and core of life, that all of the Deity which can be folded up between the sheets of any human book is to the Deity of the firmament, of the strata, of the hot aortic flood of throbbing human life, of this infinite, instantaneous consciousness in which the soul's being consists,—an incandescent point in the filament connecting the negative pole of a past eternity with the positive pole of an eternity that is to come,—that all of the Deity which any human book can hold is to this larger Deity of the working battery of the universe only as the films in a book of gold-leaf are to the broad seams and curdled lumps of ore that lie in unsunned mines and virgin placers,—— Oh!—I was saying that a man who lives out-of-doors, among live people, gets some things into his head he might not find in the index of his "Body of Divinity."

I tell you what,—the idea of the professions' digging a moat round their close corporations, like that Japanese one at Jeddo, which you could put Park-Street Church on the bottom of and look over the vane from its side, and try to stretch another such spire across it without spanning the chasm,—that idea, I say, is pretty nearly worn out. Now when a civilization or a civilized custom falls into senile *dementia*, there is commonly a judgment ripe for it, and it comes as plagues come, from a breath,—as fires come, from a spark.

Here, look at medicine. Big wigs, gold-headed canes, Latin prescriptions, shops full of abominations, recipes a yard long, "curing" patients by drugging as sailors bring a wind by whistling, selling lies at a guinea apiece,—a routine, in short, of giving unfortunate sick people a mess of things either too odious to swallow or too acrid to hold, or, if that were possible, both at once.

——You don't know what I mean, indignant and not unintelligent country-practitioner? Then you don't know the history of medicine,—and that is not my fault. But don't expose yourself in any outbreak of eloquence; for, by the mortar in which Anaxarchus was pounded! I did not bring home Schenckius and Forestus and Hildanus, and all the old folios in calf and vellum I will show you, to be bullied by the proprietor of a "Wood and Bache," and a shelf of peppered sheepskin reprints by Philadelphia Editors. Besides, many of the profession and I know a little something of each other, and you don't think I am such a simpleton as to lose their good opinion by saying what the better heads among them would condemn as unfair and untrue? Now mark how the great plague came on the generation of drugging doctors, and in what form it fell.

A scheming drug-vendor, (inventive genius,) an utterly untrustworthy and incompetent observer, (profound searcher of Nature,) a shallow dabbler in erudition, (sagacious scholar,) started the monstrous fiction (founded the immortal system) of Homœopathy. I am very fair, you see,—you can help yourself to either of these sets of phrases.

All the reason in the world would not have had

so rapid and general an effect on the public mind to disabuse it of the idea that a drug is a good thing in itself, instead of being, as it is, a bad thing, as was produced by the trick (system) of this German charlatan (theorist). Not that the wiser part of the profession needed him to teach them; but the routinists and their employers, the "general practitioners," who lived by selling pills and mixtures, and their drug-consuming customers, had to recognize that people could get well, unpoisoned. These dumb cattle would not learn it of themselves, and so the murrain of Homœopathy fell on them.

——You don't know what plague has fallen on the practitioners of theology? I will tell you, then. It is SPIRITUALISM. While some are crying out against it as a delusion of the Devil, and some are laughing at it as an hysteric folly, and some are getting angry with it as a mere trick of interested or mischievous persons, Spiritualism is quietly undermining the traditional ideas of the future state which have been and are still accepted,—not merely in those who believe in it, but in the general sentiment of the community, to a larger extent than most good people seem to be aware of. It needn't be true, to do this, any more than Homœopathy need, to do its work. The Spiritualists have some pretty strong instincts to pry over, which no doubt have been roughly handled by theologians at different times. And the Nemesis of the pulpit comes, in a shape it little thought of, beginning with the snap of a toe-joint, and ending with such a crack of old beliefs that the roar of it is heard in all the ministers' studies of Christendom! Sir, you cannot have people of cultivation, of pure character, sensible enough in common things, large-hearted women, grave judges, shrewd business-men, men of science, professing to be in communication with the spiritual world and keeping up constant intercourse with it, without its gradually reacting on the whole conception of that other life. It is the folly of the world, constantly, which confounds its wisdom. Not only out of the mouths of babes and sucklings, but out of the mouths of fools and cheats, we may often get our truest lessons. For the fool's judgment is a dog-vane that turns with a breath, and the cheat watches the clouds and sets his weathercock by them, — so that one shall often see by their pointing which way the winds of heaven are blowing, when the slow-wheeling arrows and feathers of what we call the Temples of Wisdom are turning to all points of the compass.

—— Amen! — said the young fellow called John. — Ten minutes by the watch. Those that are unanimous will please to signify by holding up their left foot!

I looked this young man steadily in the face

for about thirty seconds. His countenance was as calm as that of a reposing infant. I think it was simplicity, rather than mischief, with perhaps a youthful playfulness, that led him to this outbreak. I have often noticed that even quiet horses, on a sharp November morning, when their coats are just beginning to get the winter roughness, will give little sportive demi-kicks, with slight sudden elevation of the subsequent region of the body, and a sharp short whinny,—by no means intending to put their heels through the dasher, or to address the driver rudely, but feeling, to use a familiar word, frisky. This, I think, is the physiological condition of the young person, John. I noticed, however, what I should call a *palpebral spasm*, affecting the eyelid and muscles of one side, which, if it were intended for the facial gesture called a wink, might lead me to suspect a disposition to be satirical on his part.

——Resuming the conversation, I remarked,—I am, *ex officio*, as a Professor, a conservative. For I don't know any fruit that clings to its tree so faithfully, not even a "froze-'n'-thaw" winter-apple, as a Professor to the bough of which his chair is made. You can't shake him off, and it is as much as you can do to pull him off. Hence, by a chain of induction I need not unwind, he tends to conservatism generally.

But then, you know, if you are sailing the

Atlantic, and all at once find yourself in a current, and the sea covered with weeds, and drop your Fahrenheit over the side and find it eight or ten degrees higher than in the ocean generally, there is no use in flying in the face of facts and swearing there is no such thing as a Gulf-Stream, when you are in it.

You can't keep gas in a bladder, and you can't keep knowledge tight in a profession. Hydrogen will leak out, and air will leak in, through India-rubber; and special knowledge will leak out, and general knowledge will leak in, though a profession were covered with twenty thicknesses of sheepskin diplomas. By Jove, Sir, till common sense is well mixed up with medicine, and common manhood with theology, and common honesty with law, *We the people*, Sir, some of us with nut-crackers, and some of us with trip-hammers, and some of us with pile-drivers, and some of us coming with a whish! like air-stones out of a lunar volcano, will crash down on the lumps of nonsense in all of them till we have made powder of them like Aaron's calf!

If to be a conservative is to let all the drains of thought choke up and keep all the soul's windows down,—to shut out the sun from the east and the wind from the west,—to let the rats run free in the cellar, and the moths feed their fill in the chambers, and the spiders weave their lace before the mirrors, till the soul's typhus is bred out of oui neglect, and we begin to snore in its coma or rave in its delirium,—I, Sir, am a *bonnet-rouge*, a red-cap of the barricades, my friends, rather than a conservative.

——Were you born in Boston, Sir?—said the little man,—looking eager and excited.

I was not,—I replied.

It's a pity,—it's a pity,—said the little man;—it's the place to be born in. But if you can't fix it so as to be born here, you can come and live here. Old Ben Franklin, the father of American science and the American Union, wasn't ashamed to be born here. Jim Otis, the father of American Independence, bothered about in the Cape Cod marshes awhile, but he came to Boston as soon as he got big enough. Joe Warren, the first bloody ruffled-shirt of the Revolution, was as good as born here. Parson Channing strolled along this way from Newport, and staid here. Pity old Sam Hopkins hadn't come, too;—we'd have made a man of him,—poor, dear, good old Christian heathen! There he lies, as peaceful as a young baby, in the old burying-ground! I've stood on the slab many a time. Meant well,—meant well. Juggernaut. Parson Channing put a little oil on one linchpin, and slipped it out so softly, the first thing they knew about it was the wheel of that side was down. T'other fellow's at work now;

but he makes more noise about it. When the linchpin comes out on his side, there'll be a jerk, I tell you! Some think it will spoil the old cart, and they pretend to say that there are valuable things in it which may get hurt. Hope not,— hope not. But this is the great Macadamizing place,—always cracking up something.

Cracking up Boston folks,—said the gentleman with the *diamond*-pin, whom, for convenience' sake, I shall hereafter call the *Koh-i-noor*.

The little man turned round mechanically towards him, as Maelzel's Turk used to turn, carrying his head slowly and horizontally, as if it went by cog-wheels.—Cracking up all sorts of things,— native and foreign vermin included,—said the little man.

This remark was thought by some of us to have a hidden personal application, and to afford a fair opening for a lively rejoinder, if the Koh-i-noor had been so disposed. The little man uttered it with the distinct wooden calmness with which the ingenious Turk used to exclaim, *E-chec!* so that it *must* have been heard. The party supposed to be interested in the remark was, however, carrying a large knife-blade-full of something to his mouth just then, which, no doubt, interfered with the reply he would have made.

——My friend who used to board here was accustomed sometimes, in a pleasant way, to call himself the *Autocrat* of the table, — meaning, I suppose, that he had it all his own way among the boarders. I think our small boarder here is like to prove a refractory subject, if I undertake to use the sceptre my friend meant to bequeathe me, too magisterially. I won't deny that sometimes, on rare occasions, when I have been in company with gentlemen who *preferred* listening, I have been guilty of the same kind of usurpation which my friend openly justified. But I maintain, that I, the Professor, am a good listener. If a man can tell me a fact which subtends an appreciable angle in the horizon of thought, I am as receptive as the contribution-box in a congregation of colored brethren. If, when I am exposing my intellectual dry-goods, a man will begin a good story, I will have them all in, and my shutters up, before he has got to the fifth "says he," and listen like a three-years' child, as the author of the "Old Sailor" says. I had rather hear one of those grand elemental laughs from either of our two Georges, (fictitious names, Sir or Madam,) or listen to one of those old playbills of our College days, in which "Tom and Jerry" ("Thomas and Jeremiah," as the old Greek Professor was said to call it,) was announced to be brought on the stage with the whole force of the Faculty, read by our Frederick, (no such person, of course,) than say the best things I might by any chance find myself capable of saying. Of course, if I come across a real thinker. a suggestive, acute, illuminating, informing talker, I enjoy the luxury of sitting still for a while as much as another.

Nobody talks much that doesn't say unwise things,—things he did not mean to say; as no person plays much without striking a false note sometimes. Talk, to me, is only spading up the ground for crops of thought. I can't answer for what will turn up. If I could, it wouldn't be talking, but "speaking my piece." Better, I think, the hearty abandonment of one's self to the suggestions of the moment, at the risk of an occasional slip of the tongue, perceived the instant it escapes, but just one syllable too late, than the royal reputation of never saying a foolish thing.

——What shall I do with this little man?—There is only one thing to do,—and that is, to let him talk when he will. The day of the "Autocrat's" monologues is over.

——My friend,—said I to the young fellow whom, as I have said, the boarders call "John,"—My friend,—I said, one morning, after breakfast,—can you give me any information respecting the deformed person who sits at the other end of the table?

What! the Sculpin?—said the young fellow.

The diminutive person, with angular curvature

of the spine,—I said,—and double *talipes varus*,—I beg your pardon,—with two club-feet.

Is that long word what you call it when a fellah walks so?—said the young man, making his fists revolve round an imaginary axis, as you may have seen youth of tender age and limited pugilistic knowledge, when they show how they would punish an adversary, themselves protected by this rotating guard,—the middle knuckle, meantime, thumb-supported, fiercely prominent, death-threatening.

It is,—said I.—But would you have the kindness to tell me if you know anything about this deformed person?

About the Sculpin?—said the young fellow.

My good friend,—said I,—I am sure, by your countenance, you would not hurt the feelings of one who has been hardly enough treated by Nature to be spared by his fellows. Even in speaking of him to others, I could wish that you might not employ a term which implies contempt for what should inspire only pity.

A fellah's no business to be so——crooked,—said the young man called John.

Yes, yes,—I said, thoughtfully,—the strong hate the weak. It's all right. The arrangement has reference to the race, and not to the individual. Infirmity must be kicked out, or the stock run down. Wholesale moral arrangements are so different from retail!—I understand the instinct, my friend,—it is cosmic,—it is planetary,—it is a conservative principle in creation.

The young fellow's face gradually lost its expression as I was speaking, until it became as blank of vivid significance as the countenance of a gingerbread rabbit with two currants in the place of eyes. He had not taken my meaning.

Presently the intelligence came back with a snap that made him wink, as he answered,—Jest so. All right. A 1. Put her through. That's the way to talk. Did you speak to me, Sir?—Here the young man struck up that well-known song which I think they used to sing at Masonic festivals, beginning, "Aldiborontiphoscophornio, Where left you Chrononhotonthologos?"

I beg your pardon,—I said;—all I meant was, that men, as temporary occupants of a permanent abode called human life, which is improved or injured by occupancy, according to the style of tenant, have a natural dislike to those who, if they live the life of the race as well as of the individual, will leave lasting injurious effects upon the abode spoken of, which is to be occupied by countless future generations. This is the final cause of the underlying brute instinct which we have in common with the herds.

——The gingerbread-rabbit expression was coming on so fast, that I thought I must try again.

— It's a pity that families are kept up, where there are such hereditary infirmities. Still, let us treat this poor man fairly, and not call him names. Do you know what his name is?

I know what the rest of 'em call him, — said the young fellow. — They call him Little Boston. There's no harm in that, is there?

It is an honorable term, — I replied. — But why Little *Boston*, in a place where most are Bostonians?

Because nobody else is quite so Boston all over as he is, — said the young fellow.

"L. B. Ob. 1692." — Little Boston let him be, when we talk about him. The ring he wears labels him well enough. There is stuff in the little man, or he wouldn't stick so manfully by this crooked, crotchety old town. Give him a chance. — You will drop the Sculpin, won't you? — I said to the young fellow.

Drop him? — he answered, — I ha'n't took him up yet.

No, no, — the term, — I said, — the term. Don't call him so any more, if you please. Call him Little Boston, if you like.

All right, — said the young fellow. — I wouldn't be hard on the poor little ——

The word he used was objectionable in point of significance and of grammar. It was a frequent termination of certain adjectives among the Romans, — as of those designating a person following the sea, or given to rural pursuits. It is classed by custom among the profane words; why, it is hard to say,—but it is largely used in the street by those who speak of their fellows in pity or in wrath.

I never heard the young fellow apply the name of the odious pretended fish to the little man from that day forward.

—— Here we are, then, at our boarding-house. First, myself, the Professor, a little way from the head of the table, on the right, looking down, where the "Autocrat" used to sit. At the further end sits the Landlady. At the head of the table, just now, the Koh-i-noor, or the gentleman with the *diamond.* Opposite me is a Venerable Gentleman with a bland countenance, who as yet has spoken little. The Divinity-Student is my neighbor on the right,—and further down, that Young Fellow of whom I have repeatedly spoken. The Landlady's Daughter sits near the Koh-i-noor, as I said. The Poor Relation near the Landlady. At the right upper corner is a fresh-looking youth of whose name and history I have as yet learned nothing. Next the further left-hand corner, near the lower end of the table, sits the deformed person. The chair at his side, occupying that corner, is empty. I need not specially mention the other boarders, with the exception of Benjamin Franklin, the landlady's son, who sits near his mother. We are a tolerably assorted set,—difference enough and likeness enough; but still it seems to me there is something wanting. The Landlady's Daughter is the *prima donna* in the way of feminine attractions. I am not quite satisfied with this young lady. She wears more "jewelry," as certain young ladies call their trinkets, than I care to see on a person in her position. Her voice is strident, her laugh too much like a giggle, and she has that foolish way of dancing and bobbing like a quill-float with a "minnum" biting the hook below it, which one sees and weeps over sometimes in persons of more pretensions. I can't help hoping we shall put something into that empty chair yet which will add the missing string to our social harp. I hear talk of a rare Miss who is expected. Something in the school-girl way, I believe. We shall see.

——My friend who calls himself *The Autocrat* has given me a caution which I am going to repeat, with my comment upon it, for the benefit of all concerned.

Professor,—said he, one day,—don't you think your brain will run dry before a year's out, if you don't get the pump to help the cow? Let me tell you what happened to me once. I put a little money into a bank, and bought a check-book, so that I might draw it as I wanted, in sums to suit.

Things went on nicely for a time; scratching with a pen was as easy as rubbing Aladdin's Lamp; and my blank check-book seemed to be a dictionary of possibilities, in which I could find all the synonymes of happiness, and realize any one of them on the spot. A check came back to me at last with these two words on it, — *No funds.* My check-book was a volume of waste-paper.

Now, Professor, — said he, — I have drawn something out of your bank, you know; and just so sure as you keep drawing out your soul's currency without making new deposits, the next thing will be, *No funds,* — and then where will you be, my boy? These little bits of paper mean your gold and your silver and your copper, Professor; and you will certainly break up and go to pieces, if you don't hold on to your metallic basis.

There is something in that, — said I. — Only I rather think life can coin thought somewhat faster than I can count it off in words. What if one shall go round and dry up with soft napkins all the dew that falls of a June evening on the leaves of his garden? Shall there be no more dew on those leaves thereafter? Marry, yea, — many drops, large and round and full of moonlight as those thou shalt have absterged!

Here am I, the Professor, — a man who has lived long enough to have plucked the flowers of life and come to the berries, — which are not always sad-colored, but sometimes golden-hued as the crocus of April, or rosy-cheeked as the damask of June; a man who staggered against books as a baby, and will totter against them, if he lives to decrepitude; with a brain as full of tingling thoughts, such as they are, as a limb which we call "asleep," because it is so particularly awake, is of pricking points; presenting a key-board of nerve-pulps, not as yet tanned or ossified, to the finger-touch of all outward agencies; knowing something of the filmy threads of this web of life in which we insects buzz awhile, waiting for the gray old spider to come along; contented enough with daily realities, but twirling on his finger the key of a private Bedlam of ideals; in knowledge feeding with the fox oftener than with the stork,—loving better the breadth of a fertilizing inundation than the depth of a narrow artesian well; finding nothing too small for his contemplation in the markings of the *grammatophora subtilissima*, and nothing too large in the movement of the solar system towards the star Lambda of the constellation Hercules;—and the question is, whether there is anything left for me, the Professor, to suck out of creation, after my lively friend has had his straw in the bunghole of the Universe!

A man's mental reactions with the atmosphere of life must go on, whether he will or no, as between his blood and the air he breathes. As to catching the residuum of the process, or what we call *thought*,—the gaseous ashes of burned-out *thinking*,—the excretion of mental respiration,—that will depend on many things, as, on having a favorable intellectual temperature about one, and a fitting receptacle.—I sow more thought-seeds in twenty-four hours' travel over the desert-sand along which my lonely consciousness paces day and night, than I shall throw into soil where it will germinate, in a year. All sorts of bodily and mental perturbations come between us and the due projection of our thought. The pulse-like "fits of easy and difficult transmission" seem to reach even the transparent medium through which our souls are seen. We know our humanity by its often intercepted rays, as we tell a revolving light from a star or meteor by its constantly recurring obscuration.

An illustrious scholar once told me, that, in the first lecture he ever delivered, he spoke but half his allotted time, and felt as if he had told all he knew. Braham came forward once to sing one of his most famous and familiar songs, and for his life could not recall the first line of it;—he told his mishap to the audience, and they screamed it at him in a chorus of a thousand voices. Milton could not write to suit himself, except from the autumnal to the vernal equinox. One in the clothing-business, who, there is reason to suspect, may have inherited, by descent, the great poet's impressible temperament, let a customer slip through his fingers one day without fitting him with a new garment. "Ah!" said he to a friend of mine, who was standing by, "if it hadn't been for that confounded headache of mine this morning, I'd have had a coat on that man, in spite of himself, before he left the store." A passing throb, only,—but it deranged the nice mechanism required to persuade the accidental human being, x, into a given piece of broadcloth, a.

We must take care not to confound this frequent difficulty of transmission of our ideas with want of ideas. I suppose that a man's mind does in time form a neutral salt with the elements in the universe for which it has special elective affinities. In fact, I look upon a library as a kind of mental chemist's shop, filled with the crystals of all forms and hues which have come from the union of individual thought with local circumstances or universal principles.

When a man has worked out his special affinities in this way, there is an end of his genius as a real solvent. No more effervescence and hissing tumult as he pours his sharp thought on the world's biting alkaline unbeliefs! No more corrosion of the old monumental tablets covered with lies! No more taking up of dull earths, and turning them, first into clear solutions, and then into 'ustrous prisms!

I, the Professor, am very much like other men. I shall not find out when I have used up my affinities. What a blessed thing it is, that Nature, when she invented, manufactured, and patented her authors, contrived to make critics out of the chips that were left! Painful as the task is, they never fail to warn the author, in the most impressive manner, of the probabilities of failure in what he has undertaken. Sad as the necessity is to their delicate sensibilities, they never hesitate to advertise him of the decline of his powers, and to press upon him the propriety of retiring before he sinks into imbecility. Trusting to their kind offices, I shall endeavor to fulfil——

Bridget enters and begins clearing the table.

—— The following poem is my (The Professor's) only contribution to the great department of Ocean-Cable literature. As all the poets of this country will be engaged for the next six weeks in writing for the premium offered by the Crystal-Palace Company for the Burns Centenary, (so called, according to our Benjamin Franklin, because there will be na'ry a cent for any of us,) poetry will be very scarce and dear. Consumers may, consequently, be glad to take the present article, which, by the aid of a Latin tutor and a Professor of Chemistry, will be found intelligible to the educated classes.

DE SAUTY.

AN ELECTRO-CHEMICAL ECLOGUE.

Professor. *Blue-Nose.*

PROFESSOR.

TELL me, O Provincial! speak, Ceruleo-Nasal!
Lives there one De Sauty extant now among you,
Whispering Boanerges, son of silent thunder,
Holding talk with nations?

Is there a De Sauty ambulant on Tellus,
Bifid-cleft like mortals, dormient in night-cap,
Having sight, smell, hearing, food-receiving feature
Three times daily patent?

Breathes there such a being, O Ceruleo-Nasal?
Or is he a *mythus*,—ancient word for "humbug,"—
Such as Livy told about the wolf that wet-nursed
Romulus and Remus?

Was he born of woman, this alleged De Sauty?
Or a living product of galvanic action,
Like the *acarus* bred in Crosse's flint-solution?
Speak, thou Cyano-Rhinal!

BLUE-NOSE.

Many things thou askest, jackknife-bearing stranger,
Much-conjecturing mortal, pork-and-treacle-waster!
Pretermit thy whittling, wheel thine ear-flap toward me,
Thou shalt hear them answered.

When the charge galvanic tingled through the cable,
At the polar focus of the wire electric
Suddenly appeared a white-faced man among us:
Called himself "DE SAUTY."

As the small opossum held in pouch maternal
Grasps the nutrient organ whence the term *mammalia*,
So the unknown stranger held the wire electric,
Sucking in the current.

When the current strengthened, bloomed the pale-faced stranger,—
Took no drink nor victual, yet grew fat and rosy,—
And from time to time, in sharp articulation,
Said, "*All right!* DE SAUTY."

From the lonely station passed the utterance, spreading
Through the pines and hemlocks to the groves of steeples,
Till the land was filled with loud reverberations
Of "*All right!* DE SAUTY."

When the current slackened, drooped the mystic stranger,—
Faded, faded, faded, as the stream grew weaker,—
Wasted to a shadow, with a hartshorn odor
Of disintegration.

Drops of deliquescence glistened on his forehead,
Whitened round his feet the dust of efflorescence,
Till one Monday morning, when the flow suspended,
There was no De Sauty.

Nothing but a cloud of elements organic,
C. O. H. N. Ferrum, Chor. Flu. Sil. Potassa,

Calc. Sod. Phosph. Mag. Sulphur, Mang. (?) Alumin. (?)
Cuprum, (?)
Such as man is made of.

Born of stream galvanic, with it he had perished!
There is no De Sauty now there is no current!
Give us a new cable, then again we'll hear him
Cry, "*All right!* DE SAUTY."

II.

BACK again!—A turtle—which means a tortoise—is fond of his shell; but if you put a live coal on his back, he crawls out of it. So the boys say.

It is a libel on the turtle. He grows to his shell, and his shell is in his body as much as his body is in his shell.—I don't think there is one of our boarders quite so testudineous as I am. Nothing but a combination of motives, more peremptory than the coal on the turtle's back, could have got me to leave the shelter of my carapace; and after memorable interviews, and kindest hospitalities, and grand sights, and huge influx of patriotic pride,—for every American owns all America,—

"Creation's heir,—the world, the world is"

his, if anybody's, — I come back with the feeling which a boned turkey might experience, if, retaining his consciousness, he were allowed to resume his skeleton.

Welcome, O Fighting Gladiator, and Recumbent Cleopatra, and Dying Warrior, whose classic outlines (reproduced in the calcined mineral of Lutetia) crown my loaded shelves! Welcome, ye triumphs of pictorial art (repeated by the magic graver) that look down upon me from the walls of my sacred cell! Vesalius, as Titian drew him, high-fronted, still-eyed, thick-bearded, with signet-ring, as beseems a gentleman, with book and carelessly-held eyeglass, marking him a scholar; thou, too, Jan Kuyper, commonly called Jan Praktiseer, old man of a century and seven years besides, father of twenty sons and two daughters, cut in copper by Houbraken, bought from a portfolio on one of the Paris *quais;* and ye Three Trees of Rembrandt, black in shadow against the blaze of sunlight; and thou Rosy Cottager of Sir Joshua, — thy roses hinted by the peppery burin of Bartolozzi; ye, too, of lower grades in nature, yet not unlovely nor unrenowned, Young Bull of Paulus Potter, and Sleeping Cat of Cornelius Visscher; welcome once more to my eyes! The old books look out from the shelves, and I seem to read on their backs something besides their titles, — a kind of solemn greeting. The crimson carpet flushes warm under my feet. The arm-chair hugs me; the swivel-chair spins round with me, as if it were giddy with pleasure; the vast recumbent *fauteuil* stretches itself out under my weight, as one joyous with food and wine stretches in after-dinner laughter.

The boarders were pleased to say that they were glad to get me back. One of them ventured a compliment, namely, — that I talked as if I believed what I said. — This was apparently considered something unusual, by its being mentioned.

One who means to talk with entire sincerity, — I said, — always feels himself in danger of two things, namely, — an affectation of bluntness, like that of which Cornwall accuses Kent in "Lear," and actual rudeness. What a man wants to do, in talking with a stranger, is to get and to give as much of the best and most real life that belongs to the two talkers as the time will let him. Life is short, and conversation apt to run to mere words. Mr. Huc I think it is, who tells us some very good stories about the way in which two Chinese gentlemen contrive to keep up a long talk without saying a word which has any meaning in it. Something like this is occasionally heard on this side of the Great Wall. The best Chinese talkers I know are some pretty women whom I meet from time to time. Pleasant, airy, complimentary, the little flakes of flattery glimmering in their talk like the bits of gold-leaf in *eau-de-vie de Dantzic;* their accents flowing on in a soft ripple, — never a wave, and never a calm; words nicely fitted, but never a colored phrase or a high-flavored epithet; they turn air into syllables so gracefully, that we find meaning for the music they make as we find faces in the coals and fairy palaces in the clouds. There is something very odd, though, about this mechanical talk.

You have sometimes been in a train on the railroad when the engine was detached a long way from the station you were approaching? Well, you have noticed how quietly and rapidly the cars kept on, just as if the locomotive were drawing them? Indeed, you would not have suspected that you were travelling on the strength of a dead fact, if you had not seen the engine running away from you on a side-track. Upon my conscience, I believe some of these pretty women detach their minds entirely, sometimes, from their talk, — and, what is more, that we never know the difference. Their lips let off the fluty syllables just as their fingers would sprinkle the music-drops from their pianos; unconscious habit turns the phrase of thought into words just as it does that of music into notes. — Well, they govern the world, for all that, — these sweet-lipped women, — because beauty is the index of a larger fact than wisdom.

—— The Bombazine wanted an explanation.

Madam, — said I, — wisdom is the abstract of the past, but beauty is the promise of the future.

—— All this, however, is not what I was going to say. Here am I, suppose, seated — we will say at a dinner-table — alongside of an intelligent Englishman. We look in each other's faces, — we exchange a dozen words. One thing is settled: we mean not to offend each other, — to be perfectly courteous, — more than courteous; for we are the entertainer and the entertained, and cherish particularly amiable feelings to each other. The claret is good; and if our blood reddens a little with its warm crimson, we are none the less kind for it.

—— I don't think people that talk over their victuals are like to say anything very great, especially if they get their heads muddled with strong drink before they begin jabberin'.

The Bombazine uttered this with a sugary sourness, as if the words had been steeped in a solution of acetate of lead. — The boys of my time used to call a hit like this a "side-winder."

—— I must finish this woman. —

Madam, — I said, — the Great Teacher seems to have been fond of talking as he sat at meat. Because this was a good while ago, in a far-off place, you forget what the true fact of it was, — that those were real dinners, where people were hungry and thirsty, and where you met a very miscellaneous company. Probably there was a great deal of loose talk among the guests; at any rate, there was always wine, we may believe.

Whatever may be the hygienic advantages or disadvantages of wine, — and I for one, except for certain particular ends, believe in water, and, I blush to say it, in black tea, — there is no doubt about its being the grand specific against dull dinners. A score of people come together in all moods of mind and body. The problem is, in the space of one hour, more or less, to bring them all into the same condition of slightly exalted life. Food alone is enough for one person, perhaps, — talk, alone, for another; but the grand equalizer and fraternizer, which works up the radiators to their maximum radiation, and the absorbents to their maximum receptivity, is now just where it was when

"The conscious water saw its Lord and blushed,"

— when six great vessels containing water, the whole amounting to more than a hogshead-full, were changed into the best of wine. I once wrote a song about wine, in which I spoke so warmly of it, that I was afraid some would think it was written *inter pocula;* whereas it was composed in the bosom of my family, under the most tranquillizing domestic influences.

—— The divinity-student turned towards me, looking mischievous. — Can you tell me, — he said, — who wrote a song for a temperance celebration once, of which the following is a verse?

> Alas for the loved one, too gentle and fair
> The joys of the banquet to chasten and share!
> Her eye lost its light that his goblet might shine,
> And the rose of her cheek was dissolved in his wine!

I did, — I answered. — What are you going to do about it? — I will tell you another line I wrote long ago: —

> Don't be "consistent," — but be simply *true.*

The longer I live, the more I am satisfied of two things: first, that the truest lives are those that are cut rose-diamond-fashion, with many facets answering to the many-planed aspects of the world about them; secondly, that society is always trying in some way or other to grind us down to a single flat surface. It is hard work to resist this grinding-down action. — Now give me a chance. Better eternal and universal abstinence than the brutalities of those days that made wives and mothers and daughters and sisters blush for those whom they should have honored, as they came reeling home from their debauches! Yet better even excess than lying and hypocrisy; and if wine is upon all our tables, let us praise it for its color and fragrance and social tendency, so far as it deserves, and not hug a bottle in the closet and pretend not to know the use of a wine-glass at a public dinner! I think you will find that people who honestly mean to be true really contradict themselves much more rarely than those who try to be "consistent." But a great many things we say can be made to appear contradictory, simply because they are partial views of a truth, and may often look unlike at first, as a front view of a face and its profile often do.

Here is a distinguished divine, for whom I have great respect, for I owe him a charming hour at one of our literary anniversaries, and he has often spoken noble words; but he holds up a remark of my friend the "Autocrat,"—which I grieve to say he twice misquotes, by omitting the very word which gives it its significance,—the word *fluid*, intended to typify the mobility of the restricted will,—holds it up, I say, as if it attacked the reality of the self-determining principle, instead of illustrating its limitations by an image. Now I will not explain any farther, still less defend, and least of all attack, but simply quote a few lines from one of my friend's poems, printed more than ten years ago, and ask the distinguished gentleman where *he* has ever asserted more strongly or absolutely the independent will of the "subcreative centre," as my heretical friend has elsewhere called man.

— Thought, conscience, will, to make them all thy own
He rent a pillar from the eternal throne!
— Made in His image, thou must nobly dare
The thorny crown of sovereignty to share.
— Think not too meanly of thy low estate;
Thou hast a choice; to choose is to create!

If he will look a little closely, he will see that the profile and the full-face views of the will are both true and perfectly consistent.

Now let us come back, after this long digression, to the conversation with the intelligent Englishman. We begin skirmishing with a few light ideas,—testing for thoughts,—as our electro-chemical friend, De Sauty, if there were such a person, would test for his current; trying a little litmus-paper for acids, and then a slip of turmeric-paper for alkalies, as chemists do with unknown compounds; flinging the lead, and looking at the shells and sands it brings up to find out whether we are like to keep in shallow water, or shall have to drop the deep-sea line;—in short, seeing what we have to deal with. If the Englishman gets his Hs pretty well placed, he comes from one of the higher grades of the British social order, and we shall find him a good companion.

But, after all, here is a great fact between us. We belong to two different civilizations, and, until we recognize what separates us, we are talking like Pyramus and Thisbe, without any hole in the wall to talk through. Therefore, on the whole, if he were a superior fellow, incapable of mistaking it for personal conceit, I think I would let out the fact of the real American feeling about Old-World folks. They are children to us in certain points of view. They are playing with toys we have done with for whole generations. That silly little drum they are always beating on, and the trumpet and the feather they make so much noise and cut such a figure with, we have not quite outgrown, but play with much less seriously and constantly than they do. Then there is a whole museum of wigs, and masks, and lace-coats, and gold-sticks, and grimaces, and phrases, which we laugh at honestly, without affectation, that are still used in the Old-World puppet-shows. I don't think we on our part ever understand the Englishman's concentrated loyalty and specialized reverence. But then we do think more of a man, as such, (barring some little difficulties about race and complexion which the Englishman will touch us on presently,) than any people that ever lived did think of him. Our reverence is a great deal wider, if it is less intense. We have caste among us, to some extent, it is true; but there is never a collar on the American wolf-dog such as you often see on the English mastiff, notwithstanding his robust, hearty individuality.

This confronting of two civilizations is always a grand sensation to me; it is like cutting through the isthmus and letting the two oceans swim into each other's laps. The trouble is, it is so difficult to let out the whole American nature without its self-assertion seeming to take a personal character. But I never enjoy the Englishman so much as when he talks of church and king like Manco Capac among the Peruvians. Then you get the real British flavor, which the cosmopolite Englishman loses.

How much better this thorough interpenetration of ideas than a barren interchange of courtesies, or a bush-fighting argument, in which each man tries to cover as much of himself and expose as much of his opponent as the tangled thicket of the disputed ground will let him!

——My thoughts flow in layers or strata, at least three deep. I follow a slow person's talk, and keep a perfectly clear under-current of my own beneath it. Under both runs obscurely a consciousness belonging to a third train of reflections, independent of the two others. I will try to write out a mental movement in three parts.

A.—First voice, or Mental Soprano,—thought follows a woman talking.

B.—Second voice, or Mental Barytone,—my running accompaniment.

C.—Third voice, or Mental Basso,—low grumble of an importunate self-repeating idea.

A.—White lace, three skirts, looped with flowers, wreath of apple-blossoms, gold bracelets, diamond pin and ear-rings, the most delicious *berthe* you ever saw, white satin slippers ——

B.—Deuse take her! What a fool she is! Hear her chatter! (Look out of window just here.—Two pages and a half of description, if it were all written out, in one tenth of a second.) —Go ahead, old lady! (Eye catches picture over fireplace.) There's that infernal family nose! Came over in the "Mayflower" on the first old fool's face. Why don't they wear a ring in it?

C.—You'll be late at lecture,—late at lecture, —late,—late,—late ——

I observe that a deep layer of thought sometimes makes itself felt through the superincumbent strata, thus:—The usual single or double currents shall flow on, but there shall be an influence blending with them, disturbing them in an obscure way, until all at once I say, — Oh, there! I knew there was something troubling me, — and the thought which had been working through comes up to the surface clear, definite, and articulates itself, — a disagreeable duty, perhaps, or an unpleasant recollection.

The inner world of thought and the outer world of events are alike in this, that they are both brimful. There is no space between consecutive thoughts, or between the never-ending series of actions. All pack tight, and mould their surfaces against each other, so that in the long run there is a wonderful average uniformity in the forms of both thoughts and actions, — just as you find that cylinders crowded all become hexagonal prisms, and spheres pressed together are formed into regular polyhedra.

Every event that a man would master must be mounted on the run, and no man ever caught the reins of a thought except as it galloped by him. So, to carry out, with another comparison, my remark about the layers of thought, we may consider the mind, as it moves among thoughts or events, like a circus-rider whirling round with a great troop of horses. He can mount a fact or an idea, and guide it more or less completely, but he cannot stop it. So, as I said in another way at the beginning, he can stride two or three thoughts at once, but not break their steady walk, trot, or gallop. He can only take his foot from the saddle of one thought and put it on that of another.

—— What is the saddle of a thought? Why, a word, of course.— Twenty years after you have dismissed a thought, it suddenly wedges up to you through the press, as if it had been steadily galloping round and round all that time without a rider.

The will does not act in the interspaces of thought, for there are no such interspaces, but simply steps from the back of one moving thought upon that of another.

—— I should like to ask, — said the divinity-student, — since we are getting into metaphysics, how you can admit space, if all things are in contact, and how you can admit time, if it is always *now* to something?

— I thought it best not to hear this question.

—— I wonder if you know this class of philosophers in books or elsewhere. One of them makes his bow to the public, and exhibits an unfortunate truth bandaged up so that it cannot stir hand or foot, — as helpless, apparently, and unable to take care of itself, as an Egyptian mummy. He then proceeds, with the air and method of a master, to take off the bandages. Nothing can be neater than the way in which he does it. But as he takes off layer after layer, the truth seems to grow smaller and smaller, and some of its outlines begin to look like something we have seen before. At last, when he has got them all off, and the truth struts out naked, we recognize it as a diminutive and familiar acquaintance whom we have known in the streets all our lives. The fact is, the philosopher has coaxed the truth into his study and put all those bandages on; of course it is not very hard for him to take them off. Still, a great many people like to watch the process,—he does it so neatly!

Dear! dear! I am ashamed to write and talk, sometimes, when I see how those functions of the large-brained, thumb-opposing plantigrade are abused by my fellow-vertebrates,—perhaps by myself. How they spar for wind, instead of hitting from the shoulder!

——The young fellow called John arose and placed himself in a neat fighting attitude.—Fetch on the fellah that makes them long words!—he said,—and planted a straight hit with the right fist in the concave palm of the left hand with a click like a cup and ball.—You small boy there, hurry up that "Webster's Unabridged!"

The little gentleman with the malformation, before described, shocked the propriety of the breakfast-table by a loud utterance of three words, of which the two last were "Webster's Unabridged," and the first was an emphatic monosyllable.—Beg pardon,—he added,—forgot myself. But let us have an English dictionary, if we are to have any. I don't believe in clipping the coin of the realm, Sir! If I put a weathercock on my house, Sir, I want it to tell which way the wind blows up aloft,—off from the prairies to the ocean, or off from the ocean to the prairies, or any way it wants to blow! I don't want a weathercock with a winch in an old gentleman's study that he can take hold of and turn, so that the vane shall point west when the great wind overhead is blowing east with all its might, Sir! Wait till we give you a dictionary, Sir! It takes Boston to do that thing, Sir!

——Some folks think water can't run down-hill anywhere out of Boston,—remarked the Koh-i-noor.

I don't know what *some folks think* so well as I know what *some fools say*,—rejoined the Little Gentleman.—If importing most dry goods made the best scholars, I dare say you would know where to look for 'em.—Mr. Webster couldn't spell, Sir, or wouldn't spell, Sir,—at any rate, he didn't spell; and the end of it was a fight between the owners of some copyrights and the dignity of this noble language which we have inherited from our English fathers. Language!—the blood of the soul,

Sir! into which our thoughts run and out of which they grow! We know what a word is worth here in Boston. Young Sam Adams got up on the stage at Commencement, out at Cambridge there, with his gown on, the Governor and Council looking on in the name of his Majesty, King George the Second, and the girls looking down out of the galleries, and taught people how to spell a word that wasn't in the Colonial dictionaries! *R-e, re, s-i-s, sis, t-a-n-c-e, tance, Resistance!* That was in '43, and it was a good many years before the Boston boys began spelling it with their muskets;—but when they did begin, they spelt it so loud that the old bedridden women in the English almhouses heard every syllable! Yes, yes, yes,—it was a good while before those other two Boston boys got the class so far along that it could spell those two hard words, *Independence* and *Union!* I tell you what, Sir, there are a thousand lives, aye, sometimes a million, go to get a new word into a language that is worth speaking. We know what language means too well here in Boston to play tricks with it. We never make a new word till we have made a new thing or a new thought, Sir! When we shaped the new mould of this continent, we had to make a few. When, by God's permission, we abrogated the primal curse of maternity, we had to make a word or two. The cutwater of this great Leviathan clipper, the OCCIDENTAL,

— this thirty-masted wind-and-steam wave-crusher, — must throw a little spray over the human vocabulary as it splits the waters of a new world's destiny!

He rose as he spoke, until his stature seemed to swell into the fair human proportions. His feet must have been on the upper round of his high chair; — that was the only way I could account for it.

Puts her through fust-rate, — said the young fellow whom the boarders call John.

The venerable and kind-looking old gentleman who sits opposite said he remembered Sam Adams as Governor. An old man in a brown coat. Saw him take the Chair on Boston Common. Was a boy then, and remembers sitting on the fence in front of the old Hancock house. Recollects he had a glazed 'lection-bun, and sat eating it and looking down on to the Common. Lalocks flowered late that year, and he got a great bunch off from the bushes in the Hancock front-yard.

Them 'lection buns are no go, — said the young man John, so called. — I know the trick. Give a fellah a fo'penny bun in the mornin', an' he downs the whole of it. In about an hour it swells up in his stomach as big as a football, and *his* feelin's sp'ilt for *that* day. That's the way to stop off a young one from eatin' up all the 'lection dinner.

Salem! Salem! not Boston, — shouted the little man.

But the Koh-i-noor laughed a great rasping laugh, and the boy Benjamin Franklin looked sharp at his mother, as if he remembered the bun-experiment as a part of his past personal history.

The little gentleman was holding a fork in his left hand. He stabbed a boulder of home-made bread with it, mechanically, and looked at it as if it ought to shriek. It did not, — but he sat as if watching it.

—— Language is a solemn thing, — I said. — It grows out of life, — out of its agonies and ecstasies, its wants and its weariness. Every language is a temple, in which the soul of those who speak it is enshrined. Because time softens its outlines and rounds the sharp angles of its cornices, shall a fellow take a pickaxe to help time? Let me tell you what comes of meddling with things that can take care of themselves. — A friend of mine had a watch given him, when he was a boy, — a "bull's eye," with a loose silver case that came off like an oyster-shell from its contents; you know them, — the cases that you hang on your thumb, while the *core*, or the real watch, lies in your hand as naked as a peeled apple. Well, he began with taking off the case, and so on from one liberty to another, until he got it fairly open and there were the works, as good as if they were alive,—crown-wheel, balance-wheel, and all the rest. All right except one thing,—there was a confounded little *hair* had got tangled round the balance-wheel. So my young Solomon got a pair of tweezers, and caught hold of the *hair* very nicely, and pulled it right out, without touching any of the wheels,—when,—buzzzZZZ! and the watch had done up twenty-four hours in double magnetic-telegraph time!—The English language was wound up to run some thousands of years, I trust; but if everybody is to be pulling at everything he thinks is a *hair*, our grandchildren will have to make the discovery that it is a hair-*spring*, and the old Anglo-Norman soul's-timekeeper will run down, as so many other dialects have done before it. I can't stand this meddling any better than you, Sir. But we have a great deal to be proud of in the lifelong labors of that old lexicographer, and we mustn't be ungrateful. Besides, don't let us deceive ourselves,—the war of the dictionaries is only a disguised rivalry of cities, colleges, and especially of publishers. After all, it is likely that the language will shape itself by larger forces than phonography and dictionary-making. You may spade up the ocean as much as you like, and harrow it afterwards, if you can,—but the moon will still lead the tides, and the winds will form their surface.

—— Do you know Richardson's Dictionary? — I said to my neighbor the divinity-student.

Haöw? — said the divinity-student. — He colored, as he noticed on my face a twitch in one of the muscles which tuck up the corner of the mouth, (*zygomaticus major*,) and which I could not hold back from making a little movement on its own account.

It was too late. — A country-boy, lassoed when he was a half-grown colt. Just as good as a city-boy, and in some ways, perhaps, better, — but caught a little too old not to carry some marks of his earlier ways of life. Foreigners, who have talked a strange tongue half their lives, return to the language of their childhood in their dying hours. Gentlemen in fine linen, and scholars in large libraries, taken by surprise, or in a careless moment, will sometimes let slip a word they knew as boys in homespun and have not spoken since that time, — but it lay there under all their culture. That is one way you may know the country-boys after they have grown rich or celebrated; another is by the odd old family names, particularly those of the Hebrew prophets, which the good old people have saddled them with.

—— Boston has enough of England about it to make a good English dictionary, — said that fresh-looking youth whom I have mentioned as sitting at the right upper corner of the table.

I turned and looked him full in the face, — for the pure, manly intonations arrested me. The voice was youthful, but full of character. — I suppose some persons have a peculiar susceptibility in the matter of voice. — Hear this.

Not long after the American Revolution, a young lady was sitting in her father's chaise in a street of this town of Boston. She overheard a little girl talking or singing, and was mightily taken with the tones of her voice. Nothing would satisfy her but she must have that little girl come and live in her father's house. So the child came, being then nine years old. Until her marriage she remained under the same roof with the young lady. Her children became successively inmates of the lady's dwelling; and now, *seventy* years, or thereabouts, since the young lady heard the child singing, one of that child's children and one of her grandchildren are with her in that home, where she, no longer young, except in heart, passes her peaceful days. — Three generations linked together by so light a breath of accident!

I liked the sound of this youth's voice, I said, and his look when I came to observe him a little more closely. His complexion had something better than the bloom and freshness which had first attracted me; — it had that diffused *tone* which is a sure index of wholesome lusty life. A fine liberal style of nature it seemed to be: hair crisped moustache springing thick and dark, head firmly planted, lips finished, as one commonly sees them in gentlemen's families, a pupil well contracted, and a mouth that opened frankly with a white flash of teeth that looked as if they could serve him as they say Ethan Allen's used to serve their owner, — to draw nails with. This is the kind of fellow to walk a frigate's deck and bowl his broadsides into the "Gadlant Thudnder-bomb," or any forty-portholed adventurer who would like to exchange a few tons of iron compliments. — I don't know what put this into my head, for it was not till some time afterward I learned the young fellow had been in the naval school at Annapolis. Something had happened to change his plan of life, and he was now studying engineering and architecture in Boston.

When the youth made the short remark which drew my attention to him, the little deformed gentleman turned round and took a long look at him.

Good for the Boston boy! — he said.

I am not a Boston boy, — said the youth, smiling, — I am a Marylander.

I don't care where you come from, — we'll make a Boston man of you, — said the little gentleman. — Pray, what part of Maryland did you come from, and how shall I call you?

The poor youth had to speak pretty loud, as he

was at the right upper corner of the table, and the little gentleman next the lower left-hand corner. His face flushed a little, but he answered pleasantly, — telling who he was, as if the little man's infirmity gave him a right to ask any questions he wanted to.

Here is the place for you to sit, — said the little gentleman, pointing to the vacant chair next his own, at the corner.

You're go'n' to have a young lady next you, if you wait till to-morrow, — said the landlady to him.

He did not reply, but I had a fancy that he changed color. It can't be that *he* has susceptibilities with reference to a contingent young lady! It can't be that he has had experiences which make him sensitive! Nature could not be quite so cruel as to set a heart throbbing in that poor little cage of ribs! There is no use in wasting notes of admiration. I must ask the landlady about him.

These are some of the facts she furnished. — Has not been long with her. Brought a sight of furniture, — couldn't hardly get some of it upstairs. Hasn't seemed particularly attentive to the ladies. The Bombazine (whom she calls Cousin something or other) has tried to enter into conversation with him, but retired with the impression that he was indifferent to ladies' society. Paid his bill the other day without saying a word about it. Paid it in gold, — had a great heap of twenty-dollar pieces. Hires her best room. Thinks he is a very nice little man, but lives dreadful lonely up in his chamber. Wants the care of some capable nuss. Never pitied anybody more in her life, — never see a more interestin' person.

—— My intention was, when I began making these notes, to let them consist principally of conversations between myself and the other boarders. So they will, very probably; but my curiosity is excited about this little boarder of ours, and my reader must not be disappointed, if I sometimes interrupt a discussion to give an account of whatever fact or traits I may discover about him. It so happens that his room is next to mine, and I have the opportunity of observing many of his ways without any active movements of curiosity. That his room contains heavy furniture, that he is a restless little body and is apt to be up late, that he talks to himself, and keeps mainly to himself, is nearly all I have yet found out.

One curious circumstance happened lately, which I mention without drawing an absolute inference. — Being at the studio of a sculptor with whom I am acquainted, the other day, I saw a remarkable cast of a *left arm.* On my asking where the model came from, he said it was taken direct from the arm of a *deformed person,* who had employed one of the Italian moulders to make the cast. It was a curious case, it should seem, of one beautiful limb upon a frame otherwise singularly imperfect. — I have repeatedly noticed this little gentleman's use of his left arm. Can he have furnished the model I saw at the sculptor's?

—— So we are to have a new boarder to-morrow. I hope there will be something pretty and pleasing about her. A woman with a creamy voice, and finished in *alto rilievo*, would be a variety in the boarding-house, — a little more marrow and a little less sinew than our landlady and her daughter and the bombazine-clad female, all of whom are of the turkey-drumstick style of organization. I don't mean that these are our only female companions; but the rest being conversational non-combatants, mostly still, sad feeders, who take in their food as locomotives take in wood and water, and then wither away from the table like blossoms that never come to fruit, I have not yet referred to them as individuals.

I wonder what kind of young person we shall see in that empty chair to-morrow!

—— I read this song to the boarders after breakfast the other morning. It was written for our fellows; — you know who they are, of course.

THE BOYS.

HAS there any old fellow got mixed with the boys?
If there has, take him out, without making a noise!
Hang the Almanac's cheat and the Catalogue's spite!
Old Time is a liar! We're twenty to-night!

We're twenty! We're twenty! Who says we are more?
He's tipsy, — young jackanapes! — show him the door! —
"Gray temples at twenty?" — Yes! *white*, if we please;
Where the snow-flakes fall thickest there's nothing can freeze!

Was it snowing I spoke of? Excuse the mistake!
Look close, — you will see not a sign of a flake;
We want some new garlands for those we have shed, —
And these are white roses in place of the red!

We've a trick, we young fellows, you may have been told,
Of talking (in public) as if we were old; —
That boy we call "Doctor," and this we call "Judge;" —
It's a neat little fiction, — of course it's all fudge.

That fellow's the "Speaker," — the one on the right;
"Mr. Mayor," my young one, how are you to-night?
That's our "Member of Congress," we say when we chaff;
There's the "Reverend" What's his name? — don't make me
laugh!

That boy with the grave mathematical look
Made believe he had written a wonderful book,
And the ROYAL SOCIETY thought it was *true!*
So they chose him right in; a good joke it was, too!

There's a boy, — we pretend, — with a three-decker-brain,
That could harness a team with a logical chain;
When he spoke for our manhood in syllabled fire,
We called him "The Justice," — but now he's "The Squire."

And there's a nice youngster of excellent pith, —
Fate tried to conceal him by naming him Smith, —
But he shouted a song for the brave and the free, —
— Just read on his medal, — "My country, — of thee!"

You hear that boy laughing? — you think he's all fun, —
But the angels laugh, too, at the good he has done;
The children laugh loud as they troop to his call,
And the poor man that knows him laughs loudest of all!

Yes, we're boys, — always playing with tongue or with pen, —
And I sometimes have asked, — Shall we ever be men?
Shall we always be youthful and laughing and gay,
Till the last dear companion drops smiling away?

Then here's to our boyhood, its gold and its gray!
The stars of its Winter, the dews of its May!
And when we have done with our life-lasting toys,
Dear Father, take care of thy children, the Boys!

III.

[*The Professor talks with the Reader. He tells a Young Girl's Story.*]

When the elements that went to the making of the first man, father of mankind, had been withdrawn from the world of unconscious matter, the balance of creation was disturbed. The materials that go to the making of one woman were set free by the abstraction from inanimate nature of one man's-worth of masculine constituents. These combined to make our first mother, by a logical necessity involved in the previous creation of our common father. All this, mythically, illustratively, and by no means doctrinally or polemically.

The man implies the woman, you will understand. The excellent gentleman whom I had the pleasure of setting right in a trifling matter a few weeks ago believes in the frequent occurrence of miracles at the present day. So do I. I believe, if you could find an uninhabited coral-reef island, in the middle of the Pacific Ocean, with plenty of cocoa-palms and bread-fruit on it, and put a handsome young fellow, like our Marylander, ashore upon it, if you touched there a year afterwards, you would find him walking under the palm-trees arm in arm with a pretty woman.

Where would she come from?

Oh, that's the miracle!

——I was just as certain, when I saw that fine, high-colored youth at the upper right-hand corner of our table, that there would appear some fitting feminine counterpart to him, as if I had been a clairvoyant, seeing it all beforehand.

——I have a fancy that those Marylanders are

just about near enough to the sun to ripen well.— How some of us fellows remember Joe and Harry, Baltimoreans, both! Joe, with his cheeks like lady-apples, and his eyes like black-heart cherries, and his teeth like the whiteness of the flesh of cocoa-nuts, and his laugh that set the chandelier-drops rattling overhead, as we sat at our sparkling banquets in those gay times! Harry, champion, by acclamation, of the College heavy-weights, broad-shouldered, bull-necked, square-jawed, six feet and trimmings, a little science, lots of pluck, good-natured as a steer in peace, formidable as a red-eyed bison in the crack of hand-to-hand battle! Who forgets the great muster-day, and the collision of the classic with the democratic forces? The huge butcher, fifteen stone,—two hundred and ten pounds,—good weight,—steps out like Telamonian Ajax, defiant. No words from Harry, the Baltimorean,—one of the quiet sort, who strike first, and do the talking, if there is any, afterwards. No words, but, in the place thereof, a clean, straight, hard hit, which took effect with a spank like the explosion of a percussion-cap, knocking the slayer of beeves down a sand-bank,—followed, alas! by the too impetuous youth, so that both rolled down together, and the conflict terminated in one of those inglorious and inevitable Yankee *clinches*, followed by a general *melée*, which make our native fistic encounters so different from such admirably-ordered contests as that which I once saw at an English fair, where everything was done decently and in order, and the fight began and ended with such grave propriety, that a sporting parson need hardly have hesitated to open it with a devout petition, and, after it was over, dismiss the ring with a benediction.

I can't help telling one more story about this great field-day, though it is the most wanton and irrelevant digression. But all of us have a little speck of fight underneath our peace and good-will to men, — just a speck, for revolutions and great emergencies, you know, — so that we should not submit to be trodden quite flat by the first heavy-heeled aggressor that came along. You can tell a portrait from an ideal head, I suppose, and a true story from one spun out of the writer's invention. See whether this sounds true or not.

Admiral Sir Isaac Coffin sent out two fine blood-horses, Barefoot and Serab by name, to Massachusetts, something before the time I am talking of. With them came a Yorkshire groom, a stocky little fellow, in velvet breeches, who made that mysterious hissing noise, traditionary in English stables, when he rubbed down the silken-skinned racers, in great perfection. After the soldiers had come from the muster-field, and some of the companies were on the village-common, there was still some skirmishing between a few individuals who had not had the fight taken out of them. The little Yorkshire groom thought he must serve out somebody. So he threw himself into an approved scientific attitude, and, in brief, emphatic language, expressed his urgent anxiety to accommodate any classical young gentleman who chose to consider himself a candidate for his attentions. I don't suppose there were many of the college boys that would have been a match for him in the art which Englishmen know so much more of than Americans, for the most part. However, one of the Sophomores, a very quiet, peaceable fellow, just stepped out of the crowd, and, running straight at the groom, as he stood there, sparring away, struck him with the sole of his foot, a straight blow, as if it had been with his fist, — and knocked him heels over head and senseless, so that he had to be carried off from the field. This ugly way of hitting is the great trick of the French *savate*, which is not commonly thought able to stand its ground against English pugilistic science. — These are old recollections, with not much to recommend them, except perhaps, a dash of life, which may be worth a little something.

The young Marylander brought them all up you may remember. He recalled to my mind those two splendid pieces of vitality I told you of. Both have been long dead. How often we see these great red flaring flambeaux of life blown out, as it were, by a puff of wind,— and the little, single-wicked night-lamp of being, which some white-faced and attenuated invalid shades with trembling fingers, flickering on while they go out one after another, until its glimmer is all that is left to us of the generation it belonged to!

I told you that I was perfectly sure, beforehand, we should find some pleasing girlish or womanly shape to fill the blank at our table and match the dark-haired youth at the upper corner.

There she sits, at the very opposite corner, just as far off as accident could put her from this handsome fellow, by whose side she ought, of course, to be sitting. One of the "positive" blondes, as my friend, you may remember, used to call them. Tawny-haired, amber-eyed, full-throated, skin as white as a blanched almond. Looks dreamy to me, not self-conscious, though a black ribbon round her neck sets it off as a Marie-Antoinette's diamond-necklace could not do. So in her dress, there is a harmony of tints that looks as if an artist had run his eye over her and given a hint or two like the finishing touch to a picture. I can't help being struck with her, for she is at once rounded and fine in feature, looks calm, as blondes are apt to, and as if she might run wild, if she were trifled with.—It is just as I knew it would be,—and anybody can see that our young Marylander will be dead in love with her in a week.

Then if that little man would only turn out immensely rich and have the good-nature to die and leave them all his money, it would be as nice as a three-volume novel.

The Little Gentleman is in a flurry, I suspect, with the excitement of having such a charming neighbor next him. I judge so mainly by his silence and by a certain rapt and serious look on his face, as if he were thinking of something that had happened, or that might happen, or that ought to happen, — or how beautiful her young life looked, or how hardly Nature had dealt with him, or something which struck him silent, at any rate. I made several conversational openings for him, but he did not fire up as he often does. I even went so far as to indulge in a fling at the State House, which, as we all know, is in truth a very imposing structure, covering less ground than St. Peter's, but of similar general effect. The little man looked up, but did not reply to my taunt. He said to the young lady, however, that the State House was the Parthenon of our Acropolis, which seemed to please her, for she smiled, and he reddened a little, — so I thought. I don't think it right to watch persons who are the subjects of special infirmity, — but we all do it.

I see that they have crowded the chairs a little

at that end of the table, to make room for another new-comer of the lady sort. A well-mounted, middle-aged preparation, wearing her hair without a cap, — pretty wide in the parting, though, — contours vaguely hinted, — features very quiet, — says little as yet, but seems to keep her eye on the young lady, as if having some responsibility for her. ——

My record is a blank for some days after this. In the mean time I have contrived to make out the person and the story of our young lady, who, according to appearances, ought to furnish us a heroine for a boarding-house romance before a year is out. It is very curious that she should prove connected with a person many of us have heard of. Yet, curious as it is, I have been a hundred times struck with the circumstance that the most remote facts are constantly striking each other; just as vessels starting from ports thousands of miles apart pass close to each other in the naked breadth of the ocean, nay, sometimes even touch, in the dark, with a crack of timbers, a gurgling of water, a cry of startled sleepers, — a cry mysteriously echoed in warning dreams, as the wife of some Gloucester fisherman, some coasting skipper, wakes with a shriek, calls the name of her husband, and sinks back to uneasy slumbers upon her lonely pillow, — a widow.

Oh, these mysterious meetings! Leaving all the vague, waste, endless spaces of the washing desert, the ocean-steamer and the fishing-smack sail straight towards each other as if they ran in grooves ploughed for them in the waters from the beginning of creation! Not only things and events, but our own thoughts, are so full of these surprises, that, if there were a reader in my parish who did not recognize the familiar occurrence of what I am now going to mention, I should think it a case for the missionaries of the Society for the Propagation of Intelligence among the Comfortable Classes.

There are about as many twins in the births of thought as of children. For the first time in your lives you learn some fact or come across some idea. Within an hour, a day, a week, that same fact or idea strikes you from another quarter. It seems as if it had passed into space and bounded back upon you as an echo from the blank wall that shuts in the world of thought. Yet no possible connection exists between the two channels by which the thought or the fact arrived. Let me give an infinitesimal illustration.

One of the Boys mentioned, the other evening, in the course of a very pleasant poem he read us, a little trick of the Commons table-boarders, which I, nourished at the parental board, had never heard of. Young fellows being always hungry —— Allow me to stop dead-short, in order to utter an aphorism which has been forming itself in one of the blank interior spaces of my intelligence, like a crystal in the cavity of a geode.

Aphorism by the Professor.

In order to know whether a human being is young or old, offer it food of different kinds at short intervals. If young, it will eat anything at any hour of the day or night. If old, it observes stated periods, and you might as well attempt to regulate the time of high-water to suit a fishing-party as to change these periods.

The crucial experiment is this. Offer a bulky and boggy bun to the suspected individual just ten minutes before dinner. If this is eagerly accepted and devoured, the fact of youth is established. If the subject of the question starts back and expresses surprise and incredulity, as if you could not possibly be in earnest, the fact of maturity is no less clear.

——Excuse me,—I return to my story of the Commons-table.—Young fellows being always hungry, and tea and dry toast being the meagre fare of the evening meal, it was a trick of some of the Boys to impale a slice of meat upon a fork, at dinner-time, and stick the fork holding it beneath the table, so that they could get it at tea-time. The dragons that guarded this table of the

Hesperides found out the trick at last, and kept a sharp look-out for missing forks; — they knew where to find one, if it was not in its place. — Now the odd thing was, that, after waiting so many years to hear of this college trick, I should hear it mentioned *a second time* within the same twenty-four hours by a college youth of the present generation. Strange, but true. And so it has happened to me and to every person, often and often, to be hit in rapid succession by these twinned facts or thoughts, as if they were linked like chain-shot.

I was going to leave the simple reader to wonder over this, taking it as an unexplained marvel. I think, however, I will turn over a furrow of subsoil in it. — The explanation is, of course, that in a great many thoughts there must be a few coincidences, and these instantly arrest our attention. Now we shall probably never have the least idea of the enormous number of impressions which pass through our consciousness, until in some future life we see the photographic record of our thoughts and the stereoscopic picture of our actions. There go more pieces to make up a conscious life or a living body than you think for. Why, some of you were surprised when a friend of mine told you there were fifty-eight separate pieces in a fiddle. How many "swimming glands" — solid, organized, regularly formed, rounded disks, taking an active part in all your vital processes, part and parcel, each one of them, of your corporeal being — do you suppose are whirled along, like pebbles in a stream, with the blood which warms your frame and colors your cheeks? — A noted German physiologist spread out a minute drop of blood, under the microscope, in narrow streaks, and counted the globules, and then made a calculation. The counting by the micrometer took him *a week.* — You have, my full-grown friend, of these little couriers in crimson or scarlet livery, running on your vital errands day and night as long as you live, sixty-five billions, five hundred and seventy thousand millions. Errors excepted. — Did I hear some gentleman say, "Doubted?" — I am the Professor. I sit in my chair with a petard under it that will blow me through the sky-light of my lecture-room, if I do not know what I am talking about and whom I am quoting.

Now, my dear friends, who are putting your hands to your foreheads, and saying to yourselves that you feel a little confused, as if you had been waltzing until things began to whirl slightly round you, is it possible that you do not clearly apprehend the exact connection of all that I have been saying, and its bearing on what is now to come? Listen, then. The number of these living elements in our bodies illustrates the incalculable multitude of our thoughts; the number of our thoughts accounts for those frequent coincidences spoken of; these coincidences in the world of thought illustrate those which we constantly observe in the world of outward events, of which the presence of the young girl now at our table, and proving to be the daughter of an old acquaintance some of us may remember, is the special example which led me through this labyrinth of reflections, and finally lands me at the commencement of this young girl's story, which, as I said, I have found the time and felt the interest to learn something of, and which I think I can tell without wronging the unconscious subject of my brief delineation.

IRIS.

You remember, perhaps, in some papers published awhile ago, an odd poem written by an old Latin tutor? He brought up at the verb *amo*, I love, as all of us do, and by and by Nature opened her great living dictionary for him at the word *filia*, a daughter. The poor man was greatly perplexed in choosing a name for her. *Lucretia* and *Virginia* were the first that he thought of; but then came up those pictured stories of Titus Livius, which he could never read without crying, though he had read them a hundred times.

— Lucretia sending for her husband and her

father, each to bring one friend with him, and awaiting them in her chamber. To them her wrongs briefly. Let them see to the wretch, — she will take care of herself. Then the hidden knife flashes out and sinks into her heart. She slides from her seat, and falls dying. "Her husband and her father cry aloud." — No, — not Lucretia.

— Virginius, — a brown old soldier, father of a nice girl. She engaged to a very promising young man. Decemvir Appius takes a violent fancy to her, — must have her at any rate. Hires a lawyer to present the arguments in favor of the view that she was another man's daughter. There used to be lawyers in Rome that would do such things. — All right. There are two sides to everything. *Audi alteram partem.* The legal gentleman has no opinion, — he only states the evidence. — A doubtful case. Let the young lady be under the protection of the Honorable Decemvir until it can be looked up thoroughly. — Father thinks it best, on the whole, to give in. Will explain the matter, if the young lady and her maid will step this way. *That* is the explanation, — a stab with a butcher's knife, snatched from a stall, meant for other lambs than this poor bleeding Virginia!

The old man thought over the story. Then he must have one look at the original. So he took down the first volume and read it over. When he came to that part where it tells how the young gentleman she was engaged to and a friend of his took up the poor girl's bloodless shape and carried it through the street, and how all the women followed, wailing, and asking if that was what their daughters were coming to,—if that was what they were to get for being good girls,—he melted down into his accustomed tears of pity and grief, and, through them all, of delight at the charming Latin of the narrative. But it was impossible to call his child Virginia. He could never look at her without thinking she had a knife sticking in her bosom.

Dido would be a good name, and a fresh one. She was a queen, and the founder of a great city. Her story had been immortalized by the greatest of poets,—for the old Latin tutor clove to "Virgilius Maro," as he called him, as closely as ever Dante did in his memorable journey. So he took down his Virgil,—it was the smooth-leafed, open-lettered quarto of Baskerville,—and began reading the loves and mishaps of Dido. It wouldn't do. A lady who had not learned discretion by experience, and came to an evil end. He shook his head, as he sadly repeated,

"——misera ante diem, subitoque accensa furore;"

but when he came to the lines,

"Ergo Iris croceis per cœlum roscida pennis
Mille trahens varios adverso Sole colores,"

he jumped up with a great exclamation, which the particular recording angel who heard it pretended not to understand, or it might have gone hard with the Latin tutor some time or other.

"*Iris* shall be her name!"—he said. So her name was Iris.

—— The natural end of a tutor is to perish by starvation. It is only a question of time, just as with the burning of college libraries. These all burn up sooner or later, provided they are not housed in brick or stone and iron. I don't mean that you will see in the registry of deaths that this or that particular tutor died of well-marked, uncomplicated starvation. They *may*, even, in extreme cases, be carried off by a thin, watery kind of apoplexy, which sounds very well in the returns, but means little to those who know that it is only debility settling on the head. Generally, however, they fade and waste away under various pretexts,—calling it dyspepsia, consumption, and so on, to put a decent appearance upon the case and keep up the credit of the family and the institution where they have passed through the successive stages of inanition.

In some cases it takes a great many years to kill a tutor by the process in question. You see, they do get food and clothes and fuel, in appreciable quantities, such as they are. You will ever notice rows of books in their rooms, and a picture or two, — things that look as if they had surplus money; but these superfluities are the *water of crystallization* to scholars, and you can never get them away till the poor fellows effloresce into dust. Do not be deceived. The tutor breakfasts on coffee made of beans, edulcorated with milk watered to the verge of transparency; his mutton is tough and elastic, up to the moment when it becomes tired out and tasteless; his coal is a sullen, sulphurous anthracite, which rusts into ashes, rather than burns, in the shallow grate; his flimsy broadcloth is too thin for winter and too thick for summer. The greedy lungs of fifty hot-blooded boys suck the oxygen from the air he breathes in his recitation-room. In short, he undergoes a process of gentle and gradual starvation.

—— The mother of little Iris was not called Electra, like hers of the old story, neither was her grandfather Oceanus. Her blood-name, which she gave away with her heart to the Latin tutor, was a plain old English one, and her water-name was Hannah, beautiful as recalling the mother of Samuel, and admirable as reading equally well from the initial letter forwards and from the terminal letter backwards. The poor lady, seated with her companion at the chess-board of matrimony, had but just pushed forward her one little white pawn upon an empty square, when the Black Knight, that cares nothing for castles or kings or queens, swooped down upon her and swept her from the larger board of life.

The old Latin tutor put a modest blue stone at the head of his late companion, with her name and age and *Eheu!* upon it, — a smaller one at her feet, with initials; and left her by herself, to be rained and snowed on, — which is a hard thing to do for those whom we have cherished tenderly.

About the time that the lichens, falling on the stone, like drops of water, had spread into fair, round rosettes, the tutor had starved into a slight cough. Then he began to draw the buckle of his black pantaloons a little tighter, and took in another reef in his never-ample waistcoat. His temples got a little hollow, and the contrasts of color in his cheeks more vivid than of old. After a while his walks fatigued him, and he was tired, and breathed hard after going up a flight or two of stairs. Then came on other marks of inward trouble and general waste, which he spoke of to his physician as peculiar, and doubtless owing to accidental causes; to all which the doctor listened with deference, as if it had not been the old story that one in five or six of mankind in temperate climates tells, or has told for him, as if it were something new. As the doctor went out, he said to himself,—"On the rail at last. Accommodation train. A good many stops, but will get to the station by and by." So the doctor wrote a recipe with the astrological sign of Jupiter before it, (just as your own physician does, inestimable reader, as you will see, if you look at his next prescription,) and departed, saying he would look in occasionally. After this, the Latin tutor began the usual course of "getting better," until he got so much better that his face was very sharp, and when he smiled, three crescent lines showed at each side of his lips, and when he spoke, it was in a muffled whisper, and the white of his eye glistened as pearly as the purest porcelain,—so much better, that he hoped—by spring—he—— might be able—to—attend———to his class again.—But he was recommended not to expose himself, and so kept his chamber, and occasionally, not having anything to do, his bed. The unmarried sister with whom he lived took care of him; and the child, now old enough to be manageable, and even useful in trifling offices, sat in the chamber, or played about.

Things could not go on so forever, of course. One morning his face was sunken and his hands were very, very cold. He was "better," he whispered, but sadly and faintly. After a while he grew restless and seemed a little wandering. His mind ran on his classics, and fell back on the Latin grammar.

"Iris!" he said,—"*filiola mea!*"—The child knew this meant *my dear little daughter* as well as if it had been English.—"Rainbow!"—for he would translate her name at times,—"come to me,—*veni*"—and his lips went on automatically, and murmured, "*vel venito!*"—The child came and sat by his bedside and took his hand, which she could not warm, but which shot its rays of cold all through her slender frame. But there she sat, looking steadily at him. Presently he opened his lips feebly, and whispered, "*Moribundus.*" She did not know what that meant, but she saw that there was something new and sad. So she began to cry; but presently remembering an old book that seemed to comfort him at times, got up and brought a Bible in the Latin version, called the Vulgate. "Open it," he said,—"I will read,—*segnius irritant,*—don't put the light out, —ah! *hæret lateri,*—I am going,—*vale, vale, vale,* good-bye, good-bye,—the Lord take care of my child!—*Domine, audi*——*vel audito!*" His face whitened suddenly, and he lay still, with open eyes and mouth. He had taken his last degree.

——Little Miss Iris could not be said to begin life with a very brilliant rainbow over her, in a worldly point of view. A limited wardrobe of man's attire, such as poor tutors wear,— a few good books, principally classics,— a print or two, and a plaster model of the Pantheon, with some pieces of furniture which had seen service,— these, and a child's heart full of tearful recollections and strange doubts and questions, alternating with the cheap pleasures which are the anodynes of childish grief; such were the treasures she inherited.— No,— I forgot. With that kindly sentiment which all of us feel for old men's first children,— frost-flowers of the early winter season,— the old tutor's students had remembered him at a time when he was laughing and crying with his new parental emotions, and running to the side of the plain crib in which his *alter ego*, as he used to say, was swinging, to hang over the little heap of stirring clothes, from which looked the minute, red, downy, still, round face, with unfixed eyes and working lips,— in that unearthly gravity which has never yet been broken by a smile, and which gives to the earliest moon-year or two of an infant's life the character of a *first old age*, to counterpoise that *second childhood* which there is one chance in a dozen it may reach by and by. The boys had remembered the old man and young father at that tender period of his hard, dry life. There came to him a fair, silver goblet, embossed with classical figures, and bearing on a shield the graven words, *Ex dono pupillorum.* The handle on its side showed what use the boys had meant it for, and a kind letter in it, written with the best of feeling, in the worst of Latin, pointed delicately to its destination. Out of this silver vessel, after a long, desperate, strangling cry, which marked her first great lesson in the realities of life, the child took the blue milk, such as poor tutors and their children get, tempered with water, and sweetened a little, so as to bring it nearer the standard established by the touching indulgence and partiality of Nature,—who has mingled an extra allowance of sugar in the blameless food of the child at its mother's breast, as compared with that of its infant brothers and sisters of the bovine race.

But a willow will grow in baked sand wet with rain-water. An air-plant will grow by feeding on the winds. Nay, those huge forests that overspread great continents have built themselves up mainly from the air-currents with which they are always battling. The oak is but a foliated atmospheric crystal deposited from the aërial ocean that holds the future vegetable world in solution. The storm that tears its leaves has paid tribute to its strength, and it breasts the tornado clad in the spoils of a hundred hurricanes.

Poor little Iris! What had she in common with the great oak in the shadow of which we are losing sight of her?—She lived and grew like that, — this was all. The blue milk ran into her veins and filled them with thin, pure blood. Her skin was fair, with a faint tinge, such as the white rosebud shows before it opens. The doctor who had attended her father was afraid her aunt would hardly be able to "raise" her, — "delicate child," — hoped she was not consumptive, — thought there was a fair chance she would take after her father.

A very forlorn-looking person, dressed in black, with a white neckcloth, sent her a memoir of a child who died at the age of two years and eleven months, after having fully indorsed all the doctrines of the particular persuasion to which he not only belonged himself, but thought it very shameful that everybody else did not belong. What with foreboding looks and dreary death-bed stories, it was a wonder the child made out to live through it. It saddened her early years, of course, — it distressed her tender soul with thoughts which, as they cannot be fully taken in, should be sparingly used as instruments of torture to break down the natural cheerfulness of a healthy child, or, what is infinitely worse, to cheat a dying one out of the kind illusions with which the Father of All has strewed its downward path.

The child would have died, no doubt, and, if properly managed, might have added another to the long catalogue of wasting children who have been as cruelly played upon by spiritual physiologists, often with the best intentions, as ever the subject of a rare disease by the curious students of science.

Fortunately for her, however, a wise instinct had guided the late Latin tutor in the selection of the partner of his life, and the future mother of his child. The deceased tutoress was a tranquil, smooth woman, easily nourished, as such people are,—a quality which is inestimable in a tutor's wife,—and so it happened that the daughter inherited enough vitality from the mother to live through childhood and infancy and fight her way towards womanhood, in spite of the tendencies she derived from her other parent.

——Two and two do not always make four, in this matter of hereditary descent of qualities. Sometimes they make three, and sometimes five. It seems as if the parental traits at one time showed separate, at another blended,—that occasionally the force of two natures is represented in the derivative one by a diagonal of greater value than either original line of living movement,—that sometimes there is a loss of vitality hardly to be accounted for, and again a forward impulse of variable intensity in some new and unforeseen direction.

So it was with this child. She had glanced off from her parental probabilities at an unexpected angle. Instead of taking to classical learning like her father, or sliding quietly into household duties like her mother, she broke out early in efforts that pointed in the direction of Art. As soon as she could hold a pencil she began to sketch outlines of objects round her with a certain air and spirit. Very extraordinary horses, but their legs looked as if they could move. Birds unknown to Audubon, yet flying, as it were, with a rush. Men with impossible legs, which did yet seem to have a vital connection with their most improbable bodies. By-and-by the doctor, on his beast,—an old man with a face looking as if Time had kneaded it like dough with his knuckles, with a rhubarb tint and flavor pervading himself and his sorrel horse and all their appurtenances. A dreadful old man! Be sure she did not forget those saddle-bags that held the detestable bottles out of which he used to shake those loathsome powders which, to virgin childish palates that find heaven in strawberries and peaches, are —— Well, I suppose I had better stop. Only she wished she was dead sometimes when she heard him coming. On the next leaf would figure the gentleman with the black coat and white cravat, as he looked when he came and entertained her with stories concerning the death of various little children about her age, to encourage her, as that wicked Mr. Arouet said about shooting Admiral Byng. Then she would take her pencil, and with a few scratches there would be the outline of a child, in which you might notice how one sudden sweep gave the chubby cheek, and two dots darted at the paper looked like real eyes.

By-and-by she went to school, and caricatured the schoolmaster on the leaves of her grammars and geographies, and drew the faces of her companions, and, from time to time, heads and figures from her fancy, with large eyes, far apart, like those of Raffaelle's mothers and children, sometimes with wild floating hair, and then with wings and heads thrown back in ecstacy. This was at about twelve years old, as the dates of these drawings show, and, therefore, three or four years before she came among us. Soon after this time, the ideal figures began to take the place of portraits and caricatures, and a new feature appeared in her drawing-books in the form of fragments of verse and short poems.

It was dull work, of course, for such a young girl to live with an old spinster and go to a village school. Her books bore testimony to this; for there was a look of sadness in the faces she drew, and a sense of weariness and longing for some imaginary conditions of blessedness or other, which began to be painful. She might have gone through this flowering of the soul, and, casting her petals, subsided into a sober, human berry but for the intervention of friendly assistance and counsel.

In the town where she lived was a lady of honorable condition, somewhat past middle age, who was possessed of pretty ample means, of cultivated tastes, of excellent principles, of exemplary character, and of more than common accomplishments. The gentleman in black broadcloth and white neckerchief only echoed the common voice about her, when he called her, after enjoying, beneath her hospitable roof, an excellent cup of tea, with certain elegancies and luxuries he was unaccustomed to, "The Model of all the Virtues."

She deserved this title as well as almost any woman. She did really bristle with moral excellences. Mention any good thing she had not done; I should like to see you try! There was no handle of weakness to take hold of her by; she was as unseizable, except in her totality, as a billiard-ball; and on the broad, green, terrestrial table, where she had been knocked about, like all of us, by the cue of Fortune, she glanced from every human contact, and "caromed" from one relation to another, and rebounded from the stuffed cushion of temptation, with such exact and perfect angular movements, that the Enemy's corps of Reporters had long given up taking notes of her conduct, as there was no chance for their master.

What an admirable person for the patroness and

directress of a slightly self-willed child, with the lightning zigzag line of genius running like a glittering vein through the marble whiteness of her virgin nature! One of the lady-patroness's peculiar virtues was calmness. She was resolute and strenuous, but still. You could depend on her for every duty; she was as true as steel. She was kind-hearted and serviceable in all the relations of life. She had more sense, more knowledge, more conversation, as well as more goodness, than all the partners you have waltzed with this winter put together.

Yet no man was known to have loved her, or even to have offered himself to her in marriage. It was a great wonder. I am very anxious to vindicate my character as a philosopher and an observer of Nature by accounting for this apparently extraordinary fact.

You may remember certain persons who have the misfortune of presenting to the friends whom they meet a cold, damp hand. There are states of mind in which a contact of this kind has a depressing effect on the vital powers that makes us insensible to all the virtues and graces of the proprietor of one of these life-absorbing organs. When they touch us, virtue passes out of us, and we feel as if our electricity had been drained by a powerful negative battery, carried about by an overgrown human torpedo.

"The Model of all the Virtues" had a pair of searching eyes as clear as Wenham ice; but they were slower to melt than that fickle jewelry. Her features disordered themselves slightly at times in a surface-smile, but never broke loose from their corners and indulged in the riotous tumult of a laugh,—which, I take it, is the mob-law of the features,—and propriety the magistrate who reads the riot-act. She carried the brimming cup of her inestimable virtues with a cautious, steady hand, and an eye always on them, to see that they did not spill. Then she was an admirable judge of character. Her mind was a perfect laboratory of tests and reagents; every syllable you put into breath went into her intellectual eudiometer, and all your thoughts were recorded on litmus-paper. I think there has rarely been a more admirable woman. Of course, Miss Iris was immensely and passionately attached to her.—— Well,—these are two highly oxygenated adverbs,—grateful,—suppose we say,—yes,—grateful, dutiful, obedient to her wishes for the most part,—perhaps not quite up to the concert pitch of such a perfect orchestra of the virtues.

We must have a weak spot or two in a character before we can love it much. People that do not laugh or cry, or take more of anything than is good for them, or use anything but dictionary-words, are admirable subjects for biographies. But we don't always care most for those flat-pattern flowers that press best in the herbarium.

This immaculate woman, — why couldn't she have a fault or two? Isn't there any old whisper which will tarnish that wearisome aureole of saintly perfection? Doesn't she carry a lump of opium in her pocket? Isn't her cologne-bottle replenished oftener than its legitimate use would require? It would be such a comfort!

Not for the world would a young creature like Iris have let such words escape her, or such thoughts pass through her mind. Whether at the bottom of her soul lies any uneasy consciousness of an oppressive presence, it is hard to say, until we know more about her. Iris sits between the little gentleman and the "Model of all the Virtues," as the black-coated personage called her. — I will watch them all.

—— Here I stop for the present. What the Professor said has had to make way this time for what he saw and heard.

—— And now you may read these lines, which were written for gentle souls who love music, and read in even tones, and, perhaps, with something like a smile upon the reader's lips, at a meeting where these musical friends had gathered. Whether they were written with smiles or not, you can guess better after you have read them.

THE OPENING OF THE PIANO.

In the little southern parlor of the house you may have seen
With the gambrel-roof, and the gable looking westward to the green,
At the side toward the sunset, with the window on its right,
Stood the London-made piano I am dreaming of to-night.

Ah me! how I remember the evening when it came!
What a cry of eager voices, what a group of cheeks in flame,
When the wondrous box was opened that had come from over seas,
With its smell of mastic-varnish and its flash of ivory keys!

Then the children all grew fretful in the restlessness of joy,
For the boy would push his sister, and the sister crowd the boy,
Till the father asked for quiet in his grave paternal way,
But the mother hushed the tumult with the words, "Now, Mary, play."

For the dear soul knew that music was a very sovereign balm;
She had sprinkled it over Sorrow and seen its brow grow calm,
In the days of slender harpsichords with tapping tinkling quills,
Or carolling to her spinet with its thin metallic thrills.

So Mary, the household minstrel, who always loved to please,
Sat down to the new "Clementi," and struck the glittering keys.

Hushed were the children's voices, and every eye grew dim,
As, floating from lip and finger, arose the "Vesper Hymn."

—Catharine, child of a neighbor, curly and rosy-red,
(Wedded since, and a widow,—something like ten years dead,)
Hearing a gush of music such as none before,
Steals from her mother's chamber and peeps at the open door.

Just as the "Jubilate" in threaded whisper dies,
—"Open it! open it, lady!" the little maiden cries,
(For she thought 'twas a singing creature caged in a box she heard,)
"Open it! open it, lady! and let me see the *bird!*"

IV.

I DON'T know whether our literary or professional people are more amiable than they are in other places, but certainly quarrelling is out of fashion among them. This could never be, if they were in the habit of secret anonymous puffing of each other. That is the kind of underground machinery, which manufactures false reputations and genuine hatreds. On the other hand, I should like to know if we are not at liberty to have a good time together. and say the pleasantest things we can think of to each other, when any of us reaches his thirtieth or fortieth or fiftieth or eightieth birthday.

We don't have "scenes," I warrant you, on these occasions. No "surprise" parties! You understand these, of course. In the rural districts, where scenic tragedy and melodrama cannot be had, as in the city, at the expense of a quarter and a white pocket-handkerchief, emotional excitement has to be sought in the dramas of real life. Christenings, weddings, and funerals, especially the latter, are the main dependence; but babies, brides, and deceased citizens cannot be had at a day's notice. Now, then, for a surprise-party!

A bag of flour, a barrel of potatoes, some strings of onions, a basket of apples, a big cake and many little cakes, a jug of lemonade, a purse stuffed with bills of the more modest denominations, may, perhaps, do well enough for the properties in one of these private theatrical exhibitions. The minister of the parish, a tender-hearted, quiet, hard-working man, living on a small salary, with many children, sometimes pinched to feed and clothe them, praying fervently every day to be blest in his "basket and store," but sometimes fearing he asks amiss, to judge by the small returns, has the first *rôle,*—not, however, by his own choice, but forced upon him. The minister's wife, a sharp-eyed, unsentimental body, is first lady; the remaining parts by the rest of the family. If they only had a playbill, it would run thus: —

ON TUESDAY NEXT

WILL BE PRESENTED

THE AFFECTING SCENE

CALLED

THE SURPRISE-PARTY,

OR

THE OVERCOME FAMILY;

WITH THE FOLLOWING STRONG CAST OF CHARACTERS:

The Rev. Mr. Overcome, by the Clergyman of this Parish.

Mrs. Overcome, by his estimable lady.

Masters Matthew, Mark, Luke, and John Overcome,

Misses Dorcas, Tabitha, Rachel, and Hannah Overcome, by their interesting children.

Peggy, by the female help.

The poor man is really grateful; — it is a most welcome and unexpected relief. He tries to express his thanks, — his voice falters, — he chokes, — and bursts into tears. *That* is the great effect of the evening. The sharp-sighted lady cries a little with one eye, and counts the strings of onions, and the rest of the things, with the other. The children stand ready for a spring at the apples. The female help weeps after the noisy fashion of untutored handmaids.

Now this is all very well as charity, but do let the kind visitors remember they get their money's worth. If you pay a quarter for *dry crying*, done by a second-rate actor, how much ought you to pay for real hot, wet tears, out of the honest eyes of a gentleman who is not acting, but sobbing in earnest?

All I meant to say, when I began, was, that this was *not* a surprise-party where I read these few lines that follow:—

We will not speak of years to-night;
  For what have years to bring,
But larger floods of love and light
  And sweeter songs to sing?

We will not drown in wordy praise
  The kindly thoughts that rise;
If friendship owns one tender phrase,
  He reads it in our eyes.

We need not waste our schoolboy art
  To gild this notch of time;
Forgive me, if my wayward heart
  Has throbbed in artless rhyme.

Enough for him the silent grasp
  That knits us hand in hand,

And he the bracelet's radiant clasp
That locks our circling band.

Strength to his hours of manly toil!
Peace to his starlit dreams!
Who loves alike the furrowed soil,
The music-haunted streams!

Sweet smiles to keep forever bright
The sunshine on his lips,
And faith, that sees the ring of light
Round Nature's last eclipse!

— One of our boarders has been talking in such strong language that I am almost afraid to report it. However, as he seems to be really honest and is so very sincere in his local prejudices, I don't believe anybody will be very angry with him.

It is here, Sir! right here! — said the little deformed gentleman, — in this old new city of Boston, — this remote provincial corner of a provincial nation, that the Battle of the Standard is fighting, and was fighting before we were born, and will be fighting when we are dead and gone, — please God! The *battle* goes on everywhere throughout civilization; but here, here, here! is the broad white flag flying which proclaims, first of all, peace and good-will to men, and, next to that, the absolute, unconditional spiritual liberty of each individual immortal soul! The three-hilled city against the seven-hilled city! That is it, Sir,—nothing less than that; and if you know what that means, I don't think you'll ask for anything more. I swear to you, Sir, I believe that these two centres of civilization are just exactly the two points that close the circuit in the battery of our planetary intelligence! And I believe there are spiritual eyes looking out from Uranus and unseen Neptune,—ay, Sir, from the systems of Sirius and Arcturus and Aldebaran, and as far as that faint stain of sprinkled worlds confluent in the distance that we call the nebula of Orion,—looking on, Sir, with what organs I know not, to see which are going to melt in that fiery fusion, the accidents and hindrances of humanity or man himself, Sir,—the stupendous abortion, the illustrious failure that he is, if the three-hilled city does not ride down and trample out the seven-hilled city!

—— Steam's up!—said the young man John, so called, in a low tone.—Three hundred and sixty-five tons to the square inch. Let him blow her off, or he'll bu'st his b'iler.

The divinity-student took it calmly, only whispering that he thought there was a little confusion of images between a galvanic battery and a charge of cavalry.

But the Koh-i-noor—the gentleman, you remember, with a very large *diamond* in his shirt-front — laughed his scornful laugh, and made as if to speak.

Sail in, Metropolis! — said that same young man John, by name. And then, in a lower tone, not meaning to be heard, — Now, then, Ma'am Allen!

But he *was* heard, — and the Koh-i-noor's face turned so white with rage, that his blue-black moustache and beard looked fearful, seen against it. He grinned with wrath, and caught at a tumbler, as if he would have thrown it or its contents at the speaker. The young Marylander fixed his clear, steady eye upon him, and laid his hand on his arm, carelessly almost, but the Jewel found it was held so that he could not move it. It was of no use. The youth was his master in muscle, and in that deadly Indian hug in which men wrestle with their eyes; — over in five seconds, but breaks one of their two backs, and is good for threescore years and ten; — one trial enough, — settles the whole matter, — just as when two feathered songsters of the barnyard, game and dunghill, come together, — after a jump or two at each other, and a few sharp kicks, there is the end of it; and it is, *Après vous, Monsieur*, with the beaten party in all the social relations for all the rest of his days.

I cannot philosophically account for the Koh-i-noor's wrath. For though a cosmetic is sold, bearing the name of the lady to whom reference was made by the young person John, yet, as it is publicly asserted in respectable prints that this cosmetic is *not a dye*, I see no reason why he should have felt offended by any suggestion that he was indebted to it or its authoress. I have no doubt that there are certain exceptional complexions to which the purple tinge, above alluded to, is natural. Nature is fertile in variety. I saw an albiness in London once, for sixpence, (including the inspection of a stuffed boa-constrictor,) who looked as if she had been boiled in milk. A young Hottentot of my acquaintance had his hair all in little pellets of the size of marrowfat peas. One of my own classmates has undergone a singular change of late years,—his hair losing its original tint, and getting a remarkable discolored look; and another has ceased to cultivate any hair at all over the vertex or crown of the head. So I am perfectly willing to believe that the purple-black of the Koh-i-noor's moustache and whiskers is constitutional and not pigmentary. But I can't think why he got so angry.

The intelligent reader will understand that all this pantomine of the threatened onslaught and its suppression passed so quickly that it was all over by the time the other end of the table found out there was a disturbance; just as a man chopping wood half a mile off may be seen resting on his axe at the instant you hear the last blów he struck. So you will please to observe that the Little Gentleman was not interrupted during the time implied by these *ex-post-facto* remarks of mine, but for some ten or fifteen seconds only.

He did not seem to mind the interruption at all, for he started again. The "Sir" of his harangue was no doubt addressed to myself more than anybody else, but he often uses it in discourse as if he were talking with some imaginary opponent.

—— America, Sir, — he exclaimed, — is the only place where man is full-grown!

He straightened himself up, as he spoke, standing on the top round of his high chair, I suppose, and so presented the larger part of his little figure to the view of the boarders.

It was next to impossible to keep from laughing. The commentary was so strange an illustration of the text!

I thought it was time to put in a word; for I have lived in foreign parts, and am more or less cosmopolitan.

I doubt if we have more practical freedom in America than they have in England, — I said. — An Englishman thinks as he likes in religion and politics. Mr. Martineau speculates as freely as ever Dr. Channing did, and Mr. Bright is as independent as Mr. Seward.

Sir,—said he,—it isn't what a man thinks or says, but when and where and to whom he thinks and says it. A man with a flint and steel striking sparks over a wet blanket is one thing, and striking them over a tinder-box is another. The free Englishman is born under protest; he lives and dies under protest,—a tolerated, but not a welcome fact. Is not *freethinker* a term of reproach in England? The same idea in the soul of an Englishman who struggled up to it and still holds it *antagonistically*, and in the soul of an American to whom it is congenital and spontaneous, and often unrecognized, except as an element blended with *all* his thoughts, a natural movement, like the drawing of his breath or the beating of his heart, is a very different thing. You may teach a quadruped to walk on his hind legs, but he is always wanting to be on all-fours. Nothing that can be taught a growing youth is like the atmospheric knowledge he breathes from his infancy upwards. The American baby sucks in freedom with the milk of the breast at which he hangs.

—— That's a good joke,—said the young fellow John,—considerin' it commonly belongs to a female Paddy.

I thought—I will not be certain—that the Little Gentleman winked, as if he had been hit somewhere—as I have no doubt Dr. Darwin did when the *wooden-spoon* suggestion upset his theory about why, etc. If he winked, however, he did not dodge.

A lively comment! — he said. — But Rome, in her great founder, sucked the blood of empire out of the dugs of a brute, Sir! The Milesian wet-nurse is only a convenient vessel through which the American infant gets the life-blood of this virgin soil, Sir, that is making man over again, on the sunset pattern! You don't think what we are doing and going to do here. Why, Sir, while commentators are bothering themselves with interpretation of prophecies, *we have got* the new heavens and the new earth over us and under us! Was there ever anything in Italy, I should like to know, like a Boston sunset?

—— This time there was a laugh, and the little man himself almost smiled.

Yes, — Boston sunsets; — perhaps they're as good in some other places, but I know 'em best here. Anyhow, the American skies are different from anything they see in the Old World. Yes, and the rocks are different, and the soil is different, and everything that comes out of the soil, from grass up to Indians, is different. And now that the provisional races are dying out ——

—— What do you mean by the *provisional* races, Sir? — said the divinity-student, interrupting him.

Why, the aboriginal bipeds, to be sure, — he answered, — the red-crayon sketch of humanity laid on the canvas before the colors for the real manhood were ready.

I hope they will come to something yet, — said the divinity-student.

Irreclaimable, Sir, — irreclaimable! — said the Little Gentleman. — Cheaper to breed white men than domesticate a nation of red ones. When you can get the bitter out of the partridge's thigh, you can make an enlightened commonwealth of Indians. A provisional race, Sir, — nothing more. Exhaled carbonic acid for the use of vegetation, kept down the bears and catamounts, enjoyed themselves in scalping and being scalped, and then passed away or are passing away, according to the programme.

Well, Sir, these races dying out, the white man has to acclimate himself. It takes him a good while; but he will come all right by-and-by, Sir, — as sound as a woodchuck, — as sound as a musquash!

A new nursery, Sir, with Lake Superior and Huron and all the rest of 'em for wash-basins! A new race, and a whole new world for the new-born human soul to work in! And Boston is the brain of it, and has been any time these hundred years! That 's all I claim for Boston, — that it is the thinking centre of the continent, and therefore of the planet.

—— And the grand emporium of modesty,— said the divinity-student, a little mischievously.

Oh, don't talk to me of modesty!—answered the Little Gentleman,—I'm past that! There isn't a thing that was ever said or done in Boston, from pitching the tea overboard to the last ecclesiastical lie it tore into tatters and flung into the dock, that wasn't thought very indelicate by some fool or tyrant or bigot, and all the entrails of commercial and spiritual conservatism are twisted into colics as often as this revolutionary brain of ours has a fit of thinking come over it.—No, Sir, —show me any other place that is, or was since the megalosaurus has died out, where wealth and social influence are so fairly divided between the stationary and the progressive classes! Show me any other place where every other drawing-room is not a chamber of the Inquisition, with papas and mammas for inquisitors,—and the cold shoulder, instead of the "dry pan and the gradual fire," the punishment of "heresy"!

—— We think *Baltimore* is a pretty civilized kind of a village,—said the young Marylander, good-naturedly.— But I suppose you can't forgive it for always keeping a little ahead of Boston in point of numbers,—tell the truth now. Are we not the centre of something?

Ah, indeed, to be sure you are. You are the gastronomic metropolis of the Union. Why don't you put a canvas-back duck on the top of the Washington column? Why don't you get that lady off from Battle Monument and plant a terrapin in her place? Why will you ask for other glories when you have soft crabs? No, Sir,—you live too well to think as hard as we do in Boston. Logic comes to us with the salt-fish of Cape Ann; rhetoric is born of the beans of Beverly; but *you* —if you open your mouths to speak, Nature stops them with a fat oyster, or offers a slice of the breast of your divine bird, and silences all your aspirations.

And what of Philadelphia?—said the Marylander.

Oh, Philadelphia?—Waterworks,—killed by the Croton and Cochituate;—Ben Franklin,—borrowed from Boston;—David Rittenhouse,—made an orrery;—Benjamin Rush,—made a medical system:—both interesting to antiquarians;—great Red-river raft of medical students,—spontaneous generation of professors to match;—more widely known through the Moyamensing hose-company, and the Wistar parties;—for geological section of social strata, go to *The Club*.—Good place to live in,—first-rate market,—tip-top peaches.—What do we know about Philadelphia, except that the engine-companies are always shooting each other?

And what do you say to Ne' York?—asked the Koh-i-noor.

A great city, Sir, — replied the Little Gentleman, — a very opulent, splendid city. A point of transit of much that is remarkable, and of permanence for much that is respectable. A great money-centre. San Francisco with the mines above-ground, — and some of 'em under the sidewalks. I have seen next to nothing *grandiose*, out of New York, in all our cities. It makes 'em all look paltry and petty. Has many elements of civilization. May stop where Venice did, though, for aught we know. — The order of its development is just this: — Wealth; architecture; upholstery; painting; sculpture. Printing, as a mechanical art, — just as Nicholas Jenson and the Aldi, who were scholars too, made Venice renowned for it. Journalism, which is the accident of business and crowded populations, in great perfection. Venice got as far as Titian and Paul Veronese and Tintoretto, — great colorists, mark you, magnificent on the flesh-and-blood side of Art, — but look over to Florence and see who lie in Santa Croce, and ask out of whose loins Dante sprung!

Oh, yes, to be sure, Venice built her Ducal Palace, and her Church of St. Mark, and her Casa d' Oro, and the rest of her golden houses; and Venice had great pictures and good music; and Venice had a Golden Book, in which all the large tax-payers had their names written; — but all that did not make Venice the brain of Italy.

I tell you what, Sir,—with all these magnificent appliances of civilization, it is time we began to hear something from the *jeunesse dorée* whose names are on the Golden Book of our sumptuous, splendid, marble-palaced Venice,—something in the higher walks of literature,—something in the councils of the nation. Plenty of Art, I grant you, Sir; now, then, for vast libraries, and for mighty scholars and thinkers and statesmen,—five for every Boston one, as the population is to ours,—*ten* to one more properly, in virtue of centralizing attraction as *the* alleged metropolis,—and not call our people provincials, and have to come begging to us to write the lives of Hendrik Hudson and Gouverneur Morris!

——The Little Gentleman was on his hobby, exalting his own city at the expense of every other place. I have my doubts if he had been in either of the cities he had been talking about. I was just going to say something to sober him down, if I could, when the young Marylander spoke up.

Come, now,—he said,—what's the use of these comparisons? Didn't I hear this gentleman saying, the other day, that every American owns all America? If you have really got more brains in Boston than other folks, as you seem to think, who hates you for it, except a pack of scribbling fools? If I like Broadway better than Washington Street, what then? I own them both, as much as anybody owns either. I am an American,— and wherever I look up and see the stars and stripes overhead, that is home to me!

He spoke, and looked up as if he heard the emblazoned folds crackling over him in the breeze. We all looked up involuntarily, as if we should see the national flag by so doing. The sight of the dingy ceiling and the gas-fixture depending therefrom dispelled the illusion.

Bravo! bravo!— said the venerable gentleman on the other side of the table.— Those are the sentiments of Washington's Farewell Address. Nothing better than that since the last chapter in Revelations. Five-and-forty years ago there used to be Washington societies, and little boys used to walk in processions, each little boy having a copy of the Address, bound in red, hung round his neck by a ribbon. Why don't they now? Why don't they now? I saw enough of hating each other in the old Federal times; now let's love each other, I say,— let's love each other, and not try to make it out that there isn't any place fit to live in except the one we happen to be born in.

It dwarfs the mind, I think,— said I,— to feed it on any localism. The full stature of manhood is shrivelled ——

The color burst up into my cheeks. What was I saying,— I, who would not for the world have pained our unfortunate little boarder by an allu sion?

I will go, — he said, — and made a movement with his left arm to let himself down from his high chair.

No, — no, — he doesn't mean it, — you must not go, — said a kind voice next him; and a soft, white hand was laid upon his arm.

Iris, my dear! — exclaimed another voice, as of a female, in accents that might be considered a strong atmospheric solution of duty with very little flavor of grace.

She did not move for this address, and there was a *tableau* that lasted some seconds. For the young girl, in the glory of half-blown womanhood, and the dwarf, the cripple, the misshapen little creature covered with Nature's insults, looked straight into each other's eyes.

Perhaps no handsome young woman had ever looked at him so in his life. Certainly the young girl never had looked into eyes that reached into her soul as these did. It was not that they were in themselves supernaturally bright, — but there was the sad fire in them that flames up from the soul of one who looks on the beauty of woman without hope, but, alas! not without emotion. To him it seemed as if those amber gates had been translucent as the brown water of a mountain-brook, and through them he had seen dimly into a virgin wilderness, only waiting for the sunrise of a great passion for all its buds to blow and all its bowers to ring with melody.

That is my image, of course,—not his. It was not a simile that was in his mind, or is in anybody's at such a moment,—it was a pang of wordless passion, and then a silent, inward moan.

A lady's wish,—he said, with a certain gallantry of manner,—makes slaves of us all.—And Nature, who is kind to all her children, and never leaves the smallest and saddest of all her human failures without one little comfit of self-love at the bottom of his poor ragged pocket,—Nature suggested to him that he had turned his sentence well; and he fell into a reverie, in which the old thoughts that were always hovering just outside the doors guarded by Common Sense, and watching for a chance to squeeze in, knowing perfectly well they would be ignominiously kicked out again as soon as Common Sense saw them, flocked in pellmell,—misty, fragmentary, vague, half-ashamed of themselves, but still shouldering up against his inner consciousness till it warmed with their contact:—John Wilkes's—the ugliest man's in England—saying, that with half-an-hour's start he would cut out the handsomest man in all the land in any woman's good graces; Cadenus—old and savage—leading captive Stella and Vanessa; and then the stray line of a ballad, — "And a winning tongue had he," — as much as to say, it isn't looks, after all, but cunning words, that win our Eves over, — just as of old, when it was the worst-looking brute of the lot that got our grandmother to listen to his stuff, and so did the mischief.

Ah, dear me! We rehearse the part of Hercules with his club, subjugating man and woman in our fancy, the first by the weight of it, and the second by our handling of it, — we rehearse it, I say, by our own hearth-stones, with the *cold* poker as our club, and the exercise is easy. But when we come to real life, the poker is *in the fire*, and, ten to one, if we would grasp it, we find it too hot to hold; — lucky for us, if it is not white-hot, and we do not have to leave the skin of our hands sticking to it when we fling it down or drop it with a loud or silent cry!

—— I am frightened when I find into what a labyrinth of human character and feeling I am winding. I meant to tell my thoughts, and to throw in a few studies of manner and costume as they pictured themselves for me from day to day. Chance has thrown together at the table with me a number of persons who are worth studying, and I mean not only to look on them, but, if I can, through them. You can get any man's or woman's secret, whose sphere is circumscribed by your own, if you will only look patiently on them long enough. Nature is always applying her re-agents to character, if you will take the pains to watch her. Our studies of character, to change the image, are very much like the surveyor's triangulation of a geographical province We get a base-line in organization, always; then we get an angle by sighting some distant object to which the passions or aspirations of the subject of our observation are tending; then another; — and so we construct our first triangle. Once fix a man's ideals, and for the most part the rest is easy. *A* wants to die worth half a million. Good. *B* (female) wants to catch him, — and outlive him. All right. Minor details at our leisure.

What is it, of all your experiences, of all your thoughts, of all your misdoings, that lies at the very bottom of the great heap of acts of consciousness which make up your past life? What should you most dislike to tell your nearest friend? — Be so good as to pause for a brief space, and shut the volume you hold with your finger between the pages. —— Oh, that is it!

What a confessional I have been sitting at, with the inward ear of my soul open, as the multitudinous whisper of my involuntary confidants came back to me like the reduplicated echo of a cry among the craggy hills!

At the house of a friend where I once passed the night was one of those stately upright cabinet-desks and cases of drawers which were not rare in prosperous families during the last century. It had held the clothes and the books and the papers of generation after generation. The hands that opened its drawers had grown withered, shrivelled, and at last been folded in death. The children that played with the lower handles had got tall enough to open the desk, — to reach the upper shelves behind the folding-doors, — grown bent after a while, — and then followed those who had gone before, and left the old cabinet to be ransacked by a new generation.

A boy of ten or twelve was looking at it a few years ago, and, being a quick-witted fellow, saw that all the space was not accounted for by the smaller drawers in the part beneath the lid of the desk. Prying about with busy eyes and fingers, he at length came upon a spring, on pressing which, a secret drawer flew from its hiding-place. It had never been opened but by the maker. The mahogany shavings and dust were lying in it as when the artisan closed it, — and when I saw it, it was as fresh as if that day finished.

Is there not one little drawer in your soul, my sweet reader, which no hand but yours has ever opened, and which none that have known you seem to have suspected? What does it hold? — A sin? — I hope not.

What a strange thing an old dead sin laid

away in a secret drawer of the soul is! Must it some time or other be moistened with tears, until it comes to life again and begins to stir in our consciousness,—as the dry wheel-animalcule, looking like a grain of dust, becomes alive, if it is wet with a drop of water?

Or is it a passion? There are plenty of withered men and women walking about the streets who have the secret drawer in their hearts, which, if it were opened, would show as fresh as it was when they were in the flush of youth and its first trembling emotions. What it held will, perhaps, never be known, until they are dead and gone, and some curious eye lights on an old yellow letter with the fossil footprints of the extinct passion trodden thick all over it.

There is not a boarder at our table, I firmly believe, excepting the young girl, who has not a story of the heart to tell, if one could only get the secret drawer open. Even this arid female, whose armor of black bombazine looks stronger against the shafts of love than any cuirass of triple brass, has had her sentimental history, if I am not mistaken. I will tell you my reason for suspecting it.

Like many other old women, she shows a great nervousness and restlessness whenever I venture to express any opinion upon a class of subjects which can hardly be said to belong to any man or set of men as their strictly private property,—not even to the clergy, or the newspapers commonly called "religious." Now, although it would be a great luxury to me to obtain my opinions by contract, ready-made, from a professional man, and although I have a constitutional kindly feeling to all sorts of good people which would make me happy to agree with all their beliefs, if that were possible, still I must have an idea, now and then, as to the meaning of life; and though the only condition of peace in this world is to have no ideas, or, at least, not to express them, with reference to such subjects, I can't afford to pay quite so much as that even for peace.

I find that there is a very prevalent opinion among the dwellers on the shores of Sir Isaac Newton's Ocean of Truth, that *salt fish*, which have been taken from it a good while ago, split open, cured and dried, are the only proper and allowable food for reasonable people. I maintain, on the other hand, that there are a number of live fish still swimming in it, and that every one of us has a right to see if he cannot catch some of them. Sometimes I please myself with the idea that I have landed an actual living fish, small, perhaps, but with rosy gills and silvery scales. Then I find the consumers of nothing but the salted and dried article insist that it is poisonous, simply because it is alive, and cry out to people not to touch it. I have not found, however, that people mind them much.

The poor boarder in bombazine is my dynamometer. I try every questionable proposition on her. If she winces, I must be prepared for an outcry from the other old women. I frightened her, the other day, by saying that *faith, as an intellectual state, was self-reliance*, which, if you have a metaphysical turn, you will find is not so much of a paradox as it sounds at first. So she sent me a book to read which was to cure me of that error. It was an old book, and looked as if it had not been opened for a long time. What should drop out of it, one day, but a small heart-shaped paper, containing a lock of that straight, coarse, brown hair which sets off the sharp faces of so many thin-flanked, large-handed bumpkins? I read upon the paper the name "Hiram." — Love! love! love! — everywhere! everywhere! — under diamonds and housemaids' "jewelry," — lifting the marrowy camel's-hair, and rustling even the black bombazine! — No, no, — I think she never was pretty, but she was young once, and wore bright ginghams, and, perhaps, gay merinos. We shall find that the poor little crooked man has been in love, or is in love, or will be in love before we have done with him, for aught that I know!

Romance! Was there ever a boarding-house in

the world where the seemingly prosaic table had not a living fresco for its background, where you could see, if you had eyes, the smoke and fire of some upheaving sentiment, or the dreary craters of smouldering or burnt-out passions? You look on the black bombazine and high-necked decorum of your neighbor, and no more think of the real life that underlies this despoiled and dismantled womanhood than you think of a stone trilobite as having once been full of the juices and the nervous thrills of throbbing and self-conscious being. There is a wild creature under that long yellow pin which serves as brooch for the bombazine cuirass, — a wild creature, which I venture to say would leap in his cage, if I should stir him, quiet as you think him. A heart which has been domesticated by matrimony and maternity is as tranquil as a tame bulfinch; but a wild heart which has never been fairly broken in flutters fiercely long after you think time has tamed it down, — like that purple finch I had the other day, which could not be approached without such palpitations and frantic flings against the bars of his cage, that I had to send him back and get a little orthodox canary which had learned to be quiet and never mind the wires or his keeper's handling. I will tell you my wicked, but half involuntary experiment on the wild heart under the faded bombazine.

Was there ever a person in the room with you, marked by any special weakness or peculiarity, with whom you could be two hours and not touch the infirm spot? I confess the most frightful tendency to do just this thing. If a man has a brogue, I am sure to catch myself imitating it. If another is lame, I follow him, or, worse than that, go before him, limping. I could never meet an Irish gentleman — if it had been the Duke of Wellington himself — without stumbling upon the word "Paddy," — which I use rarely in my common talk.

I have been worried to know whether this was owing to some innate depravity of disposition on my part, some malignant torturing instinct, which, under different circumstances, might have made a Fijian anthropophagus of me, or to some law of thought for which I was not answerable. It is, I am convinced, a kind of physical fact like *endosmosis*, with which some of you are acquainted. A thin film of politeness separates the unspoken and unspeakable current of thought from the stream of conversation. After a time one begins to soak through and mingle with the other.

We were talking about names, one day. — Was there ever anything, — I said, — like the Yankee for inventing the most uncouth, pretentious, detestable appellations, — inventing or finding them, — since the time of Praise-God Barebones? I heard a country-boy once talking of another whom he called *Elpit*, as I understood him. *Elbridge* is common enough, but this sounded oddly. It seems the boy was christened *Lord Pitt*,—and called, for convenience, as above. I have heard a charming little girl, belonging to an intelligent family in the country, called *Angēs* invariably; doubtless intended for Agnes. Names are cheap. How can a man name an innocent new-born child, that never did him any harm, *Hiram?* —— The poor relation, or whatever she is, in bombazine, turned toward me, but I was stupid, and went on.— To think of a man going through life saddled with such an abominable name as that!—— The poor relation grew very uneasy.—I continued; for I never thought of all this till afterwards.—I knew one young fellow, a good many years ago, by the name of Hiram——

——What's got into you, Cousin,—said our landlady,—to look so?—There! you've upset your teacup!

It suddenly occurred to me what I had been doing, and I saw the poor woman had her hand at her throat; she was half-choking with the "hysteric ball,"—a very odd symptom, as you know, which nervous women often complain of. What business had I to be trying experiments on this forlorn old soul? I had a great deal better be watching that young girl.

Ah, the young girl! I am sure that she can hide nothing from me. Her skin is so transparent that one can almost count her heart-beats by the flushes they send into her cheeks. She does not seem to be shy, either. I think she does not know enough of danger to be timid. She seems to me like one of those birds that travellers tell of, found in remote, uninhabited islands, who, having never received any wrong at the hand of man, show no alarm at and hardly any particular consciousness of his presence.

The first thing will be to see how she and our little deformed gentleman get along together; for, as I have told you, they sit side by side. The next thing will be to keep an eye on the duenna, — the "Model" and so forth, as the white-neckcloth called her. The intention of that estimable lady is, I understand, to launch her and leave her. I suppose there is no help for it, and I don't doubt this young lady knows how to take care of herself, but I do not like to see young girls turned loose in boarding-houses. Look here now! There is that jewel of his race, whom I have called for convenience the Koh-i-noor, (you understand it is quite out of the question for me to use the family names of our boarders, unless I want to get into trouble,) — I say, the gentleman with the *diamond* is looking very often and very intently, it seems to me, down toward the farther corner of the table, where sits our amber-eyed blonde. The landlady's daughter does not look pleased, it seems to me, at this, nor at those other attentions which the gentleman referred to has, as I have learned, pressed upon the newly-arrived young person. The landlady made a communication to me, within a few days after the arrival of Miss Iris, which I will repeat to the best of my remembrance.

He, (the person I have been speaking of,) — she said, — seemed to be kinder hankerin' round after that young woman. It had hurt her daughter's feelin's a good deal, that the gentleman she was a-keepin' company with should be offerin' tickets and tryin' to send presents to them that he'd never know'd till jest a little spell ago, — and he as good as merried, so fur as solemn promises went, to as respectable a young lady, if she did say so, as any there was round, whosomever they might be.

Tickets! presents! — said I. — What tickets, what presents has he had the impertinence to be offering to that young lady?

Tickets to the Múseum, — said the landlady. — There is them that's glad enough to go to the Múseum, when tickets is given 'em; but some of 'em ha'n't had a ticket sence Cenderilla was played, — and now he must be offerin' 'em to this ridiculous young paintress, or whatever she is, that's come to make more mischief than her board's worth. But it a'n't her fault,—said the landlady, relenting;—and that aunt of hers, or whatever she is, served him right enough.

Why, what did she do?

Do? Why, she took it up in the tongs and dropped it out o' winder.

Dropped? dropped what?—I said.

Why, the *soap*,—said the landlady.

It appeared that the Koh-i-noor, to ingratiate himself, had sent an elegant package of perfumed soap, directed to Miss Iris, as a delicate expression of a lively sentiment of admiration, and that, after having met with the unfortunate treatment referred to, it was picked up by Master Benjamin Franklin, who appropriated it, rejoicing, and indulged in most unheard-of and inordinate ablutions in consequence, so that his hands were a frequent subject of maternal congratulation, and he smelt like a civet-cat for weeks after his great acquisition.

After watching daily for a time, I think I can see clearly into the relation which is growing up between the little gentleman and the young lady. She shows a tenderness to him that I can't help being interested in. If he was her crippled child, instead of being more than old enough to be her father, she could not treat him more kindly. The landlady's daughter said, the other day, she believed that girl was settin' her cap for the Little Gentleman.

Some of them young folks is very artful, — said her mother, — ana there is them that would merry Lazarus, if he'd only picked up crumbs enough. I don't think, though, this is one of that sort; she's kinder childlike, — said the landlady, — and maybe never had any dolls to play with; for they say her folks was poor before Ma'am undertook to see to her teachin' and board her and clothe her.

I could not help overhearing this conversation. "Board her and clothe her!" — speaking of such a young creature! Oh, dear! — Yes, — she must be fed, — just like Bridget, maid-of-all-work at this establishment. Somebody must pay for it. Somebody has a right to watch her and see how much it takes to "keep" her, and growl at her, if she has too good an appetite. Somebody has a right to keep an eye on her and take care that she does not dress too prettily. No mother to see her own youth over again in those fresh features and rising reliefs of half-sculptured womanhood, and, seeing its loveliness, forget her lessons of neutral-tinted propriety, and open the cases that hold her own ornaments to find for her a necklace or a bracelet or a pair of ear-rings, — .hose golden lamps that light up the deep, shadowy dimples on the cheeks of young beauties, — swinging in a semibarbaric splendor that carries the wild fancy to Abyssinian queens and musky Odalisques! I don't believe any woman has utterly given up the great firm of Mundus & Co., so long as she wears ear-rings.

I think Iris loves to hear the Little Gentleman talk. She smiles sometimes at his vehement statements, but never laughs at him. When he speaks to her, she keeps her eye always steadily upon him. This may be only natural good-breeding, so to speak, but it is worth noticing. I have often observed that vulgar persons, and public audiences of inferior collective intelligence, have this in common: the least thing draws off their minds, when you are speaking to them. I love this young creature's rapt attention to her diminutive neighbor while he is speaking.

He is evidently pleased with it. For a day or two after she came, he was silent and seemed nervous and excited. Now he is fond of getting the talk into his own hands, and is obviously conscious that he has at least one interested listener. Once or twice I have seen marks of special attention to personal adornment,—a ruffled shirt-bosom, one day, and a diamond pin in it,—not so *very* large as the Koh-i-noor's, but more lustrous. I mentioned the death's-head ring he wears on his right hand. I was attracted by a very handsome red stone, a ruby or carbuncle or something of the sort, to notice his left hand, the other day. It is a handsome hand, and confirms my suspicion that the cast mentioned was taken from his arm. After all, this is just what I should expect. It is not very uncommon to see the upper limbs, or one of them, running away with the whole strength, and, therefore, with the whole beauty, which we should never have noticed, if it had been divided equally between all four extremities. If it is so, of course he is proud of his one strong and beautiful arm; that is human nature. I am afraid he can hardly help betraying his favoritism, as people who have any one showy point are apt to do, — especially dentists with handsome teeth, who always smile back to their last molars.

Sitting, as he does, next to the young girl, and next but one to the calm lady who has her in charge, he cannot help seeing their relations to each other.

That is an admirable woman, Sir, — he said to me one day, as we sat alone at the table after breakfast, — an admirable woman, Sir, — and I hate her.

Of course, I begged an explanation.

An admirable woman, Sir, because she does good things, and even kind things, — takes care of this — this — young lady — we have here, talks like a sensible person, and always looks as if she was doing her duty with all her might. I hate her because her voice sounds as if it never trembled, and her eyes look as if she never knew what it was to cry. Besides, she looks at me, Sir, stares at me, as if she wanted to get an image of me for some gallery in her brain, — and we don't love to be looked at in this way, we that have —— I hate her, — I hate her, — her eyes kill me, — it is like being stabbed with icicles to be looked at so, — the sooner she goes home, the better. I don't want a woman to weigh me in a balance; there are men enough for that sort of work. The judicial character isn't captivating in females, Sir. A woman fascinates a man quite as often by what she overlooks as by what she sees. Love prefers twilight to daylight; and a man doesn't think much of, nor care much for, a woman outside of his household, unless he can couple the idea of love, past, present, or future, with her. I don't believe the Devil would give half as much for the services of a sinner as he would for those of one of these folks that are always doing virtuous acts in a way to make them unpleasing. — That young girl wants a tender nature to cherish her and give her a chance to put out her leaves, — sunshine, and not east winds.

He was silent, — and sat looking at his handsome left hand with the red stone ring upon it. — Is he going to fall in love with Iris?

Here are some lines I read to the boarders the other day: —

THE CROOKED FOOTPATH.

Ah, here it is! the sliding rail
 That marks the old remembered spot, —
The gap that struck our schoolboy trail, —
 The crooked path across the lot.

It left the road by school and church,
 A pencilled shadow, nothing more,
That parted from the silver birch
 And ended at the farmhouse door.

No line or compass traced its plan;
 With frequent bends to left or right,
In aimless, wayward curves it ran,
 But always kept the door in sight.

The gabled porch, with woodbine green, —
 The broken millstone at the sill, —
Though many a rood might stretch between,
 The truant child could see them still.

No rocks across the pathway lie, —
 No fallen trunk is o'er it thrown, —
And yet it winds, we know not why,
 And turns as if for tree or stone.

Perhaps some lover trod the way
 With shaking knees and leaping heart, —
And so it often runs astray
 With sinuous sweep or sudden start.

Or one, perchance, with clouded brain
  From some unholy banquet reeled, —
And since, our devious steps maintain
  His track across the trodden field.

Nay, deem not thus, — no earthborn will
  Could ever trace a faultless line;
Our truest steps are human still, —
  To walk unswerving were divine!

Truants from love, we dream of wrath; —
  Oh, rather let us trust the more!
Through all the wanderings of the path,
  We still can see our Father's door!

V.

The Professor finds a Fly in his Teacup.

I HAVE a long theological talk to relate, which must be dull reading to some of my young and vivacious friends. I don't know, however, that any of them have entered into a contract to read all that I write, or that I have promised always to write to please them. What if I should sometimes write to please myself?

Now you must know that there are a great many things which interest me, to some of which this or that particular class of readers may be totally indifferent. I love Nature, and human nature, its thoughts, affections, dreams, aspirations, delusions, — Art in all its forms, — *virtu* in all its eccentricities, — old stories from black-letter volumes and yellow manuscripts, and new projects out of hot brains not yet imbedded in the snows of age. I love the generous impulses of the reformer; but not less does my imagination feed itself upon the old litanies, so often warmed by the human breath upon which they were wafted to Heaven that they glow through our frames like our own heart's blood. I hope I love good men and women; I know that they never speak a word to me, even if it be of question or blame, that I do not take pleasantly, if it is expressed with a reasonable amount of human kindness.

I have before me at this time a beautiful and affecting letter, which I have hesitated to answer, though the postmark upon it gave its direction, and the name is one which is known to all, in some of its representatives. It contains no reproach, only a delicately-hinted fear. Speak gently, as this dear lady has spoken, and there is no heart so insensible that it does not answer to the appeal, no intellect so virile that it does not own a certain deference to the claims of age, of childhood, of sensitive and timid natures, when they plead with it not to look at those sacred things by the broad daylight which they see in mystic shadow. How grateful would it be to make perpetual peace with these pleading saints and their confessors, by the simple act that silences all complainings! Sleep, sleep, sleep! says the Arch-Enchantress of them all, — and pours her dark and potent anodyne, distilled over the fires that consumed her foes, — its large, round drops changing, as we look, into the beads of her convert's rosary! Silence! the pride of reason! cries another, whose whole life is spent in reasoning down reason.

I hope I love good people, not for their sake, but for my own. And most assuredly, if any deed of wrong or word of bitterness led me into an act of disrespect towards that enlightened and excellent class of men who make it their calling to teach goodness and their duty to practise it, I should feel that I had done myself an injury rather than them. Go and talk with any professional man holding any of the mediæval creeds, choosing one who wears upon his features the mark of inward and outward health, who looks cheerful, intelligent, and kindly, and see how all your prejudices melt away in his presence! It is impossible to come into intimate relations with a large, sweet nature, such as you may often find in this class, without longing to be at one with it in all its modes of being and believing. But does it not occur to you that one may love truth as he sees it, and his race as he views it, better than even the sympathy and approbation of many good men whom he honors,—better than sleeping to the sound of the Miserere or listening to the repetition of an effete Confession of Faith?

The three learned professions have but recently emerged from a state of *quasi* barbarism. None of them like too well to be told of it, but it must be sounded in their ears whenever they put on airs. When a man has taken an overdose of laudanum, the doctors tell us to place him between two persons who shall make him walk up and down incessantly; and if he still cannot be kept from going to sleep, they say that a lash or two over his back is of great assistance.

So we must keep the doctors awake by telling them that they have not yet shaken off astrology and the doctrine of signatures, as is shown by the form of their prescriptions, and their use of nitrate of silver, which turns epileptics into Ethiopians. If that is not enough, they must be given over to the scourgers, who like their task and get good fees for it. A few score years ago, sick people were made to swallow burnt toads and powdered earthworms and the expressed juice of wood-lice. The physician of Charles I. and II. prescribed abominations not to be named. Barbarism, as bad as that of Congo or Ashantee. Traces of this barbarism linger even in the greatly improved medical science of our century. So while the solemn farce of over-drugging is going on, the world over, the harlequin pseudo-science jumps on to the stage, whip in hand, with half-a-dozen somersets, and begins laying about him.

In 1817, perhaps you remember, the law of wager by battle was unrepealed, and the rascally murderous, and worse than murderous, clown, Abraham Thornton, put on his gantlet in open court and defied the appellant to lift the other which he threw down. It was not until the reign of George II. that the statutes against witchcraft were repealed. As for the English Court of Chancery, we know that its antiquated abuses form one of the staples of common proverbs and popular literature. So the laws and the lawyers have to be watched perpetually by public opinion as much as the doctors do.

I don't think the other profession is an exception. When the Reverend Mr. Cauvin and his associates burned my distinguished scientific brother, — he was burned with green fagots, which made it rather slow and painful, — it appears to me they were in a state of religious barbarism. The dogmas of such people about the Father of Mankind and his creatures are of no more account in my opinion than those of a council of Aztecs. If a man picks your pocket, do you not consider him thereby disqualified to pronounce any authoritative opinion on matters of ethics? If a man hangs my ancient female relatives for sorcery, as they did in this neighborhood a little while ago, or burns my instructor for not believing as he does, I care no more for his religious edicts than I should for those of any other barbarian.

Of course, a barbarian may hold many true opinions; but when the ideas of the healing art, of the administration of justice, of Christian love, could not exclude systematic poisoning, judicial duelling, and murder for opinion's sake, I do not see how we can trust the verdict of that time relating to any subject which involves the primal instincts violated in these abominations and absurdities. — What if we are even now in a state of *semi*-barbarism?

Perhaps some think we ought not to talk at table about such things. — I am not so sure of that. Religion and government appear to me the two subjects which of all others should belong to the common talk of people who enjoy the blessings of freedom. Think, one moment. The earth is a great factory-wheel, which, at every revolution on its axis, receives fifty thousand raw souls and turns off nearly the same number worked up more or less completely. There must be somewhere a population of two hundred thousand million, perhaps ten or a hundred times as many, earth-born intelligences. *Life*, as we call it, is nothing but the edge of the boundless ocean of existence where it comes on soundings. In this view, I do not see anything so fit to talk about, or half so interesting, as that which relates to the innumerable majority of our fellow-creatures, the dead-living, who are hundreds of thousands to one of the live-living, and with whom we all potentially belong, though we have got tangled for the present in some parcels of fibrine, albumen, and phosphates, that keep us on the minority side of the house. In point of fact, it is one of the many results of *Spiritualism* to make the permanent destiny of the race a matter of common reflection and discourse, and a vehicle for the prevailing disbelief of the Middle-Age doctrines on the subject. I cannot help thinking, when I remember how many conversations my friend and myself have reported, that it would be very extraordinary, if there were no mention of that class of subjects which involves all that we have and all that we hope, not merely for ourselves, but for the dear people whom we love best,—noble men, pure and lovely women, ingenuous children,—about the destiny of nine tenths of whom you know the opinions that would have been taught by those old man-roasting, woman-strangling dogmatists.—However, I fought this matter with one of our boarders the other day, and I am going to report the conversation.

The divinity-student came down, one morning, looking rather more serious than usual. He said little at breakfast-time, but lingered after the others, so that I, who am apt to be long at the table, found myself alone with him.

When the rest were all gone, he turned his chair round towards mine, and began.

I am afraid, — he said, — you express yourself a little too freely on a most important class of subjects. Is there not danger in introducing discussions or allusions relating to matters of religion into common discourse?

Danger to what? — I asked.

Danger to truth, — he replied, after a slight pause.

I didn't know Truth was such an invalid, — I said. — How long is it since she could only take the air in a close carriage, with a gentleman in a black coat on the box? Let me tell you a story, adapted to young persons, but which won't hurt older ones.

—— There was a very little boy who had one of those balloons you may have seen, which are filled with light gas, and are held by a string to keep them from running off in aeronautic voyages on their own account. This little boy had a naughty brother, who said to him, one day, — Brother, pull down your balloon, so that I can look at it and take hold of it. Then the little boy pulled it down. Now the naughty brother had a sharp pin in his hand, and he thrust it into the balloon, and all the gas oozed out, so that there was nothing left but a shrivelled skin.

One evening, the little boy's father called him to the window to see the moon, which pleased him very much; but presently he said, — Father, do not pull the string and bring down the moon, for my naughty brother will prick it, and then it will all shrivel up and we shall not see it any more.

Then his father laughed, and told him how the moon had been shining a good while, and would shine a good while longer, and that all we could do was to keep our windows clean, never letting the dust get too thick on them, and especially to keep our eyes open, but that we could not pull the moon down with a string, nor prick it with a pin. — Mind you this, too, the moon is no man's private property, but is seen from a good many parlor-windows.

—— Truth is tough. It will not break, like a bubble, at a touch; nay, you may kick it about all day, like a football, and it will be round and full at evening. Does not Mr. Bryant say, that Truth gets well if she is run over by a locomotive, while Error dies of lockjaw if she scratches her finger? I never heard that a mathematician was alarmed for the safety of a demonstrated proposition. I think, generally, that fear of open discussion implies feebleness of inward conviction, and great sensitiveness to the expression of individual opinion is a mark of weakness.

—— I am not so much afraid for truth, — said the divinity-student, — as for the conceptions of truth in the minds of persons not accustomed to judge wisely the opinions uttered before them.

Would you, then, banish all allusions to matters of this nature from the society of people who come together habitually?

I would be very careful in introducing them, — said the divinity-student.

Yes, but friends of yours leave pamphlets in people's entries, to be picked up by nervous misses and hysteric housemaids, full of doctrines these people do not approve. Some of your friends stop little children in the street, and give them books, which their parents, who have had them baptized into the Christian fold and give them what they consider proper religious instruction, do not think fit for them. One would say it was fair enough to talk about matters thus forced upon people's attention.

The divinity-student could not deny that this was what might be called opening the subject to the discussion of intelligent people.

But, — he said, — the greatest objection is this, that persons who have not made a professional study of theology are not competent to speak on such subjects. Suppose a minister were to undertake to express opinions on medical subjects, for instance, would you not think he was going beyond his province?

I laughed, — for I remembered John Wesley's "sulphur and supplication," and so many other cases where ministers had meddled with medicine, — sometimes well and sometimes ill, but, as a general rule, with a tremendous lurch to quackery, owing to their very loose way of admitting evidence, — that I could not help being amused.

I beg your pardon, — I said, — I do not wish to be impolite, but I was thinking of their certificates to patent medicines. Let us look at this matter.

If a minister had attended lectures on the theory and practice of medicine, delivered by those who had studied it most deeply, for thirty or forty years, at the rate of from fifty to one hundred a year, — if he had been constantly reading and hearing read the most approved text-books on the subject, — if he had seen medicine actually practised according to different methods, daily, for the same length of time, — I should think, that if a person of average understanding, he *was* entitled to express an opinion on the subject of medicine, or else that his instructors were a set of ignorant and incompetent charlatans.

If, before a medical practitioner would allow me to enjoy the full privileges of the healing art, he expected me to affirm my belief in a considerable number of medical doctrines, drugs, and formulæ, I should think that he thereby implied my right to discuss the same, and my ability to do so, if I knew how to express myself in English.

Suppose, for instance, the Medical Society should refuse to give us an opiate, or to set a broken limb, until we had signed our belief in a certain number of propositions, — of which we will say this is the first:.—

I. All men's teeth are naturally in a state of total decay or caries, and, therefore, no man can bite until every one of them is extracted and a new set is inserted according to the principles of dentistry adopted by this Society.

I, for one, should want to discuss that before signing my name to it, and I should say this: — Why, no, that isn't true. There are a good many bad teeth, we all know, but a great many more good ones. You mustn't trust the *dentists;* they are all the time looking at the people who have bad teeth, and such as are suffering from toothache. The idea that you must pull out every one of every nice young man and young woman's natural teeth! Poh, poh! Nobody believes that. This tooth must be straightened, that must be filled with gold, and this other perhaps extracted;

but it must be a very rare case, if they are all so bad as to require extraction; and if they are, don't blame the poor soul for it! Don't tell us, as some old dentists used to, that everybody not only always has every tooth in his head good for nothing, but that he ought to have his head cut off as a punishment for that misfortune! No, I can't sign Number One. Give us Number Two.

II. We hold that no man can be well who does not agree with our views of the efficacy of calomel, and who does not take the doses of it prescribed in our tables, as there directed.

To which I demur, questioning why it should be so, and get for answer the two following: —

III. Every man who does not take our prepared calomel, as prescribed by us in our Constitution and By-Laws, is and must be a mass of disease from head to foot; it being self-evident that he is simultaneously affected with Apoplexy, Arthritis, Ascites, Asphyxia, and Atrophy; with Borborygmus, Bronchitis, and Bulimia; with Cachexia, Carcinoma, and Cretinismus; and so on through the alphabet, to Xerophthalmia and Zona, with all possible and incompatible diseases which are necessary to make up a totally morbid state; and he will certainly die, if he does not take freely of our prepared calomel, to be obtained only of one of our authorized agents.

IV. No man shall be allowed to take our prepared calomel who does not give in his solemn adhesion to each and all of the above-named and the following propositions (from ten to a hundred) and show his mouth to certain of our apothecaries, who have *not* studied dentistry, to examine whether all his teeth have been extracted and a new set inserted according to our regulations.

Of course, the doctors have a right to say we shan't have any rhubarb, if we don't sign their articles, and that, if, after signing them, we express doubts (in public) about any of them, they will cut us off from our jalap and squills, — but then to ask a fellow not to discuss the propositions before he signs them is what I should call boiling it down a little *too* strong!

If we understand them, why can't we discuss them? If we can't understand them, because we haven't taken a medical degree, what the Father of Lies do they ask us to sign them for?

Just so with the graver profession. Every now and then some of its members seem to lose common sense and common humanity. The laymen have to keep setting the divines right constantly. Science, for instance, — in other words, knowledge, — is not the enemy of religion; for, if so, then religion would mean ignorance. But it is often the antagonist of school-divinity.

Everybody knows the story of early astronomy and the school-divines. Come down a little later.

Archbishop Usher, a very learned Protestant prelate, tells us that the world was created on Sunday, the twenty-third of October, four thousand and four years before the birth of Christ. Deluge, December 7th, two thousand three hundred and forty-eight years B. C. — Yes, and the earth stands on an elephant, and the elephant on a tortoise. One statement is as near the truth as the other.

Again, there is nothing so brutalizing to some natures as *moral surgery.* I have often wondered that Hogarth did not add one more picture to his four stages of Cruelty. Those wretched fools, reverend divines and others, who were strangling men and women for imaginary crimes a little more than a century ago among us, were set right by a layman, and very angry it made them to have him meddle.

The good people of Northampton had a very remarkable man for their clergyman, — a man with a brain as nicely adjusted for certain mechanical processes as Babbage's calculating machine. The commentary of the laymen on the preaching and practising of Jonathan Edwards was, that, after twenty-three years of endurance, they turned him out by a vote of twenty to one, and passed a resolve that he should never preach for them again. A man's logical and analytical adjustments are of little consequence, compared to his primary relations with Nature and truth; and people have sense enough to find it out in the long run; they know what "logic" is worth.

In that miserable delusion referred to above, the reverend Aztecs and Fijians argued rightly enough from their premises, no doubt, for many men can do this. But common sense and common humanity were unfortunately left out from their premises, and a layman had to supply them. A hundred more years and many of the barbarisms still lingering among us will, of course, have disappeared like witch-hanging. But people are sensitive now, as they were then. You will see by this extract that the Rev. Cotton Mather did not like intermeddling with his business very well. "Let the *Levites* of the Lord keep close to their Instructions," he says, "and *God will smite thro' the loins of those that rise up against them.* I will report unto you a Thing which many Hundreds among us know to be true. The *Godly Minister* of a certain Town in Connecticut, when he had occasion to be absent on a *Lord's Day* from his Flock, employ'd an honest *Neighbour* of some small Talents for a *Mechanick*, to read a *Sermon* out of some *good Book* unto 'em. This *Honest*, whom they ever counted also a *Pious Man*, had so much conceit of his *Talents*, that instead of *Reading a Sermon* appointed, he to the *Surprize* of the People, fell to *preaching one of his own.* For his Text he took these Words, '*Despise not*

Prophecyings'; and in his Preachment he betook himself to bewail the *Envy of the Clergy* in the Land, in that they did not wish *all the Lord's People to be Prophets*, and call forth *Private Brethren* publickly to *prophesie.* While he was thus in the midst of his Exercise, God smote him with horrible *Madness;* he was taken ravingly distracted; the People were forc'd with violent Hands to carry him home. . . . I will not mention his Name: He was reputed a Pious Man. — This is one of Cotton's "Remarkable Judgments of God, on Several Sorts of Offenders," — and the next cases referred to are the Judgments on the "Abominable Sacrilege" of not paying the Ministers' Salaries.

This sort of thing doesn't do here and now, you see, my young friend! We talk about our free institutions; — they are nothing but a coarse outside machinery to secure the freedom of individual thought. The President of the United States is only the engine-driver of our broad-gauge mail-train; and every honest, independent thinker has a seat in the first-class cars behind him.

——There is something in what you say, — replied the divinity-student; — and yet it seems to me there are places and times where disputed doctrines of religion should not be introduced. You would not attack a church dogma — say,

Total Depravity — in a lyceum-lecture, for instance?

Certainly not; I should choose another place, — I answered. — But, mind you, at this table I think it is very different. I shall express my ideas on any subject I like. The laws of the lecture-room, to which my friends and myself are always amenable, do not hold here. I shall not often give arguments, but frequently opinions, — I trust with courtesy and propriety, but, at any rate, with such natural forms of expression as it has pleased the Almighty to bestow upon me.

A man's opinions, look you, are generally of much more value than his arguments. These last are made by his brain, and perhaps he does not believe the proposition they tend to prove, — as is often the case with paid lawyers; but opinions are formed by our whole nature, — brain, heart, instinct, brute life, everything all our experience has shaped for us by contact with the whole circle of our being.

—— There is one thing more, — said the divinity-student, — that I wished to speak of; I mean that idea of yours, expressed some time since, of *depolarizing* the text of sacred books in order to judge them fairly. May I ask why you do no try the experiment yourself?

Certainly, — I replied, — if it gives you any pleasure to ask foolish questions. I think the ocean telegraph-wire ought to be laid and will be laid, but I don't know that you have any right to ask me to go and lay it. But, for that matter, I have heard a good deal of Scripture depolarized in and out of the pulpit. I heard the Rev. Mr. F once depolarize the story of the Prodigal Son in Park-Street Church. Many years afterwards, I heard him repeat the same or a similar depolarized version in Rome, New York. I heard an admiiable depolarization of the story of the young man who "had great possessions" from the Rev. Mr. H. in another pulpit, and felt that I had never half understood it before. All paraphrases are more or less perfect depolarizations. But I tell you this: the faith of our Christian community is not robust enough to bear the turning of our most sacred language into its depolarized equivalents. You have only to look back to Dr. Channing's famous Baltimore discourse and remember the shrieks of blasphemy with which it was greeted, to satisfy yourself on this point. Time, time only, can gradually wean us from our *Epeolatry*, or word-worship, by spiritualizing our ideas of the thing signified. Man is an idolater or symbol-worshipper by nature, which, of course, is no fault of his; but sooner or later all his local and temporary symbols must be ground to powder, like the golden calf, — word-images as well as metal and wooden ones. Rough work, iconoclasm, — but the only way to get at truth. It is, indeed, as that quaint and rare old discourse, "A Summons for Sleepers," hath it, "no doubt a thankless office, and a verie unthriftie occupation; *veritas odium parit*, truth never goeth without a scratcht face; he that will be busie with *væ vobis*, let him looke shortly for *coram nobis*."

The very aim and end of our institutions is just this: that we may think what we like and say what we think.

——Think what we like! — said the divinity-student; — think what we like! What! against all human and divine authority?

Against all human versions of its own or any other authority. At our own peril always, if we do not *like* the right, — but not at the risk of being hanged and quartered for political heresy, or broiled on green fagots for ecclesiastical treason! Nay, we have got so far, that the very word *heresy* has fallen into comparative disuse among us.

And now, my young friend, let us shake hands and stop our discussion, which we will not make a quarrel. I trust you know, or will learn, a great many things in your profession which we common scholars do not know; but mark this: when the common people of New England stop talking politics and theology, it will be because they have got an Emperor to teach them the one, and a Pope to teach them the other!

That was the end of my long conference with the divinity-student. The next morning we got talking a little on the same subject, very good-naturedly, as people return to a matter they have talked out.

You must look to yourself, — said the divinity-student, — if your democratic notions get into print. You will be fired into from all quarters.

If it were only a bullet, with the marksman's name on it! — I said. — I can't stop to pick out the peep-shot of the anonymous scribblers.

Right, Sir! right! — said the Little Gentleman. — The scamps! I know the fellows. They can't give fifty cents to one of the Antipodes, but they must have it jingled along through everybody's palms all the way, till it reaches him, — and forty cents of it get spilt, like the water out of the fire-buckets passed along a "lane" at a fire; — but when it comes to anonymous defamation, putting lies into people's mouths, and then advertising those people through the country as the authors of them, — oh, then it is that they let not their left hand know what their right hand doeth!

I don't like Ehud's style of doing business, Sir. He comes along with a very sanctimonious look, Sir, with his "secret errand unto thee," and his "message from God unto thee," and then pulls out his hidden knife with that unsuspected left hand of his, — (the Little Gentleman lifted his clenched left hand with the blood-red jewel on the ring-finger,) — and runs it, blade and haft, into a man's stomach! Don't meddle with these fellows, Sir. They are read mostly by persons whom you would not reach, if you were to write ever so much. Let 'em alone. A man whose opinions are not attacked is beneath contempt.

I hope so, — I said. — I got three pamphlets and innumerable squibs flung at my head for attacking one of the pseudo-sciences, in former years. When, by the permission of Providence, I held up to the professional public the damnable facts connected with the conveyance of poison from one young mother's chamber to another's, — for doing which humble office I desire to be thankful that I have lived, though nothing else good should ever come of my life, — I had to bear the sneers of those whose position I had assailed, and, as I believe, have at last demolished, so that nothing but the ghosts of dead women stir among the ruins. — What would you do, if the folks without names kept at you, trying to get a San Benito on to your shoulders that would fit you? — Would you stand still in fly-time, or would you give a kick now and then?

Let 'em bite! — said the Little Gentleman; — let 'em bite! It makes 'em hungry to shake 'em off, and they settle down again as thick as ever and twice as savage. Do you know what med dling with the folks without names, as you call 'em, is like? — It is like riding at the *quintain.* You run full tilt at the board, but the board is on a pivot, with a bag of sand on an arm that balances it. The board gives way as soon as you touch it; and before you have got by, the bag of sand comes round whack on the back of your neck. "Ananias," for instance, pitches into your lecture, we will say, in some paper taken by the people in your kitchen. Your servants get saucy and negligent. If their newspaper calls you names, they need not be so particular about shutting doors softly or boiling potatoes. So you lose your temper, and come out in an article which you think is going to finish "Ananias," proving him a booby who doesn't know enough to understand even a lyceum-lecture, or else a person that tells lies. Now you think you've got him! Not so fast. "Ananias" keeps still and winks to "Shimei," and "Shimei" comes out in the paper which they take in your neighbor's kitchen, ten times worse than t'other fellow. If you meddle with "Shimei," he steps out, and next week appears "Rab-shakeh," an unsavory wretch; and now, at any rate, you find out what good sense there was in Hezekiah's "Answer him not." — No, no, — keep your temper. — So saying, the Little Gentleman doubled his left fist and looked at it, as if he should like to hit something or somebody a most pernicious punch with it.

Good!—said I.—Now let me give you some axioms I have arrived at, after seeing something of a great many kinds of good folks.

——Of a hundred people of each of the different leading religious sects, about the same proportion will be safe and pleasant persons to deal and to live with.

——There are, at least, three real saints among the women to one among the men, in every denomination.

——The spiritual standard of different classes I would reckon thus:—

1. The comfortably rich.
2. The decently comfortable
3. The very rich, who are apt to be irreligious.
4. The very poor, who are apt to be immoral.

——The cut nails of machine-divinity may be driven in, but they won't clinch.

——The arguments which the greatest of our schoolmen could not refute were two: the blood in men's veins, and the milk in women's breasts.

——Humility is the first of the virtues—for other people.

——Faith always implies the disbelief of a lesser fact in favor of a greater. A little mind often sees the unbelief, without seeing the belief, of a large one.

The Poor Relation had been fidgeting about and working her mouth while all this was going on. She broke out in speech at this point.

I hate to hear folks talk so. I don't see that you are any better than a heathen.

I wish I were half as good as many heathens have been, — I said. — Dying for a principle seems to me a higher degree of virtue than scolding for it; and the history of heathen races is full of instances where men have laid down their lives for the love of their kind, of their country, of truth, nay, even for simple manhood's sake, or to show their obedience or fidelity. What would not such beings have done for the souls of men, for the Christian commonwealth, for the King of Kings, if they had lived in days of larger light? Which seems to you nearest heaven, Socrates drinking his hemlock, Regulus going back to the enemy's camp, or that old New England divine sitting comfortably in his study and chuckling over his conceit of certain poor women, who had been burned to death in his own town, going "roaring out of one fire into another"?

I don't believe he said any such thing, — replied the Poor Relation.

It is hard to believe, — said I, — but it is true for all that. In another hundred years it will be as incredible that men talked as we sometimes hear them now.

Pectus est quod facit theologum. The heart makes the theologian. Every race, every civilization, either has a new revelation of its own or a new interpretation of an old one. Democratic America has a different humanity from feudal Europe, and so must have a new divinity. See, for one moment, how intelligence reacts on our faiths. The Bible was a divining-book to our ancestors, and is so still in the hands of some of the vulgar. The Puritans went to the Old Testament for their laws; the Mormons go to it for their patriarchal institution. Every generation dissolves something new and precipitates something once held in solution from that great storehouse of temporary and permanent truths.

You may observe this: that the conversation of intelligent men of the stricter sects is strangely in advance of the formulæ that belong to their organizations. So true is this, that I have doubts whether a large proportion of them would not have been rather pleased than offended, if they could have overheard our talk. For, look you, I think there is hardly a professional teacher who will not in private conversation allow a large part of what we have said, though it may frighten him in print; and I know well what an under-current of secret sympathy gives vitality to those poor words of mine which sometimes get a hearing.

I don't mind the exclamation of any old stager

who drinks Madeira worth from two to six Bibles a bottle, and burns, according to his own premises, a dozen souls a year in the cigars with which he muddles his brains. But as for the good and true and intelligent men whom we see all around us, laborious, self-denying, hopeful, helpful, — men who know that the active mind of the century is tending more and more to the two poles, Rome and Reason, the sovereign church or the free soul, authority or personality, God in us or God in our masters, and that, though a man may by accident *stand* half-way between these two points, he must *look* one way or the other, — I don't believe they would take offence at anything I have reported of our late conversation.

But supposing any one *do* take offence at first sight, let him look over these notes again, and see whether he is quite sure he does not agree with most of these things that were said amongst us. If he agrees with most of them, let him be patient with an opinion he does not accept, or an expression or illustration a little too vivacious. I don't know that I shall report any more conversations on these topics; but I do insist on the right to express a civil opinion on this class of subjects without giving offence, just when and where I please, — unless, as in the lecture-room, there is an implied contract to keep clear of doubtful matters. You didn't think a man could sit at a breakfast-table doing nothing but making puns every morning for a year or two, and never give a thought to the two thousand of his fellow-creatures who are passing into another state during every hour that he sits talking and laughing! Of course, the *one* matter that a real human being cares for is what is going to become of them and of him. And the plain truth is, that a good many people are saying one thing about it and believing another.

——How do I know that? Why, I have known and loved to talk with good people, all the way from Rome to Geneva in doctrine, as long as I can remember. Besides, the real religion of the world comes from women much more than from men,—from mothers most of all, who carry the key of our souls in their bosoms. It is in their hearts that the "sentimental" religion some people are so fond of sneering at has its source. The sentiment of love, the sentiment of maternity, the sentiment of the paramount obligation of the parent to the child as having called it into existence, enhanced just in proportion to the power and knowledge of the one and the weakness and ignorance of the other,—these are the "sentiments" that have kept our soulless systems from driving men off to die in holes like those that riddle the sides of the hill opposite the Monastery of St. Saba, where the miserable victims of a falsely-interpreted religion starved and withered in their delusion.

I have looked on the face of a saintly woman this very day, whose creed many dread and hate but whose life is lovely and noble beyond all praise. When I remember the bitter words I have heard spoken against her faith, by men who have an Inquisition which excommunicates those who ask to leave their communion in peace, and an *Index Expurgatorius* on which this article may possibly have the honor of figuring, — and, far worse than these, the reluctant, pharisaical confession, that it might perhaps be *possible* that one who so believed should be accepted of the Creator, — and then recall the sweet peace and love that show through all her looks, the price of untold sacrifices and labors, — and again recollect how thousands of women, filled with the same spirit, die, without a murmur, to earthly life, die to their own names even, that they may know nothing but their holy duties, — while men are torturing and denouncing their fellows, and while we can hear day and night the clinking of the hammers that are trying, like the brute forces in the "Prometheus," to rivet their adamantine wedges right through the breast of human nature, — I have been ready to believe that we have even now a new revelation, and the name of its Messiah is WOMAN!

——I should be sorry,—I remarked, a day or two afterwards, to the divinity-student,—if anything I said tended in any way to foster any jealousy between the professions, or to throw disrespect upon that one on whose counsel and sympathies almost all of us lean in our moments of trial. But we are false to our new conditions of life, if we do not resolutely maintain our religious as well as our political freedom, in the face of any and all supposed monopolies. Certain men will, of course, say two things, if we do not take their views: first, that we don't know anything about these matters; and, secondly, that we are not so good as they are. They have a polarized phraseology for saying these things, but it comes to precisely that. To which it may be answered, in the first place, that we have good authority for saying that even babes and sucklings know *something;* and, in the second, that, if there is a mote or so to be removed from our premises, the courts and councils of the last few years have found beams enough in some other quarters to build a church that would hold all the good people in Boston and have sticks enough left to make a bonfire for all the heretics.

As to that terrible depolarizing process of mine, of which we were talking the other day, I will give you a specimen of one way of managing it, if you like. I don't believe it will hurt you or anybody. Besides, I had a great deal rather finish our talk with pleasant images and gentle words than with sharp sayings, which will only afford a text, if anybody repeats them, for endless relays of attacks from Messrs. Ananias, Shimei, and Rab-shakeh.

[I must leave such gentry, if any of them show themselves, in the hands of my clerical friends, many of whom are ready to stand up for the rights of the laity, — and to those blessed souls, the good women, to whom this version of the story of a mother's hidden hopes and tender anxieties is dedicated by their peaceful and loving servant.]

A MOTHER'S SECRET.

How sweet the sacred legend — if unblamed
In my slight verse such holy things are named —
Of Mary's secret hours of hidden joy,
Silent, but pondering on her wondrous boy!
Ave, Maria! Pardon, if I wrong
Those heavenly words that shame my earthly song!

The choral host had closed the angel's strain
Sung to the midnight watch on Bethlehem's plain;
And now the shepherds, hastening on their way,
Sought the still hamlet where the Infant lay.
They passed the fields that gleaning Ruth toiled o'er, —
They saw afar the ruined threshing-floor

Where Moab's daughter, homeless and forlorn,
Found Boaz slumbering by his heaps of corn;
And some remembered how the holy scribe,
Skilled in the lore of every jealous tribe,
Traced the warm blood of Jesse's royal son
To that fair alien, bravely wooed and won.
So fared they on to seek the promised sign
That marked the anointed heir of David's line.
At last, by forms of earthly semblance led,
They found the crowded inn, the oxen's shed.
No pomp was there, no glory shone around
On the coarse straw that strewed the reeking ground;
One dim retreat a flickering torch betrayed,—
In that poor cell the Lord of Life was laid!
The wondering shepherds told their breathless tale
Of the bright choir that woke the sleeping vale;
Told how the skies with sudden glory flamed;
Told how the shining multitude proclaimed
"Joy, joy to earth! Behold the hallowed morn!
In David's city Christ the Lord is born!
'Glory to God!' let angels shout on high,—
'Good-will to men!' the listening Earth reply!"
They spoke with hurried words and accents wild;
Calm in his cradle slept the heavenly child.
No trembling word the mother's joy revealed,—
One sigh of rapture, and her lips were sealed;
Unmoved she saw the rustic train depart,
But kept their words to ponder in her heart.

Twelve years had passed; the boy was fair and tall,
Growing in wisdom, finding grace with all.
The maids of Nazareth, as they trooped to fill
Their balanced urns beside the mountain-rill,—
The gathered matrons, as they sat and spun,

Spoke in soft words of Joseph's quiet son.
No voice had reached the Galilean vale
Of star-led kings or awe-struck shepherds' tale:
In the meek, studious child they only saw
The future Rabbi, learned in Israel's law.
So grew the boy; and now the feast was near,
When at the holy place the tribes appear.
Scarce had the home-bred child of Nazareth seen
Beyond the hills that girt the village-green,
Save when at midnight, o'er the star-lit sands,
Snatched from the steel of Herod's murdering bands,
A babe, close-folded to his mother's breast,
Through Edom's wilds he sought the sheltering West.
Then Joseph spake: "Thy boy hath largely grown
Weave him fine raiment, fitting to be shown;
Fair robes beseem the pilgrim, as the priest:
Goes he not with us to the holy feast?"
And Mary culled the flaxen fibres white;
Till eve she spun; she spun till morning light;
The thread was twined; its parting meshes through
From hand to hand her restless shuttle flew,
Till the full web was wound upon the beam,—
Love's curious toil,—a vest without a seam!
They reach the holy place, fulfil the days
To solemn feasting given, and grateful praise.
At last they turn, and far Moriah's height
Melts in the southern sky and fades from sight.
All day the dusky caravan has flowed
In devious trails along the winding road,—
(For many a step their homeward path attends,
And all the sons of Abraham are as friends).
Evening has come,—the hour of rest and joy;—
Hush! hush!—that whisper,—"Where is Mary's boy?
O weary hour! O aching days that passed

Filled with strange fears, each wilder than the last:
The soldier's lance, — the fierce centurion's sword, —
The crushing wheels that whirl some Roman lord, —
The midnight crypt that sucks the captive's breath, —
The blistering sun on Hinnom's vale of death!
  Thrice on his cheek had rained the morning light,
Thrice on his lips the mildewed kiss of night,
Crouched by some porphyry column's shining plinth,
Or stretched beneath the odorous terebinth.
  At last, in desperate mood, they sought once more
The Temple's porches, searched in vain before;
They found him seated with the ancient men, —
The grim old rufflers of the tongue and pen, —
Their bald heads glistening as they clustered near,
Their gray beards slanting as they turned to hear,
Lost in half-envious wonder and surprise
That lips so fresh should utter words so wise.
  And Mary said, — as one who, tried too long,
Tells all her grief and half her sense of wrong, —
"What is this thoughtless thing which thou hast done?
Lo, we have sought thee sorrowing, O my son!"
Few words he spake, and scarce of filial tone, —
Strange words, their sense a mystery yet unknown;
Then turned with them and left the holy hill,
To all their mild commands obedient still.
  The tale was told to Nazareth's sober men,
And Nazareth's matrons told it oft again;
The maids retold it at the fountain's side;
The youthful shepherds doubted or denied;
It passed around among the listening friends,
With all that fancy adds and fiction lends,
Till newer marvels dimmed the young renown
Of Joseph's son, who talked the Rabbis down.
  But Mary, faithful to its lightest word,

Kept in her heart the sayings she had heard,
Till the dread morning rent the Temple's veil,
And shuddering Earth confirmed the wondrous tale.

Youth fades; love droops; the leaves of friendship fall;
A mother's secret hope outlives them all.

VI.

You don't look so dreadful poor in the face as you did a while back. Bloated some, I expect.

This was the cheerful and encouraging and elegant remark with which the Poor Relation greeted the divinity-student one morning.

Of course every good man considers it a great sacrifice on his part to continue living in this transitory, unsatisfactory, and particularly unpleasant world. This is so much a matter of course, that I was surprised to see the divinity-student change color. He took a look at a small and uncertain-minded glass which hung slanting forward over the chapped sideboard. The image it returned to him had the color of a very young pea somewhat over-boiled. The scenery of a long tragic drama flashed through his mind as the lightning-express-train *whishes* by a station: the gradual dismantling process of disease; friends looking on, sympathetic, but secretly chuckling over their own stomachs of iron and lungs of caoutchouc; nurses attentive, but calculating their crop, and thinking how soon it will be ripe, so that they can go to your neighbor, who is good for a year or so longer; doctors assiduous, but giving themselves a mental shake, as they go out of your door, which throws off your particular grief as a duck sheds a raindrop from his oily feathers; undertakers solemn, but happy; then the great subsoil cultivator, who plants, but never looks for fruit in his garden; then the stone-cutter, who finds the lie that has been waiting for you on a slab ever since the birds or beasts made their tracks on the new red sandstone; then the grass and the dandelions and the buttercups, — Earth saying to the mortal body, with her sweet symbolism, "You have scarred my bosom, but you are forgiven"; then a glimpse of the soul as a floating consciousness without very definite form or place, but dimly conceived of as an upright column of vapor or mist several times larger than life-size, so far as it could be said to have any size at all, wandering about and living a thin and half-awake life for want of good old-fashioned solid *matter* to come down upon with foot and fist, — in fact, having neither foot nor fist, nor conveniences for taking the sitting posture.

And yet the divinity-student was a good Christian, and those heathen images which remind one of the childlike fancies of the dying Adrian were only the efforts of his imagination to give shape to the formless and position to the placeless. Neither did his thoughts spread themselves out and link themselves as I have displayed them. They came confusedly into his mind like a heap of broken mosaics, — sometimes a part of the picture complete in itself, sometimes connected fragments, and sometimes only single severed stones.

They did not diffuse a light of celestial joy over his countenance. On the contrary, the Poor Relation's remark turned him pale, as I have said; and when the terrible wrinkled and jaundiced looking-glass turned him green in addition, and he saw himself in it, it seemed to him as if it were all settled, and his book of life were to be shut not yet half-read, and go back to the dust of the under-ground archives. He coughed a mild short cough, as if to point the direction in which his downward path was tending. It was an honest little cough enough, so far as appearances went. But coughs are ungrateful things. You find one out in the cold, take it up and nurse it and make everything of it, dress it up warm, give it all sorts of balsams and other food it likes, and carry it round in your bosom as if it were a miniature lapdog. And by-and-by its little bark grows sharp and savage, and — confound the thing! — you find it is a wolf's whelp that you have got there, and he is gnawing in the breast where he has been nestling so long. — The Poor Relation said that somebody's surrup was good for folks that were gettin' into a bad way. — The landlady had heard of desperate cases cured by cherry-pictorial.

Whiskey's the fellah, — said the young man John. — Make it into punch, cold at dinner-time 'n' hot at bed-time. I'll come up 'n' show you how to mix it. Haven't any of you seen the wonderful fat man exhibitin' down in Hanover Street?

Master Benjamin Franklin rushed into the dialogue with a breezy exclamation, that he had seen a great picter outside of the place where the fat man was exhibitin'. Tried to get in at half-price, but the man at the door looked at his teeth and said he was more'n ten year old.

It isn't two years, — said the young man John, — since that fat fellah was exhibitin' here as the Livin' Skeleton. Whiskey — that's what did it, — real Burbon's the stuff. Hot water, sugar, 'n' jest a little shavin' of lemon-skin in it, — *skin*, mind you, none o' your juice; take it off thin, — shape of one of them flat curls the factory-girls wear on the sides of their foreheads.

But I am a teetotaller, — said the divinity-student, in a subdued tone; — not noticing the enormous length of the bow-string the young fellow had just drawn.

He took up his hat and went out.

I think you have worried that young man more than you meant, — I said. — I don't believe he will jump off one of the bridges, for he has too much principle; but I mean to follow him and see where he goes, for he looks as if his mind were made up to something.

I followed him at a reasonable distance. He walked doggedly along, looking neither to the right nor the left, turned into State Street, and made for a well-known Life-Insurance Office. Luckily, the doctor was there and overhauled him on the spot. There was nothing the matter with him, he said, and he could have his life insured as a sound one. He came out in good spirits, and told me this soon after.

This led me to make some remarks the next morning on the manners of well-bred and ill-bred people.

I began, — The whole essence of true gentle-breeding (one does not like to say gentility) lies in the wish and the art to be agreeable. Good-breeding is *surface-Christianity.* Every look, movement, tone, expression, subject of discourse, that may give pain to another is habitually excluded from conversational intercourse. This is the reason why rich people are apt to be so much more agreeable than others.

——I thought you were a great champion of equality,—said the discreet and severe lady who had accompanied our young friend, the Latin Tutor's daughter.

I go politically for *e*quality,—I said,—and socially for *the* quality.

Who are the "quality,"—said the Model, etc., —in a community like ours?

I confess I find this question a little difficult to answer,—I said.—Nothing is better known than the distinction of social ranks which exists in every community, and nothing is harder to define. The great gentlemen and ladies of a place are its real lords and masters and mistresses; they are the *quality*, whether in a monarchy or a republic; mayors and governors and generals and senators and ex-presidents are nothing to them. How well we know this, and how seldom it finds a distinct expression! Now I tell you truly, I believe in man as man, and I disbelieve in all distinctions except such as follow the natural lines of cleavage in a society which has crystallized according to its own true laws. But the essence of equality is to be able to say the truth; and there is nothing more curious than these truths relating to the stratification of society.

Of all the facts in this world that do not take hold of immortality, there is not one so intensely real, permanent, and engrossing as this of social position, — as you see by the circumstance that the core of all the great social orders the world has seen has been, and is still, for the most part, a privileged class of gentlemen and ladies arranged in a regular scale of precedence among themselves, but superior as a body to all else.

Nothing but an ideal Christian equality, which we have been getting farther away from since the days of the Primitive Church, can prevent this subdivision of society into classes from taking place everywhere, — in the great centres of our republic as much as in old European monarchies. Only there position is more absolutely hereditary, — here it is more completely elective.

—— Where is the election held? and what are the qualifications? and who are the electors? — said the Model.

Nobody ever sees when the vote is taken; there never is a formal vote. The women settle it mostly; and they know wonderfully well what is presentable, and what can't stand the blaze of the chandeliers and the critical eye and ear of people trained to know a staring shade in a ribbon, a false light in a jewel, an ill-bred tone, an angular movement, everything that betrays a coarse fibre and cheap training. As a general thing, you do not get elegance short of two or three removes from the soil, out of which our best blood doubtless comes, — quite as good, no doubt, as if it came from those old prize-fighters with iron pots on their heads, to whom some great people are so fond of tracing their descent through a line of small artisans and petty shopkeepers whose veins have held "base" fluid enough to fill the Cloaca Maxima!

Does not money go everywhere? — said the Model.

Almost. And with good reason. For though there are numerous exceptions, rich people are, as I said, commonly altogether the most agreeable companions. The influence of a fine house, graceful furniture, good libraries, well-ordered tables, trim servants, and, above all, a position so secure that one becomes unconscious of it, gives a harmony and refinement to the character and manners which we feel, even if we cannot explain their charm. Yet we can get at the reason of it by thinking a little.

All these appliances are to shield the sensibility from disagreeable contacts, and to soothe it by varied natural and artificial influences. In this way the mind, the taste, the feelings, grow delicate, just as the hands grow white and soft when saved from toil and incased in soft gloves. The whole nature becomes subdued into suavity. I confess I like the quality-ladies better than the common kind even of literary ones. They haven't read the last book, perhaps, but they attend better to you when you are talking to them. If they are never learned, they make up for it in tact and elegance. Besides, I think, on the whole, there is less self-assertion in diamonds than in dogmas. I don't know where you will find a sweeter portrait of humility than in Esther, the poor play-girl of King Ahasuerus; yet Esther put on her royal apparel when she went before her lord. I have no doubt she was a more gracious and agreeable person than Deborah, who judged the people and wrote the story of Sisera. The wisest woman you talk with is ignorant of something that you know, but an elegant woman never forgets her elegance.

Dowdyism is clearly an expression of imperfect vitality. The highest fashion is intensely alive,—not alive necessarily to the truest and best things, but with its blood tingling, as it were, in all its extremities and to the farthest point of its surface, so that the feather in its bonnet is as fresh as the crest of a fighting-cock, and the rosette on its slipper as clean-cut and *pimpant* (pronounce it English fashion,—it is a good word) as a dahlia. As a general rule, that society where flattery is acted is much more agreeable than that where it is spoken. Don't you see why? Attention and deference don't require you to make fine speeches expressing your sense of unworthiness (lies) and returning all the compliments paid you. This is one reason.

—— A woman of sense ought to be above flattering any man, — said the Model.

[*My reflection.* Oh! oh! no wonder you didn't get married. Served you right.] *My remark.* Surely, Madam, — if you mean by flattery telling people boldly to their faces that they are this or that, which they are not. But a woman who does not carry a halo of good feeling and desire to make everybody contented about with her wherever she goes, — an atmosphere of grace, mercy, and peace, of at least six feet radius, which wraps every human being upon whom she voluntarily bestows her presence, and so flatters him with the comfortable thought that she is rather glad he is alive than otherwise, isn't worth the trouble of talking to, *as a woman;* she may do well enough to hold discussions with.

—— I don't think the Model exactly liked this. She said, — a little spitefully, I thought, — that a sensible man might stand a little praise, but would of course soon get sick of it, if he were in the habit of getting much.

Oh, yes, — I replied, — just as men get sick of tobacco. It is notorious how apt they are to get tired of that vegetable.

—— That's so! — said the young fellow John. — I've got tired of my cigars and burnt 'em all up.

I am heartily glad to hear it, — said the Model.

— I wish they were all disposed of in the same way.

So do I, — said the young fellow John.

Can't you get your friends to unite with you in committing those odious instruments of debauchery to the flames in which you have consumed your own?

I wish I could, — said the young fellow John.

It would be a noble sacrifice, — said the Model, — and every American woman would be grateful to you. Let us burn them all in a heap out in the yard.

That a'n't my way, — said the young fellow John; — I burn 'em one 't' time, — little end in my mouth and big end outside.

—— I watched for the effect of this sudden change of programme, when it should reach the calm stillness of the Model's interior apprehension, as a boy watches for the splash of a stone which he has dropped into a well. But before it had fairly reached the water, poor Iris, who had followed the conversation with a certain interest until it turned this sharp corner, (for she seems rather to fancy the young fellow John,) laughed out such a clear, loud laugh, that it started us all off, as the locust-cry of some full-throated soprano drags a multitudinous chorus after it. It was plain that some dam or other had broken in the soul of this young girl, and she was squaring up old scores of laughter, out of which she had been cheated, with a grand flood of merriment that swept all before it. So we had a great laugh all round, in which the Model — who, if sne had as many virtues as there are spokes to a wheel, all compacted with a personality as round and complete as its tire, yet wanted that one little addition of grace, which seems so small, and is as important as the linch-pin in trundling over the rough ways of life — had not the tact to join. She seemed to be "stuffy" about it, as the young fellow John said. In fact, I was afraid the joke would have cost us both our new lady-boarders. It had no effect, however, except, perhaps, to hasten the departure of the elder of the two, who could, on the whole, be spared.

—— I had meant to make this note of our conversation a text for a few axioms on the matter of breeding. But it so happened, that, exactly at this point of my record, a very distinguished philosopher, whom several of our boarders and myself go to hear, and whom no doubt many of my readers follow habitually, treated this matter of *manners*. Up to this point, if I have been so fortunate as to coincide with him in opinion, and so unfortunate as to try to express what he has more felicitously said, nobody is to blame; for what has been given thus far was all written before the lecture was delivered. But what shall I do now? He told us it was childish to lay down rules for deportment, — but he could not help laying down a few.

Thus, — *Nothing so vulgar as to be in a hurry.* — True, but hard of application. People with short legs step quickly, because legs are pendulums, and swing more times in a minute the shorter they are. Generally a natural rhythm runs through the whole organization: quick pulse, fast breathing, hasty speech, rapid trains of thought, excitable temper. *Stillness* of person and steadiness of features are signal marks of good-breeding. Vulgar persons can't sit still, or, at least, they must work their limbs or features.

Talking of one's own ails and grievances. — Bad enough, but not so bad as insulting the person you talk with by remarking on his ill-looks, or appearing to notice any of his personal peculiarities.

Apologizing. — A very desperate habit, — one that is rarely cured. Apology is only egotism wrong side out. Nine times out of ten, the first thing a man's companion knows of his shortcoming is from his apology. It is mighty presumptuous on your part to suppose your small failures of so much consequence that you must make a talk about them.

Good dressing, quiet ways, low tones of voice, lips that can wait, and eyes that do not wander, — shyness of personalities, except in certain intimate communions,—to be *light in hand* in conversation, to have ideas, but to be able to make talk, if necessary, without them,—to belong to the company you are in, and not to yourself,—to have nothing in your dress or furniture so fine that you cannot afford to spoil it and get another like it, yet to preserve the harmonies throughout your person and dwelling: I should say that this was a fair capital of manners to begin with.

Under bad manners, as under graver faults, lies very commonly an overestimate of our special individuality, as distinguished from our generic humanity. It is just here that the very highest society asserts its superior breeding. Among truly elegant people of the highest *ton*, you will find more real equality in social intercourse than in a country village. As nuns drop their birth-names and become Sister Margaret and Sister Mary, so high-bred people drop their personal distinctions and become brothers and sisters of conversational charity. Nor are fashionable people without their heroism. I believe there are men who have shown as much self-devotion in carrying a lone wall-flower down to the supper-table as ever saint or martyr in the act that has canonized his name. There are Florence Nightingales of the ballroom, whom nothing can hold back from their errands of mercy. They find out the red-handed, glove-less undergraduate of bucolic antecedents, as he squirms in his corner, and distil their soft words upon him like dew upon the green herb. They reach even the poor relation, whose dreary apparition saddens the perfumed atmosphere of the sumptuous drawing-room. I have known one of these angels ask, *of her own accord*, that a desolate middle-aged man, whom nobody seemed to know, should be presented to her by the hostess. He wore no shirt-collar, — he had on black gloves, — and was flourishing a red bandanna handkerchief! Match me this, ye proud children of poverty, who boast of your paltry sacrifices for each other! Virtue in humble life! What is that to the glorious self-renunciation of a martyr in pearls and diamonds? As I saw this noble woman bending gracefully before the social mendicant, — the white billows of her beauty heaving under the foam of the traitorous laces that half revealed them, — I should have wept with sympathetic emotion, but that tears, except as a private demonstration, are an ill-disguised expression of self-consciousness and vanity, which is inadmissible in good society.

I have sometimes thought, with a pang, of the position in which political chance or contrivance might hereafter place some one of our fellow-citizens. It has happened hitherto, so far as my limited knowledge goes, that the President of the United States has always been what might be called in general terms a gentleman. But what if at some future time the choice of the people should fall upon one on whom that lofty title could not, by any stretch of charity, be bestowed? This may happen, — how soon the future only knows. Think of this miserable man of coming political possibilities, — an unpresentable boor, sucked into office by one of those eddies in the flow of popular sentiment which carry straws and chips into the public harbor, while the prostrate trunks of the monarchs of the forest hurry down on the senseless stream to the gulf of political oblivion! Think of him, I say, and of the concentrated gaze of good society through its thousand eyes, all confluent, as it were, in one great burning-glass of ice that shrivels its wretched object in fiery torture, itself cold as the glacier of an unsunned cavern! No, — there will be angels of good-breeding then as now, to shield the victim of free institutions from himself and from his torturers. I can fancy a lovely woman playfully withdrawing the knife which he would abuse by making it an instrument for the conveyance of food, — or, failing in this kind artifice, sacrificing herself by imitating his use of that implement; how much harder than to plunge it into her bosom, like Lucretia! I can see her studying his provincial dialect until she becomes the Champollion of New England or Western or Southern barbarisms. She has learned that *häow* means *what;* that *thinkin'* is the same thing as *thinking;* or she has found out the meaning of that extraordinary monosyllable, which no single-tongued phonographer can make legible, prevailing on the banks of the Hudson and at its embouchure, and elsewhere, — what they say when they think they say *first,* (*fe-eest,* —*fe* as in the French *le*), — or that *cheer* means *chair,* — or that *urritation* means *irritation,* — and so of other enormities. Nothing surprises her. The highest breeding, you know, comes round to the Indian standard, — to take everything coolly, — *nil admirari,* — if you happen to be learned and like the Roman phrase for the same thing.

If you like the company of people that stare at you from head to foot to see if there is a hole in your coat, or if you have not grown a little older, or if your eyes are not yellow with jaundice, or if your complexion is not a little faded, and so on, and then convey the fact to you, in the style in which the Poor Relation addressed the divinity-student, — go with them as much as you like. I hate the sight of the wretches. Don't for mercy's sake think I hate *them;* the distinction is one my friend or I drew long ago. No matter where you find such people; they are clowns. The rich woman who looks and talks in this way is not half so much a lady as her Irish servant, whose pretty "saving your presence," when she has to say something which offends her natural sense of good manners, has a hint in it of the breeding of courts, and the blood of old Milesian kings, which very likely runs in her veins,—thinned by two hundred years of potato, which, being an underground fruit, tends to drag down the generations that are made of it to the earth from which it came, and, filling their veins with starch, turn them into a kind of human vegetable.

I say, if you like such people, go with them. But I am going to make a practical application of the example at the beginning of this particular record, which some young people who are going to choose professional advisers by-and-by may remember and thank me for. If you are making choice of a physician, be sure you get one, if possible, with a cheerful and serene countenance. A physician is not—at least, ought not to be—an executioner; and a sentence of death on his face is as bad as a warrant for execution signed by the Governor. As a general rule, no man has a right to tell another by word or look that he is going to die. It may be necessary in some extreme cases; but as a rule, it is the last extreme of impertinence which one human being can offer to another. "You have killed me," said a patient once to a physician who had rashly told him he was incurable. He ought to have lived six months, but he was dead in six weeks. If we will only let Nature and the God of Nature alone, persons will commonly learn their condition as early as they ought to know it, and not be cheated out of their natural birthright of hope of recovery, which is intended to accompany sick people as long as life is comfortable, and is graciously replaced by the hope of heaven, or at least of rest, when life has become a burden which the bearer is ready to let fall.

Underbred people tease their sick and dying friends to death. The chance of a gentleman or lady with a given mortal ailment to live a certain time is as good again as that of the common sort of coarse people. As you go down the social scale, you reach a point at length where the common talk in sick rooms is of churchyards and sepulchres, and a kind of perpetual vivisection is forever carried on, upon the person of the miserable sufferer.

And so, in choosing your clergyman, other things being equal, prefer the one of a wholesome and cheerful habit of mind and body. If you can get along with people who carry a certificate in their faces that their goodness is so great as to make them very miserable, your children cannot. And whatever offends one of these little ones cannot be right in the eyes of Him who loved them so well.

After all, as *you* are a gentleman or a lady, you will probably select gentlemen for your bodily and spiritual advisers, and then all will be right.

This repetition of the above words,—*gentleman and lady*,—which could not be conveniently avoided, reminds me what strange uses are made of them by those who ought to know what they mean. Thus, at a marriage ceremony, once, of two very excellent persons who had been at service, instead of, Do you take this man, etc.? and, Do you take this woman? how do you think the officiating clergyman put the questions? It was, Do you, MISS So and So, take this GENTLEMAN? and, Do you, MR. This or That, take this LADY?! What would any English duchess, ay, or the Queen of England herself, have thought, if the Archbishop of Canterbury had called her and her bridegroom anything but plain woman and man at such a time?

I don't doubt the Poor Relation thought it was all very fine, if she happened to be in the church; but if the worthy man who uttered these monstrous words—monstrous in such a connection—had known the ludicrous surprise, the convulsion of inward disgust and contempt, that seized upon many of the persons who were present,—had guessed what a sudden flash of light it threw on the Dutch gilding, the pinchbeck, the shabby, perking pretension belonging to certain social layers, — so inherent in their whole mode of being, that the holiest offices of religion cannot exclude its impertinences, — the good man would have given his marriage-fee twice over to recall that superb and full-blown vulgarism. Any persons whom it could please could have no better notion of what the words referred to signify than of the meaning of *apsides* and *asymptotes.*

MAN! Sir! WOMAN! Sir! Gentility is a fine thing, not to be undervalued, as I have been trying to explain; but humanity comes before that.

> "When Adam delved and Eve span,
> Who was then the gentleman?"

The beauty of that plainness of speech and manners which comes from the finest training is not to be understood by those whose *habitat* is below a certain level. Just as the exquisite sea-anemones and all the graceful ocean-flowers die out at some fathoms below the surface, the elegances and suavities of life die out one by one as we sink through the social scale. Fortunately, the virtues are more tenacious of life, and last pretty well until we get down to the mud of absolute pauperism, where they do not flourish greatly.

——I had almost forgotten about our boarders. As the Model of all the Virtues is about to leave us, I find myself wondering what is the reason we are not all very sorry. Surely we all like good persons. She is a good person. Therefore we like her. — Only we don't.

This brief syllogism, and its briefer negative, involving the principle which some English conveyancer borrowed from a French wit and embodied in the lines by which *Dr. Fell* is made unamiably immortal, — this syllogism, I say, is one that most persons have had occasion to construct and demolish, respecting somebody or other, as I have done for the Model. "Pious and painefull." Why has that excellent old phrase gone out of use? Simply because these good *painefull* or painstaking persons proved to be such nuisances in the long run, that the word "painefull" came, before people thought of it, to mean *paingiving* instead of *painstaking*.

—— So, the old fellah's off to-morrah, — said the young man John.

Old fellow? — said I, — whom do you mean?

Why, the one that came with our little beauty, — the old fellah in petticoats.

—— Now that means something, — said I to myself. — These rough young rascals very often hit the nail on the head, if they do strike with their eyes shut. A real woman does a great many things without knowing why she does them; but these pattern machines mix up their intellects with everything they do, just like men. They can't help it, no doubt; but we can't help getting sick of them, either. Intellect is to a woman's nature what her watch-spring skirt is to her dress; it ought to underlie her silks and embroideries, but not to show itself too staringly on the outside.— You don't know, perhaps, but I will tell you;— the brain is the palest of all the internal organs, and the heart the reddest. Whatever comes from the brain carries the hue of the place it came from, and whatever comes from the heart carries the heat and color of its birthplace.

The young man John did not hear my *soliloque*, of course, but sent up one more bubble from our sinking conversation, in the form of a statement, that she was at liberty to go to a personage who receives no visits, as is commonly supposed, from virtuous people.

Why, I ask again, (of my reader,) should a person who never did anybody any wrong, but, on the contrary, is an estimable and intelligent, nay, a particularly enlightened and exemplary member of society, fail to inspire interest, love, and devotion? Because of the *reversed current* in the flow of thought and emotion. The red heart sends all its instincts up to the white brain to be analyzed, chilled, blanched, and so become pure reason, which is just exactly what we do not want of woman as woman. The current should run the other way. The nice, calm, cold thought, which in women shapes itself so rapidly that they hardly know it as thought, should always travel to the lips *viâ* the heart. It does so in those women whom all love and admire. It travels the wrong way in the Model. That is the reason why the Little Gentleman said, "I hate her, I hate her." That is the reason why the young man John called her the "old fellah," and banished her to the company of the great Unpresentable. That is the reason why I, the Professor, am picking her to pieces with scalpel and forceps. That is the reason why the young girl whom she has befriended repays her kindness with gratitude and respect, rather than with the devotion and passionate fondness which lie sleeping beneath the calmness of her amber eyes. I can see her, as she sits between this estimable and most correct of personages and the misshapen, crotchety, often violent and explosive little man on the other side of her, leaning and swaying towards him as she speaks, and looking into his sad eyes as if she found some fountain in them at which her soul could quiet its thirst.

Women like the Model are a natural product of a chilly climate and high culture. It is not

> "The frolic wind that breathes the spring,
> Zephyr with Aurora playing,"

when the two meet

> —— "on beds of violets blue,
> And fresh-blown roses washed in dew,"

that claim such women as their offspring. It is rather the east wind, as it blows out of the fogs of Newfoundland, and clasps a clear-eyed wintry noon on the chill bridal couch of a New England ice-quarry. — Don't throw up your cap now, and hurrah as if this were giving up everything, and turning against the best growth of our latitudes, — the daughters of the soil. The brain-women never interest us like the heart-women; white roses please less than red. But our Northern seasons have a narrow green streak of spring, as well as a broad white zone of winter, — they have a glowing band of summer and a golden stripe of autumn in their many-colored wardrobe; and women are born to us that wear all these hues of earth and heaven in their souls. Our ice-eyed brain-women are really admirable, if we only ask of them just what they can give, and no more. Only compare them, talking or writing, with one of those babbling, chattering dolls, of warmer latitudes, who do not know enough even to keep out of print, and who are interesting to us only as specimens of *arrest of development* for our psychological cabinets.

Good-bye, Model of all the Virtues! We can spare you now. A little clear perfection, undiluted with human weakness, goes a great way. Go! be useful, be honorable and honored, be just, be charitable, talk pure reason, and help to disenchant the world by the light of an achromatic understanding. Good-bye! Where is my Béranger? I must read a verse or two of "Frétillon."

Fair play for all. But don't claim incompatible qualities for anybody. Justice is a very rare virtue in our community. Everything that public sentiment cares about is put into a Papin's digester, and boiled under high pressure till all is turned into one homogeneous pulp, and the very bones give up their jelly. What are all the strongest epithets of our dictionary to us now? The critics and politicians, and especially the philanthropists, have chewed them, till they are mere wads of syllable-fibre, without a suggestion of their old pungency and power.

Justice! A good man respects the rights even of brute matter and arbitrary symbols. If he writes the same word twice in succession, by accident, he always erases the one that stands *second;* has not the first-comer the prior right? This act of abstract justice, which I trust many of my readers, like myself, have often performed, is a curious anti-illustration, by the way, of the absolute wickedness of human dispositions. Why doesn't a man always strike out the *first* of the two words, to gratify his diabolical love of *injustice*?

So, I say, we owe a genuine, substantial tribute of respect to these filtered intellects which have left their womanhood on the strainer. They are so clear that it is a pleasure at times to look at the world of thought through them. But the rose and purple tints of richer natures they cannot give us, and it is not just to them to ask it.

Fashionable society gets at these rich natures very often in a way one would hardly at first think of. It loves vitality above all things, sometimes disguised by affected languor, always well kept under by the laws of good-breeding, — but still it loves abundant life, opulent and showy organizations, — the spherical rather than the plane trigonometry of female architecture, — plenty of red blood, flashing eyes, tropical voices, and forms that bear the splendors of dress without growing pale beneath their lustre. Among these you will find the most delicious women you will ever meet, — women whom dress and flattery and the round of city gayeties cannot spoil, — talking with whom, you forget their diamonds and laces, — and around whom all the nice details of elegance, which the cold-blooded beauty next them is scanning so nicely, blend in one harmonious whole, too perfect to be disturbed by the petulant sparkle of a jewel, or the yellow glare of a bangle, or the gay toss of a feather.

There are many things that I, personally, love better than fashion or wealth. Not to speak of those highest objects of our love and loyalty, I think I love ease and independence better than the golden slavery of perpetual *matinées* and *soirées*, or the pleasures of accumulation.

But fashion and wealth are two very solemn realities, which the frivolous class of moralists have talked a great deal of silly stuff about. Fashion is only the attempt to realize Art in living forms and social intercourse. What business has a man who knows nothing about the beautiful, and cannot pronounce the word *view*, to talk about fashion to a set of people who, if one of the quality left a card at their doors, would contrive to keep it on the very top of their heap of the names of their two-story acquaintances, till it was as yellow as the Codex Vaticanus?

Wealth, too, — what an endless repetition of the same foolish trivialities about it! Take the single fact of its alleged uncertain tenure and transitory character. In old times, when men were all the time fighting and robbing each other, — in those tropical countries where the Sabeans and the Chaldeans stole all a man's cattle and camels, and there were frightful tornadoes and rains of fire from heaven, it was true enough that riches took wings to themselves not unfrequently in a very unexpected way. But, with common prudence in investments, it is not so now. In fact, there is nothing earthly that lasts so well, on the whole, as money. A man's learning dies with him; even his virtues fade out of remembrance:

but the dividends on the stocks he bequeathes to his children live and keep his memory green.

I do not think there is much courage or originality in giving utterance to truths that everybody knows, but which get overlaid by conventional trumpery. The only distinction which it is necessary to point out to feeble-minded folk is this: that, in asserting the breadth and depth of that significance which gives to fashion and fortune their tremendous power, we do not indorse the extravagances which often disgrace the one, nor the meanness which often degrades the other.

A remark which seems to contradict a universally current opinion is not generally to be taken "neat," but watered with the ideas of common-sense and commonplace people. So, if any of my young friends should be tempted to waste their substance on white kids and "all-rounds," or to insist on becoming millionnaires at once, by anything I have said, I will give them references to some of the class referred to, well known to the public as providers of literary diluents, who will weaken any truth so that there is not an old woman in the land who cannot take it with perfect impunity.

I am afraid some of the blessed saints in diamonds will think I mean to flatter them. I hope not; — if I do, set it down as a weakness. But there is so much foolish talk about wealth and fashion, (which, of course, draw a good many heartless and essentially vulgar people into the glare of their candelabra, but which have a real respectability and meaning, if we will only look at them stereoscopically, with both eyes instead of one,) that I thought it a duty to speak a few words for them. Why can't somebody give us a list of things that everybody thinks and nobody says, and another list of things that everybody says and nobody thinks?

Lest my parish should suppose we have forgotten graver matters in these lesser topics, I beg them to drop these trifles and read the following lesson for the day.

THE TWO STREAMS.

Behold the rocky wall
That down its sloping sides
Pours the swift rain-drops, blending, as they fall,
In rushing river-tides!

Yon stream, whose sources run
Turned by a pebble's edge,
Is Athabasca, rolling toward the sun
Through the cleft mountain-ledge.

The slender rill had strayed,
But for the slanting stone,

To evening's ocean, with the tangled braid
    Of foam-flecked Oregon.

    So from the heights of Will
    Life's parting stream descends,
And, as a moment turns its slender rill,
    Each widening torrent bends,—

    From the same cradle's side,
    From the same mother's knee,—
One to long darkness and the frozen tide,
    One to the Peaceful Sea!

VII.

OUR landlady's daughter is a young lady of some pretensions to gentility. She wears her bonnet well back on her head, which is known by all to be a mark of high breeding. She wears her trains very long, as the great ladies do in Europe. To be sure, their dresses are so made only to sweep the tapestried floors of châteaux and palaces; as those odious aristocrats of the other side do not go draggling through the mud in silks and satins, but, forsooth, must ride in coaches when they are in full dress. It is true, that, considering various habits of the American people, also the little accidents which the best-kept sidewalks are liable to, a lady who has swept a mile of them is not exactly in such a condition that one would care to be her neighbor. But then there is no need of being so hard on these slight weaknesses of the poor, dear women as our little deformed gentleman was the other day.

——There are no such women as the Boston women, Sir,—he said. Forty-two degrees, north latitude, Rome, Sir, Boston, Sir! They had grand women in old Rome, Sir,—and the women bore such men-children as never the world saw before. And so it was here, Sir. I tell you, the revolution the Boston boys started had to run in woman's milk before it ran in man's blood, Sir!

But confound the make-believe women we have turned loose in our streets!—where do *they* come from? Not out of Boston parlors, I trust. Why, there isn't a beast or a bird that would drag its tail through the dirt in the way these creatures do their dresses. Because a queen or a duchess wears long robes on great occasions, a maid-of-all-work or a factory-girl thinks she must make herself a nuisance by trailing through the street, picking up and carrying about with her——pah! that's what I call getting vulgarity into your bones and marrow. Making believe be what you are not is the essence of vulgarity. Show over dirt is the one attribute of vulgar people. If any man can walk behind one of these women and see what she rakes up as she goes, and not feel squeamish, he has got a tough stomach. I wouldn't let one of 'em into my room without serving 'em as David served Saul at the cave in the wilderness, — cut off his skirts, Sir! cut off his skirts!

I suggested, that I had seen some pretty stylish ladies who offended in the way he condemned.

Stylish *women*, I don't doubt, — said the Little Gentleman. — Don't tell me that a true lady ever sacrifices the duty of keeping all about her sweet and clean to the wish of making a vulgar show. I won't believe it of a lady. There are some things that no fashion has any right to touch, and cleanliness is one of those things. If a woman wishes to show that her husband or her father has got money, which she wants and means to spend, but doesn't know how, let her buy a yard or two of silk and pin it to her dress when she goes out to walk, but let her unpin it before she goes into the house; — there may be poor women that will think it worth disinfecting. It is an insult to a respectable laundress to carry such things into a house for her to deal with. I don't like the Bloomers any too well, — in fact, I never saw but one, and she — or he, or it — had a mob of boys after her, or whatever you call the creature, as if she had been a ———

The Little Gentleman stopped short, — flushed somewhat, and looked round with that involuntary, suspicious glance which the subjects of any bodily misfortune are very apt to cast round them. His eye wandered over the company, none of whom, excepting myself and one other, had, probably, noticed the movement. They fell at last on Iris,—his next neighbor, you remember.

——We know in a moment, on looking suddenly at a person, if that person's eyes have been fixed on us. Sometimes we are conscious of it *before* we turn so as to see the person. Strange secrets of curiosity, of impertinence, of malice, of love, leak out in this way. There is no need of Mrs. Felix Lorraine's reflection in the mirror, to tell us that she is plotting evil for us behind our backs. We know it, as we know by the ominous stillness of a child that some mischief or other is going on. A young girl betrays, in a moment, that her eyes have been feeding on the face where you find them fixed, and not merely brushing over it with their pencils of blue or brown light.

A certain involuntary adjustment assimilates us, you may also observe, to that upon which we look. Roses redden the cheeks of her who stoops to gather them, and buttercups turn little people's chins yellow. When we look at a vast landscape, our chests expand as if we would enlarge to fill it. When we examine a minute object, we naturally contract, nor only our foreheads, but all our dimensions. If I *see* two men wrestling, I wrestle too, with my limbs and features. When a country-fellow comes upon the stage, you will see twenty faces in the boxes putting on the bumpkin expression. There is no need of multiplying instances to reach this generalization; every person and thing we look upon puts its special mark upon us. If this is repeated often enough, we get a permanent resemblance to it, or, at least, a fixed aspect which we took from it. Husband and wife come to look alike at last, as has often been noticed. It is a common saying of a jockey, that he is "all horse"; and I have often fancied that milkmen get a stiff, upright carriage, and an angular movement of the arm, that remind one of a pump and the working of its handle.

All this came in by accident, just because I happened to mention that the Little Gentleman found that Iris had been looking at him with her soul in her eyes, when his glance rested on her after wandering round the company. What he thought, it is hard to say; but the shadow of suspicion faded off from his face, and he looked calmly into the amber eyes, resting his cheek upon the hand that wore the red jewel.

——If it were a possible thing,—women are such strange creatures! Is there any trick that love and their own fancies do not play them? Just see how they marry! A woman that gets hold of a bit of manhood is like one of those

Chinese wood-carvers who work on any odd, fantastic root that comes to hand, and, if it is only bulbous above and bifurcated below, will always contrive to make a man — such as he is — out of it. I should like to see any kind of a man, distinguishable from a Gorilla, that some good and even pretty woman could not shape a husband out of.

—— A child, — yes, if you choose to call her so, — but such a child! Do you know how Art brings all ages together? There is no age to the angels and ideal human forms among which the artist lives, and he shares their youth until his hand trembles and his eye grows dim. The youthful painter talks of white-bearded Leonardo as if he were a brother, and the veteran forgets that Raphael died at an age to which his own is of patriarchal antiquity.

But why this lover of the beautiful should be so drawn to one whom Nature has wronged so deeply seems hard to explain. Pity, I suppose. They say that leads to love.

—— I thought this matter over until I became excited and curious, and determined to set myself more seriously at work to find out what was going on in these wild hearts and where their passionate lives were drifting. I say wild hearts and passionate lives, because I think I can look through this seeming calmness of youth and this apparent feebleness of organization, and see that Nature, whom it is very hard to cheat, is only waiting as the sapper waits in his mine, knowing that all is in readiness and the slow-match burning quietly down to the powder. He will leave it by-and-by, and then it will take care of itself.

One need not wait to see the smoke coming through the roof of a house and the flames breaking out of the windows to know that the building is on fire. Hark! There is a quiet, steady, unobtrusive, crisp, not loud, but very knowing little creeping crackle that is tolerably intelligible. There is a whiff of something floating about, suggestive of toasting shingles. Also a sharp pyroligneous-acid pungency in the air that stings one's eyes. Let us get up and see what is going on. — Oh, — oh, — oh! do you know what has got hold of you? It is the great red dragon that is born of the little red eggs we call *sparks*, with his hundred blowing red manes, and his thousand lashing red tails, and his multitudinous red eyes glaring at every crack and key-hole, and his countless red tongues lapping the beams he is going to crunch presently, and his hot breath warping the panels and cracking the glass and making old timber sweat that had forgotten it was ever alive with sap. Run for your life! leap! or you will be a cinder in five minutes, that nothing but a coroner would take for the wreck of a human being!

If any gentleman will have the kindness to stop this run-away comparison, I shall be much obliged to him. All I intended to say was, that we need not wait for hearts to break out in flames to know that they are full of combustibles and that a spark has got among them. I don't pretend to say or know what it is that brings these two persons together;—and when I say together, I only mean that there is an evident affinity of some kind or other which makes their commonest intercourse strangely significant, as that each seems to understand a look or a word of the other. When the young girl laid her hand on the Little Gentleman's arm,—which so greatly shocked the Model, you may remember,—I saw that she had learned the lion-tamer's secret. She masters him, and yet I can see she has a kind of awe of him, as the man who goes into the cage has of the monster that he makes a baby of.

One of two things must happen. The first is love, downright love, on the part of this young girl, for the poor little misshapen man. You may laugh, if you like. But women are apt to love the men who they think have the largest capacity of loving;—and who can love like one that has thirsted all his life long for the smile of youth and beauty, and seen it fly his presence as the wave ebbed from the parched lips of him whose fabled punishment is the perpetual type of human longing and disappointment? What would become of *him*, if this fresh soul should stoop upon him in her first young passion, as the flamingo drops out of the sky upon some lonely and dark lagoon in the marshes of Cagliari, with a flutter of scarlet feathers and a kindling of strange fires in the shadowy waters that hold her burning image?

—— Marry her, of course? — Why, no, not *of course.* I should think the chance less, on the whole, that he would be willing to marry her than she to marry him.

There is one other thing that might happen. If the interest he awakes in her gets to be a deep one, and yet has nothing of love in it, she will glance off from him into some great passion or other. All excitements run to love in women of a certain — let us not say age, but youth. An electrical current passing through a coil of wire makes a magnet of a bar of iron lying within it, but not touching it. So a woman is turned into a love-magnet by a tingling current of life running round her. I should like to see one of them balanced on a pivot properly adjusted, and watch if she did not turn so as to point north and south, — as she would, if the love-currents are like those of the earth our mother.

Pray, do you happen to remember Wordsworth's "Boy of Windermere"? This boy used to put his hands to his mouth, and shout aloud, mimicking the hooting of the owls, who would answer him

> "with quivering peals,
> And long halloos and screams, and echoes loud
> Redoubled and redoubled."

When they failed to answer him, and he hung listening intently for their voices, he would sometimes catch the faint sound of far distant waterfalls, or the whole scene around him would imprint itself with new force upon his perceptions.—Read the sonnet, if you please;—it is Wordsworth all over,—trivial in subject, solemn in style, vivid in description, prolix in detail, true metaphysically, but immensely suggestive of "imagination," to use a mild term, when related as an actual fact of a sprightly youngster.

All I want of it is to enforce the principle, that, when the door of the soul is once opened to a guest, there is no knowing who will come in next.

——Our young girl keeps up her early habit of sketching heads and characters. Nobody is, I should think, more faithful and exact in the drawing of the academical figures given her as lessons; but there is a perpetual arabesque of fancies that runs round the margin of her drawings, and there is one book which I know she keeps to run riot in, where, if anywhere, a shrewd eye would be most likely to read her thoughts. This book of hers I mean to see, if I can get at it honorably.

I have never yet crossed the threshold of the Little Gentleman's chamber. How he lives, when he once gets within it, I can only guess. His hours are late, as I have said; often, on waking late in the night, I see the light through cracks in his window-shutters on the wall of the house opposite. If the times of witchcraft were not over, I should be afraid to be so close a neighbor to a place from which there come such strange noises. Sometimes it is the dragging of something heavy over the floor, that makes me shiver to hear it, — it sounds so like what people that kill other people have to do now and then. Occasionally I hear very sweet strains of music, — whether of a wind or stringed instrument, or a human voice, strange as it may seem, I have often tried to find out, but through the partition I could not be quite sure. If I have not heard a woman cry and moan, and then again laugh as though she would die laughing, I have heard sounds so like them that — I am a fool to confess it — I have covered my head with the bedclothes; for I have had a fancy in my dreams, that I could hardly shake off when I woke up, about that so-called witch that was his great-grandmother, or whatever it was,—a sort of fancy that she visited the Little Gentleman,—a young woman in old-fashioned dress, with a red ring round her white neck,—not a necklace, but a dull stain.

Of course you don't suppose that I have any foolish superstitions about the matter,—I, the Professor, who have seen enough to take all that nonsense out of any man's head! It is not our beliefs that frighten us half so much as our fancies. A man not only believes, but knows he runs a risk, whenever he steps into a railroad car; but it doesn't worry him much. On the other hand, carry that man across a pasture a little way from some dreary country-village, and show him an old house where there were strange deaths a good many years ago, and there are rumors of ugly spots on the walls,——the old man hung himself in the garret, that is certain, and ever since the country-people have called it "the haunted house,"—the owners haven't been able to let it since the last tenants left on account of the noises,—so it has fallen into sad decay, and the moss grows on the rotten shingles of the roof, and the clapboards have turned black, and the windows rattle like teeth that chatter with fear, and the walls of the house begin to lean as if its knees were shaking,——take the man who didn't mind the real risk of the cars to that old house, on some dreary

November evening, and ask him to sleep there alone, — how do you think he will like it? He doesn't believe one word of ghosts, — but then he knows, that, whether waking or sleeping, his imagination will people the haunted chambers with ghostly images. It is not what we *believe*, as I said before, that frightens us commonly, but what we *conceive*. A principle that reaches a good way, if I am not mistaken. I say, then, that, if these odd sounds coming from the Little Gentleman's chamber sometimes make me nervous, so that I cannot get to sleep, it is not because I suppose he is engaged in any unlawful or mysterious way. The only wicked suggestion that ever came into my head was one that was founded on the landlady's story of his having a pile of gold; it was a ridiculous fancy; besides, I suspect the story of *sweating* gold was only one of the many fables got up to make the Jews odious and afford a pretext for plundering them. As for the sound like a woman laughing and crying, I never said it *was* a woman's voice; for, in the first place, I could only hear indistinctly; and, secondly, he may have an organ, or some queer instrument or other, with what they call the *vox humana* stop. If he moves his bed round to get away from the window, or for any such reason, there is nothing very frightful in that simple operation. Most of our foolish conceits explain themselves in some such simple way. And yet, for all that, I confess, that, when I woke up the other evening, and heard, first a sweet complaining cry, and then footsteps, and then the dragging sound, — nothing but his bed, I am quite sure, — I felt a stirring in the roots of my hair as the feasters did in Keats's terrible poem of "Lamia."

There is nothing very odd in my feeling nervous when I happen to lie awake and get listening for sounds. Just keep your ears open any time after midnight, when you are lying in bed in a lone attic of a dark night. What horrid, strange, suggestive, unaccountable noises you will hear! The *stillness* of night is a vulgar error. All the dead things seem to be alive. Crack! That is the old chest of drawers; you never hear it crack in the daytime. Creak! There's a door ajar; *you know you shut them all.* Where can that latch be that rattles so? Is anybody trying it softly? or, worse than any *body*, is ——? (Cold shiver.) Then a sudden gust that jars all the windows; — very strange! — there does not seem to be any wind about that it belongs to. When it stops, you hear the worms boring in the powdery beams overhead. Then steps outside, — a stray animal no doubt. All right, — but a gentle moisture breaks out all over you; and then something like a whistle or a cry, — another gust of wind, perhaps; that accounts for the rustling that just made your heart roll over and tumble about, so that it felt more like a live rat under your ribs than a part of your own body; then a crash of something that has fallen, — blown over, very likely ——— *Pater noster, qui es in cœlis!* for you are damp and cold, and sitting bolt upright, and the bed trembling so that the death-watch is frightened and has stopped ticking!

No, — night is an awful time for strange noises and secret doings. Who ever dreamed, till one of our sleepless neighbors told us of it, of that Walpurgis gathering of birds and beasts of prey, — foxes, and owls, and crows, and eagles, that come from all the country round on moonshiny nights to crunch the clams and muscles, and pick out the eyes of dead fishes that the storm has thrown on Chelsea Beach? Our old mother Nature has pleasant and cheery tones enough for us when she comes in her dress of blue and gold over the eastern hill-tops; but when she follows us up-stairs to our beds in her suit of black velvet and diamonds, every creak of her sandals and every whisper of her lips is full of mystery and fear.

You understand, then, distinctly, that I do not believe there is anything about this singular little neighbor of mine which is as it should not be. Probably a visit to his room would clear up all that has puzzled me, and make me laugh at the notions which began, I suppose, in nightmares, and ended by keeping my imagination at work so as almost to make me uncomfortable at times. But it is not so easy to visit him as some of our other boarders, for various reasons which I will not stop to mention. I think some of them are rather pleased to get "the Professor" under their ceilings.

The young man John, for instance, asked me to come up one day and try some "old Burbon," which he said was A 1. On asking him what was the number of his room, he answered, that it was forty-'leven, sky-parlor floor, but that I shouldn't find it, if he didn't go ahead to show me the way. I followed him to his *habitat*, being very willing to see in what kind of warren he burrowed, and thinking I might pick up something about the boarders who had excited my curiosity.

Mighty close quarters they were where the young man John bestowed himself and his furniture; this last consisting of a bed, a chair, a bureau, a trunk, and numerous pegs with coats and "pants" and "vests,"—as he was in the habit of calling waistcoats and pantaloons or trousers,—hanging up as if the owner had melted out of them. Several prints were pinned up unframed,—among them that grand national portrait-piece, "Barnum presenting Ossian E. Dodge to Jenny Lind," and a picture of a famous trot, in which I admired anew the cabalistic air of that imposing array of expressions, and especially the Italicized word, "Dan Mace *names* b. h. Major Slocum," and "Hiram Woodruff *names* g. m. Lady Smith." "Best three in five. Time: 2.40, 2.46, 2.50."

That set me thinking how very odd this matter of trotting horses is, as an index of the mathematical exactness of the laws of living mechanism. I saw Lady Suffolk trot a mile in 2.26. Flora Temple has trotted close down to 2.20; and Ethan Allen in 2.25, or less. Many horses have trotted their mile under 2.30; none that I remember in public as low down as 2.20. From five to ten *seconds*, then, in about a hundred and sixty is the whole range of the maxima of the present race of trotting-horses. The same thing is seen in the running of men. Many can run a mile in five minutes; but when one comes to the fractions below, they taper down until somewhere about 4.30 the maximum is reached. Averages of masses have been studied more than averages of maxima and minima. We know from the Registrar-General's Reports, that a certain number of children — say from one to two dozen — die every year in England from drinking hot water out of spouts of teakettles. We know, that, among suicides, women and men past a certain age almost never use fire-arms. A woman who has made up her mind to die is still afraid of a pistol or a gun. Or is it that the explosion would derange her costume? I say, averages of masses we have; but our tables of maxima we owe to the sporting men more than to the philosophers. The lesson their experience teaches is, that Nature makes no leaps,—does nothing *per saltum.* The greatest brain that ever lived, no doubt, was only a small fraction of an idea ahead of the second best. Just look at the chess-players. Leaving out the phenomenal exceptions, the nice shades that separate the skilful ones show how closely their brains approximate,—almost as closely as chronometers. Such a person is a "*knight*-player,"—he must have that piece given him. Another must have two pawns. Another, "pawn and two," or one pawn and two moves. Then we find one who claims "pawn and move," holding himself, with this fractional advantage, a match for one who would be pretty sure to beat him playing even.—So much are minds alike; and you and I think we are "peculiar,"—that Nature broke her jelly-mould after shaping our cerebral convolutions! So I reflected, standing and looking at the picture.

——I say, Governor,—broke in the young man John,—them hosses 'll stay jest as well, if you'll only set down. I've had 'em this year, and they haven't stirred. — He spoke, and handed the chair towards me, — seating himself, at the same time, on the end of the bed.

You have lived in this house some time? — I said, — with a note of interrogation at the end of the statement.

Do I look as if I'd lost much flesh? — said he, — answering my question by another.

No, — said I; — for that matter, I think you do credit to "the bountifully furnished table of the excellent lady who provides so liberally for the company that meets around her hospitable board."

[The sentence in quotation-marks was from one of those disinterested editorials in small type, which I suspect to have been furnished by a friend of the landlady's, and paid for as an advertisement. This impartial testimony to the superior qualities of the establishment and its head attracted a number of applicants for admission, and a couple of new boarders made a brief appearance at the table. One of them was of the class of people who grumble if they don't get canvas-backs and woodcocks every day, for three-fifty per week. The other was subject to somnambulism, or walking in the night, when he ought to have been asleep in his bed. In this state he walked into several of the boarders' chambers, his eyes wide open, as is usual with somnambulists, and, from some odd instinct or other, wishing to know what the hour was, got together a number of their watches, for the purpose of comparing them, as it would seem. Among them was a repeater, belonging to our young Marylander. He happened to wake up while the somnambulist was in his chamber, and, not knowing his infirmity, caught hold of him and gave him a dreadful shaking, after which he tied his hands and feet, and so left him till morning, when he introduced him to a gentleman used to taking care of such cases of somnambulism.]

If you, my reader, will please to skip backward, over this parenthesis, you will come to our conversation, which it has interrupted.

It a'n't the feed, — said the young man John, — it's the old woman's looks when a fellah lays it in too strong. The feed's well enough. After geese have got tough, 'n' turkeys have got strong, 'n' lamb's got old, 'n' veal's pretty nigh beef, 'n' sparragrass's growin' tall 'n' slim 'n' scattery about the head, 'n' green peas are gettin' so big 'n' hard they'd be dangerous if you fired 'em out of a revolver, we get hold of all them delicacies of the season. But it's too much like feedin' on live folks and devourin' widdah's substance, to lay yourself out in the eatin' way, when a fellah's as hungry as the chap that said a turkey was too much for one 'n' not enough for two. I can't help lookin' at the old woman. Corned-beef-days she's tolerable calm. Roastin'-days she worries some, 'n' keeps a sharp eye on the chap that carves. But when there's anything in the poultry line, it seems to hurt her feelin's so to see the knife goin' into the breast and joints comin' to pieces, that there's no comfort in eatin'. When I cut up an old fowl and help the boarders, I always feel as if I ought to say, Won't you have a slice of widdah? — instead of chicken.

The young man John fell into a train of reflections which ended in his producing a Bologna sausage, a plate of "crackers," as we Boston folks call certain biscuits, and the bottle of whiskey described as being A 1.

Under the influence of the crackers and sausage, he grew cordial and communicative.

It was time, I thought, to sound him as to those of our boarders who had excited my curiosity.

What do you think of our young Iris? — I began.

Fust-rate little filly; — he said. — Pootiest and nicest little chap I've seen since the schoolma'am left. Schoolma'am was a brown-haired one, — eyes coffee-color. This one has got wine-colored eyes, — 'n' that's the reason they turn a fellah's head, I suppose.

This is a splendid blonde, — I said, — the other was a brunette. Which style do you like best?

Which do I like best, boiled mutton or roast mutton? — said the young man John. Like 'em both, — it a'n't the color of 'em makes the goodness. I've been kind of lonely since schoolma'am went away. Used to like to look at her. I never said anything particular to her, that I remember, but ——

I don't know whether it was the cracker and sausage, or that the young fellow's feet were treading on the hot ashes of some longing that had not had time to cool, but his eye glistened as he stopped.

I suppose she wouldn't have looked at a fellah like me, — he said, — but I come pretty near tryin'. If she had said, Yes, though, I shouldn't have known what to have done with her. Can't marry a woman now-a-days till you're so deaf you have to cock your head like a parrot to hear what she says, and so long-sighted you can't see what she looks like nearer than arm's-length.

Here is another chance for you, — I said. — What do you want nicer than such a young lady as Iris?

It's no use, — he answered. — I look at them girls and feel as the fellah did when he missed catchin' the trout. — 'To'od 'a' cost more butter to cook him 'n' he's worth, — says the fellah. — Takes a whole piece o' goods to cover a girl up now-a-days. I'd as lief undertake to keep a span of elephants, — and take an ostrich to board, too, — as to marry one of 'em. What's the use? Clerks and counter-jumpers a'n't anything. Sparragrass and green peas a'n't for them, — not while they're young and tender. Hossback-ridin' a'n't for them, — except once a year, — on Fast-day. And marryin' a'n't for them. Sometimes a fellah feels lonely, and would like to have a nice young woman, to tell her how lonely he feels. And sometimes a fellah, — here the young man John looked very confidential, and, perhaps, as if a little ashamed of his weakness, — sometimes a fellah would like to have one o' them small young ones to trot on his knee and push about in a little wagon, — a kind of a little Johnny, you know; — it's odd enough, but, it seems to me, nobody can afford them little articles, except the folks that are so rich they can buy everything, and the folks that are so poor they don't want anything. It makes nice boys of us young fellahs, no doubt! And it's pleasant to see fine young girls sittin', like shopkeepers behind their goods, waitin', and waitin', and waitin', 'n' no customers, — and the men lingerin' round and lookin' at the goods, like folks that want to be customers, but haven't got the money!

Do you think the deformed gentleman means to make love to Iris? — I said.

What! Little Boston ask that girl to marry him! Well, now, that's comin' of it a little too strong. Yes, I guess she will marry him and carry him round in a basket, like a lame bantam! Look here! — he said, mysteriously; — one of the boarders swears there's a woman comes to see him, and that he has heard her singin' and screechin'. I should like to know what he's about in that den of his. He lays low 'n' keeps dark, — and, I tell you, there's a good many of the boarders would like to get into his chamber, but he don't seem to want 'em. Biddy could tell somethin' about what she's seen when she's been to put his room to rights. She's a Paddy 'n' a fool, but she knows enough to keep her tongue still. All I know is, I saw her crossin' herself one day when she came out of that room. She looked pale enough, 'n' I heard her mutterin' somethin' or other about the Blessed Virgin. If it hadn't been for the double doors to that chamber of his, I'd have had a squint inside before this; but, somehow or other, it never seems to happen that they're both open at once.

What do you think he employs himself about? — said I.

The young man John winked.

I waited patiently for the thought, of which this wink was the blossom, to come to fruit in words.

I don't believe in witches, — said the young man John.

Nor I.

We were both silent for a few minutes.

——Did you ever see the young girl's drawing-books,—I said, presently.

All but one,—he answered;—she keeps a lock on that, and won't show it. Ma'am Allen, (the young rogue sticks to that name, in speaking of the gentleman with the *diamond*,) Ma'am Allen tried to peek into it one day when she left it on the sideboard. "If you please," says she,—'n' took it from him, 'n' gave him a look that made him curl up like a caterpillar on a hot shovel. I only wished he hadn't, and had jest given her a little saas, for I've been takin' boxin'-lessons, 'n' I've got a new way of counterin' I want to try on to somebody.

——The end of all this was, that I came away from the young fellow's room, feeling that there were two principal things that I had to live for, for the next six weeks or six months, if it should take so long. These were, to get a sight of the young girl's drawing-book, which I suspected had her heart shut up in it, and to get a look into the Little Gentleman's room.

I don't doubt you think it rather absurd that I should trouble myself about these matters. You tell me, with some show of reason, that all I shall find in the young girl's book will be some outlines of angels with immense eyes, traceries of flowers, rural sketches, and caricatures, among which I shall probably have the pleasure of seeing my own features figuring. Very likely. But I'll tell you what *I* think I shall find. If this child has idealized the strange little bit of humanity over which she seems to have spread her wings like a brooding dove, — if, in one of those wild vagaries that passionate natures are so liable to, she has fairly sprung upon him with her clasping nature, as the sea-flowers fold about the first stray shell-fish that brushes their outspread tentacles, depend upon it, I shall find the marks of it in this drawing-book of hers, — if I can ever get a look at it, — fairly, of course, for I would not play tricks to satisfy my curiosity.

Then, if I can get into this Little Gentleman's room under any fair pretext, I shall, no doubt, satisfy myself in five minutes that he is just like other people, and that there is no particular mystery about him.

The night after my visit to the young man John, I made all these and many more reflections. It was about two o'clock in the morning, — bright starlight, — so light that I could make out the time on my alarm-clock, — when I woke up trembling and very moist. It was the heavy dragging sound, as I had often heard it before, that waked me. Presently a window was softly closed. I had just begun to get over the agitation with which we always awake from nightmare dreams, when I heard the sound which seemed to me as of a woman's voice, — the clearest, purest soprano which one could well conceive of. It was not loud, and I could not distinguish a word, if it was a woman's voice; but there were recurring phrases of sound and snatches of rhythm that reached me, which suggested the idea of complaint, and sometimes, I thought, of passionate grief and despair. It died away at last, — and then I heard the opening of a door, followed by a low, monotonous sound, as of one talking, — and then the closing of a door, — and presently the light on the opposite wall disappeared and all was still for the night.

By George! this gets interesting, — I said, as I got out of bed for a change of night-clothes.

I had this in my pocket the other day, but thought I wouldn't read it at our celebration. So I read it to the boarders instead, and print it to finish off this record with.

ROBINSON OF LEYDEN.

He sleeps not here; in hope and prayer
His wandering flock had gone before,
But he, the shepherd, might not share
Their sorrows on the wintry shore.

Before the Speedwell's anchor swung,
Ere yet the Mayflower's sail was spread,
While round his feet the Pilgrims clung,
The pastor spake, and thus he said:—

"Men, brethren, sisters, children dear!
God calls you hence from over sea;
Ye may not build by Haerlem Meer,
Nor yet along the Zuyder-Zee.

"Ye go to bear the saving word
To tribes unnamed and shores untrod:
Heed well the lessons ye have heard
From those old teachers taught of God.

"Yet think not unto them was lent
All light for all the coming days,
And Heaven's eternal wisdom spent
In making straight the ancient ways.

"The living fountain overflows
For every flock, for every lamb,
Nor heeds, though angry creeds oppose
With Luther's dike or Calvin's dam."

He spake; with lingering, long embrace,
With tears of love and partings fond,
They floated down the creeping Maas,
Along the isle of Ysselmond.

They passed the frowning towers of Briel,
The "Hook of Holland's" shelf of sand,
And grated soon with lifting keel
The sullen shores of Fatherland.

No home for these! — too well they knew
The mitred king behind the throne; —
The sails were set, the pennons flew,
And westward ho! for worlds unknown.

— And these were they who gave us birth,
The Pilgrims of the sunset wave,
Who won for us this virgin earth,
And freedom with the soil they gave.

The pastor slumbers by the Rhine, —
In alien earth the exiles lie, —
Their nameless graves our holiest shrine,
His words our noblest battle-cry!

Still cry them, and the world shall hear,
Ye dwellers by the storm-swept sea!
Ye *have* not built by Haerlem Meer,
Nor on the land-locked Zuyder-Zee!

VIII.

There has been a sort of stillness in the atmosphere of our boarding-house since my last record, as if something or other were going on. There is no particular change that I can think of in the aspect of things; yet I have a feeling as if some game of life were quietly playing and strange forces were at work, underneath this smooth surface of every-day boarding-house life, which would show themselves some fine morning or other in events, if not in catastrophes. I have been watchful, as I said I should be, but have little to tell as yet. You may laugh at me, and very likely think me foolishly fanciful to trouble myself about what is going on in a middling-class household like ours. Do as you like. But here is that terrible fact to begin with, — a beautiful young girl, with the blood and the nerve-fibre that belong to Nature's women, turned loose among live men.

—— *Terrible* fact?

Very terrible. Nothing more so. Do you forget the angels who lost heaven for the daughters of men? Do you forget Helen, and the fair women who made mischief and set nations by the ears before Helen was born? If jealousies that gnaw men's hearts out of their bodies, — if pangs that waste men to shadows and drive them into raving madness or moping melancholy, — if assassination and suicide are dreadful possibilities, then there is always something frightful about a lovely young woman. — I love to look at this "Rainbow," as her father used sometimes to call her, of ours. Handsome creature that she is in forms and colors, — the very picture, as it seems to me, of that "golden blonde" my friend whose book you read last year fell in love with when he was a boy, (as you remember, no doubt,) — handsome as she is, fit for a sea-king's bride, it is not her beauty alone that holds my eyes upon her. Let me tell you one of my fancies, and then you will understand the strange sort of fascination she has for me.

It is in the hearts of many men and women — let me add children — that there is a *Great Secret* waiting for them, — a secret of which they get hints now and then, perhaps oftener in early than in later years. These hints come sometimes in dreams, sometimes in sudden startling flashes, — second wakings, as it were, — a waking out of the waking state, which last is very apt to be a half-sleep. I have many times stopped short and held my breath, and felt the blood leaving my cheeks, in one of these sudden clairvoyant flashes. Of course I cannot tell what kind of a secret this is; but I think of it as a disclosure of certain relations of our personal being to time and space, to other intelligences, to the procession of events, and to their First Great Cause. This secret seems to be broken up, as it were, into fragments, so that we find here a word and there a syllable, and then again only a letter of it; but it never is written out for most of us as a complete sentence, in this life. I do not think it could be; for I am disposed to consider our beliefs about such a possible disclosure rather as a kind of premonition of an enlargement of our faculties in some future state than as an expectation to be fulfilled for most of us in this life. Persons, however, have fallen into trances, — as did the Reverend William Tennent, among many others, — and learned some things which they could not tell in our human words.

Now among the visible objects which hint to us fragments of this infinite secret for which our souls are waiting, the faces of women are those that carry the most legible hieroglyphics of the great mystery. There are women's faces, some real, some ideal, which contain something in them that becomes a positive element in our creed, so direct and palpable a revelation is it of the infinite purity and love. I remember two faces of women with wings, such as they call angels, of Fra Angelico, — and I just now came across a print of Raphael's Santa Apollina, with something of the same quality, — which I was sure had their prototypes in the world above ours. No wonder the Catholics pay their vows to the Queen of Heaven! The unpoetical side of Protestantism is, that it has no women to be worshipped.

But mind you, it is not every beautiful face that hints the Great Secret to us, nor is it only in beautiful faces that we find traces of it. Sometimes it looks out from a sweet sad eye, the only beauty of a plain countenance; sometimes there is so much meaning in the lips of a woman, not otherwise fascinating, that we know they have a message for us, and wait almost with awe to hear their accents. But this young girl has at once the beauty of feature and the unspoken mystery of expression. Can she tell me anything? Is her life a complement of mine, with the missing element in it which I have been groping after through so many friendships that I have tired of, and through —— Hush! Is the door fast? Talking loud is a bad trick in these curious boarding-houses.

You must have sometimes noted this fact that I am going to remind you of and to use for a special illustration. Riding along over a rocky road, suddenly the slow monotonous grinding of the crushing gravel changes to a deep heavy rumble. There is a great hollow under your feet, — a huge unsunned cavern. Deep, deep beneath you, in the core of the living rock, it arches its awful vault, and far away it stretches its winding galleries, their roofs dripping into streams where fishes have been swimming and spawning in the dark until their scales are white as milk and their eyes have withered out, obsolete and useless.

So it is in life. We jog quietly along, meeting the same faces, grinding over the same thoughts, — the gravel of the soul's highway, — now and then jarred against an obstacle we cannot crush, but must ride over or round as we best may, sometimes bringing short up against a disappointment, but still working along with the creaking and rattling and grating and jerking that belong to the journey of life, even in the smoothest-rolling vehicle. Suddenly we hear the deep under-ground reverberation that reveals the unsuspected depth of some abyss of thought or passion beneath us.——

I wish the girl would go. I don't like to look at her so much, and yet I cannot help it. Always that same expression of something that I ought to know, — something that she was made to tell and I to hear, — lying there ready to fall off from her lips, ready to leap out of her eyes and make a saint of me, or a devil or a lunatic, or perhaps a prophet to tell the truth and be hated of men, or a poet whose words shall flash upon the dry stubble-field of worn-out thoughts and burn over an age of lies in an hour of passion.

It suddenly occurs to me that I may have put you on the wrong track. The Great Secret that I refer to has nothing to do with the Three Words. Set your mind at ease about that, — there are reasons I could give you which settle all that matter. I don't wonder, however, that you confounded the Great Secret with the Three Words.

I LOVE YOU *is* all the secret that many, nay, most women have to tell. When that is said, they are like China-crackers on the morning of the fifth of July. And just as that little patriotic implement is made with a slender train which leads to the magazine in its interior, so a sharp eye can almost always see the train leading from a young girl's eye or lip to the "I love you" in her heart. But the Three Words are not the Great Secret I mean. No, women's faces are only one of the tablets on which that is written in its partial, fragmentary symbols. It lies deeper than Love, though very probably Love is a part of it. Some, I think, — Wordsworth might be one of them, — spell out a portion of it from certain beautiful natural objects, landscapes, flowers, and others. I can mention several poems of his that have shadowy hints which seem to me to come near the region where I think it lies. I have known two persons who pursued it with the passion of the old alchemists, — all wrong evidently, but infatuated, and never giving up the daily search for it until they got tremulous and feeble, and their dreams changed to visions of things that ran and crawled about their floor and ceilings, and so they died. The vulgar called them drunkards.

I told you that I would let you know the mystery of the effect this young girl's face produces on me. It is akin to those influences a friend of mine has described, you may remember, as coming from certain *voices.* I cannot translate it into words,—only into feelings; and these I have attempted to shadow by showing that her face hinted that revelation of something we are close to knowing, which all imaginative persons are looking for either in this world or on the very threshold of the next.

You shake your head at the vagueness and fanciful incomprehensibleness of my description of the expression in a young girl's face. You forget what a miserable surface-matter this language is in which we try to reproduce our interior state of being. Articulation is a shallow trick. From the light Poh! which we toss off from our lips as we fling a nameless scribbler's impertinences into our waste-baskets, to the gravest utterance which comes from our throats in our moments of deepest need, is only a space of some three or four inches. Words, which are a set of clickings, hissings, lispings, and so on, mean very little, compared to tones and expression of the features. I give it up; I thought I could shadow forth in some feeble way, by their aid, the effect this young girl's face produces on my imagination; but it is of no use. No doubt your head aches, trying to make something of my description. If there is here and there one that can make anything intelligible out of my talk about the Great Secret, and who has spelt out a syllable or two of it on some woman's face, dead or living, that is all I can expect. One should see the person with whom he converses about such matters. There are dreamy-eyed people to whom I should say all these things with a certainty of being understood; —

> That moment that his face I see,
> I know the man that must hear me:
> To him my tale I teach.

——I am afraid some of them have not got a spare quarter of a dollar for this August number, so that they will never see it.

——Let us start again, just as if we had not made this ambitious attempt, which may go for nothing, and you can have your money refunded, if you will make the change.

This young girl, about whom I have talked so unintelligibly, is the unconscious centre of attraction to the whole solar system of our breakfast-table. The Little Gentleman leans towards her, and she again seems to be swayed as by some invisible gentle force towards him. That slight inclination of two persons with a strong affinity towards each other, throwing them a little out of plumb when they sit side by side, is a physical fact I have often noticed. Then there is a tendency in all the men's eyes to converge on her; and I do firmly believe, that, if all their chairs were examined, they would be found a little obliquely placed, so as to favor the direction in which their occupants love to look.

That bland, quiet old gentleman, of whom I have spoken as sitting opposite to me, is no exception to the rule. She brought down some mignonette one morning, which she had grown in her chamber. She gave a sprig to her little neighbor, and one to the landlady, and sent another by the hand of Bridget to this old gentleman.

—— Sarvant, Ma'am! Much obleeged,—he said, and put it gallantly in his button-hole.— After breakfast he must see some of her drawings. Very fine performances,—very fine!—truly elegant productions,—truly elegant!—Had seen Miss Linley's needle-work in London, in the year (eighteen hundred and little or nothing, I think he said,)—patronized by the nobility and gentry, and Her Majesty,—elegant, truly elegant productions, very fine performances; these drawings reminded him of them; — wonderful resemblance to Nature; an extraordinary art, painting; Mr. Copley made some very fine pictures that he remembered seeing when he was a boy. Used to remember some lines about a portrait written by Mr. Cowper, beginning, —

> "Oh that those lips had language! Life has pass'd
> With me but roughly since I heard thee last."

And with this the old gentleman fell to thinking about a dead mother of his that he remembered ever so much younger than he now was, and looking, not as his mother, but as his daughter should look. The dead young mother was looking at the old man, her child, as she used to look at him so many, many years ago. He stood still as if in a waking dream, his eyes fixed on the drawings till their outlines grew indistinct and they ran into each other, and a pale, sweet face shaped itself out of the glimmering light through which he saw them. — What is there quite so profoundly human as an old man's memory of a mother who died in his earlier years? Mother she remains till manhood, and by-and-by she grows to be as a sister; and at last, when, wrinkled and bowed and broken, he looks back upon her in her fair youth, he sees in the sweet image he caresses, not his parent, but, as it were, his child.

If I had not seen all this in the old gentleman's

face, the words with which he broke his silence would have betrayed his train of thought.

—— If they had only taken pictures then as they do now! — he said. — All gone! all gone! nothing but her face as she leaned on the arms of her great chair; and I would give a hundred pound for the poorest little picture of her, such as you can buy for a shilling of anybody that you don't want to see. — The old gentleman put his hand to his forehead so as to shade his eyes. I saw he was looking at the dim photograph of memory, and turned from him to Iris.

How many drawing-books have you filled, — I said, — since you began to take lessons? —— This was the first, — she answered, — since she was here; and it was not full, but there were many separate sheets of large size she had covered with drawings.

I turned over the leaves of the book before us. Academic studies, principally of the human figure. Heads of sibyls, prophets, and so forth. Limbs from statues. Hands and feet from Nature. What a superb drawing of an arm! I don't remember it among the figures from Michel Angelo, which seem to have been her patterns mainly. From Nature, I think, or after a cast from Nature. — Oh! ——

—— Your smaller studies are in this, I suppose, — I said, taking up the drawing-book with a lock on it.—— Yes,—she said.——I should like to see her style of working on a small scale.—— There was nothing in it worth showing,—she said; and presently I saw her try the lock, which proved to be fast. We are all caricatured in it, I haven't the least doubt. I think, though, I could tell by her way of dealing with us what her fancies were about us boarders. Some of them act as if they were bewitched with her, but she does not seem to notice it much. Her thoughts seem to be on her little neighbor more than on anybody else. The young fellow John appears to stand second in her good graces. I think he has once or twice sent her what the landlady's daughter calls bó-kays of flowers,—somebody has, at any rate.—I saw a book she had, which must have come from the divinity-student. It had a dreary title-page, which she had enlivened with a fancy portrait of the author,—a face from memory, apparently,—one of those faces that small children loathe without knowing why, and which give them that inward disgust for heaven so many of the little wretches betray, when they hear that these are "good men," and that heaven is full of such.—The gentleman with the *diamond*—the Koh-i-noor, so called by us—was not encouraged, I think, by the reception of his packet of perfumed soap. He pulls his purple moustache and looks appreciatingly at Iris, who never sees him as it should seem. The young Marylander, who I thought would have been in love with her before this time, sometimes looks from his corner across the long diagonal of the table, as much as to say, I wish you were up here by me, or I were down there by you, — which would, perhaps, be a more natural arrangement than the present one. But nothing comes of all this, — and nothing has come of my sagacious idea of finding out the girl's fancies by looking into her locked drawing-book.

Not to give up all the questions I was determined to solve, I made an attempt also to work into the Little Gentleman's chamber. For this purpose, I kept him in conversation, one morning, until he was just ready to go up-stairs, and then, as if to continue the talk, followed him as he toiled back to his room. He rested on the landing and faced round toward me. There was something in his eye which said, Stop there! So we finished our conversation on the landing. The next day, I mustered assurance enough to knock at his door, having a pretext ready. — No answer. — Knock again. A door, as if of a cabinet, was shut softly and locked, and presently I heard the peculiar dead beat of his thick-soled, misshapen boots. The bolts and the lock of the inner door were unfastened, — with unnecessary noise, I thought, — and he came into the passage. He pulled the inner door after him and opened the outer one at which I stood. He had on a flowered silk dressing-gown, such as "Mr. Copley" used to paint his old-fashioned merchant-princes in; and a quaint-looking key in his hand. Our conversation was short, but long enough to convince me that the Little Gentleman did not want my company in his chamber, and did not mean to have it.

I have been making a great fuss about what is no mystery at all, — a schoolgirl's secrets and a whimsical man's habits. I mean to give up such nonsense and mind my own business. — Hark! What the deuse is that odd noise in his chamber?

—— I think I am a little superstitious. There were two things, when I was a boy, that diabolized my imagination, — I mean, that gave me a distinct apprehension of a formidable bodily shape which prowled round the neighborhood where I was born and bred. The first was a series of marks called the "Devil's footsteps." These were patches of sand in the pastures, where no grass grew, where even the low-bush blackberry, the "dewberry," as our Southern neighbors call it, in prettier and more Shakspearian language, did not spread its clinging creepers, — where even the pale, dry, sadly-sweet "everlasting" could not grow, but all was bare and blasted. The second was a mark in one of the public buildings near my home, — the college dormitory named after a Colonial Governor. I do not think many persons are aware of the existence of this mark, — little having been said about the story in print, as it was considered very desirable, for the sake of the Institution, to hush it up. In the northwest corner, and on the level of the third or fourth story, there are signs of a breach in the walls, mended pretty well, but not to be mistaken. A considerable portion of that corner must have been carried away, from within outward. It was an unpleasant affair; and I do not care to repeat the particulars; but some young men had been using sacred things in a profane and unlawful way, when the occurrence, which was variously explained, took place. The story of the Appearance in the chamber was, I suppose, invented afterwards; but of the injury to the building there could be no question; and the zig-zag line, where the mortar is a little thicker than before, is still distinctly visible. The queer burnt spots, called the "Devil's footsteps," had never attracted attention before this time, though there is no evidence that they had not existed previously, except that of the late Miss M., a "Goody," so called, or sweeper, who was positive on the subject, but had a strange horror of referring to an affair of which she was thought to know something. — I tell you it was not so pleasant for a little boy of impressible nature to go up to bed in an old gambrel-roofed house, with untenanted, locked upper-chambers, and a most ghostly garret, — with the "Devil's footsteps" in the fields behind the house, and in front of it the patched dormitory where the unexplained occurrence had taken place which startled those godless youths at their mock devotions, so that one of them was epileptic from that day forward, and another, after a dreadful season of mental conflict, took holy orders and became renowned for his ascetic sanctity.

There were other circumstances that kept up the impression produced by these two singular facts I have just mentioned. There was a dark storeroom, on looking through the key-hole of which, I could dimly see a heap of chairs and tables, and other four-footed things, which seemed to me to have rushed in there, frightened, and in their fright to have huddled together and climbed up on each other's backs, — as the people did in that awful crush where so many were killed, at the execution of Holloway and Haggerty. Then the Lady's portrait, up-stairs, with the sword-thrusts through it, — marks of the British officers' rapiers, — and the tall mirror in which they used to look at their red coats, — confound them for smashing its mate! — and the deep, cunningly wrought arm-chair in which Lord Percy used to sit while his hair was dressing;—he was a gentleman, and always had it covered with a large *peignoir*, to save the silk covering my grandmother embroidered. Then the little room down-stairs, from which went the orders to throw up a bank of earth on the hill yonder, where you may now observe a granite obelisk, — "the study," in my father's time, but in those days the council-chamber of armed men, — sometimes filled with soldiers; — come with me, and I will show you the "dents" left by the butts of their muskets all over the floor. — With all these suggestive objects round me, aided by the wild stories those awful country-boys that came to live in our service brought with them, — of contracts written in blood and left out over night, not to be found the next morning, (removed by the Evil One, who takes his nightly round among our dwellings, and filed away for future use,) — of dreams coming true, — of death-signs, — of apparitions, — no wonder that my imagination got excited, and I was liable to superstitious fancies.

Jeremy Bentham's logic, by which he proved that he couldn't possibly see a ghost, is all very well — in the day-time. All the reason in the world will never get those impressions of childhood, created by just such circumstances as I have been telling, out of a man's head. That is the only excuse I have to give for the nervous kind of curiosity with which I watch my little neighbor, and the obstinacy with which I lie awake whenever I hear anything going on in his chamber after midnight.

But whatever further observations I may have made must be deferred for the present. You will see in what way it happened that my thoughts were turned from spiritual matters to bodily ones, and how I got my fancy full of material images, — faces, heads, figures, muscles, and so forth, — in such a way that I should have no chance in this number to gratify any curiosity you may feel, if I had the means of so doing.

Indeed, I have come pretty near omitting my periodical record this time. It was all the work of a friend of mine, who would have it that I should sit to him for my portrait. When a soul draws a body in the great lottery of life, where every one is sure of a prize, such as it is, the said soul inspects the said body with the same curious interest with which one who has ventured into a "gift enterprise" examines the "massive silver pencil-case" with the coppery smell and impressible tube, or the "splendid gold ring" with the questionable specific gravity, which it has been his fortune to obtain in addition to his purchase.

The soul, having studied the article of which it finds itself proprietor, thinks, after a time, it knows it pretty well. But there is this difference between its view and that of a person looking at us: — we look from within, and see nothing but the mould formed by the elements in which we are incased; other observers look from without, and see us as living statues. To be sure, by the aid of mirrors, we get a few glimpses of our outside aspect; but this occasional impression is always modified by that look of the soul from within outward which none but ourselves can take. A portrait is apt, therefore, to be a surprise to us. The artist looks only from without. He sees us, too, with a hundred aspects on our faces we are never likely to see. No genuine expression can be studied by the subject of it in the looking-glass.

More than this; he sees us in a way in which many of our friends or acquaintances never see us. Without wearing any mask we are conscious of, we have a special face for each friend. For, in the first place, each puts a special reflection of himself upon us, on the principle of assimilation you found referred to in my last record, if you happened to read that document. And secondly, each of our friends is capable of seeing just so far, and no farther, into our face, and each sees in it the particular thing that he looks for. Now the artist, if he is truly an artist, does not take any one of these special views. Suppose he should copy you as you appear to the man who wants your name to a subscription-list, you could hardly expect a friend who entertains you to recognize the likeness to the smiling face which sheds its radiance at his board. Even within your own family, I am afraid there is a face which the rich uncle knows, that is not so familiar to the poor relation. The artist must take one or the other, or something compounded of the two, or something different from either. What the daguerreotype and photograph do is to give the features and one particular look, the very look which kills all expression, that of self-consciousness. The artist throws you off your guard, watches you in movement and in repose, puts your face through its exercises, observes its transitions, and so gets the whole range of its expression. Out of all this he forms an ideal portrait, which is not a copy of your exact look at any one time or to any particular person. Such a portrait cannot be to everybody what the ungloved call "as nat'ral as .ife." Every good picture, therefore, must be considered wanting in resemblance by many persons.

There is one strange revelation which comes out, as the artist shapes your features from his outline. It is that you resemble so many relatives to whom you yourself never had noticed any particular likeness in your countenance.

He is at work at me now, when I catch some of these resemblances, thus: —

There! that is just the look my father used to have sometimes; I never thought I had a sign of it. The mother's eyebrow and grayish-blue eye, those I knew I had. But there is a something which recalls a smile that faded away from my sister's lips — how many years ago! I thought it so pleasant in her, that I love myself better for having a trace of it.

Are we not young? Are we not fresh and blooming? Wait a bit. The artist takes a mean little brush and draws three fine lines, diverging outwards from the eye over the temple. Five years. — The artist draws one tolerably distinct and two faint lines, perpendicularly between the eyebrows. Ten years. — The artist breaks up the contours round the mouth, so that they look a little as a hat does that has been sat upon and recovered itself, ready, as one would say, to crumple up again in the same creases, on smiling or other change of feature. — Hold on! Stop that! Give a young fellow a chance! Are we not whole years short of that interesting period of life when Mr. Balzac says that a man, etc., etc., etc.?

There now! That is ourself, as we look after finishing an article, getting a three-mile pull with the ten-foot sculls, redressing the wrongs of the toilet, and standing with the light of hope in our eye and the reflection of a red curtain on our cheek. Is he not a Poet that painted us?

"Blest be the art that can immortalize!"
COWPER.

—— Young folks look on a face as a unit; children who go to school with any given little John Smith see in his name a distinctive appellation, and in his features as special and definite an expression of his sole individuality as if he were the first created of his race. As soon as we are old enough to get the range of three or four generations well in hand, and to take in large family histories, we never see an individual in a face of any stock we know, but a mosaic copy of a pattern, with fragmentary tints from this and that ancestor. The analysis of a face into its ancestral elements requires that it should be examined in the very earliest infancy, before it has lost that ancient and solemn look it brings with it out of the past eternity; and again in that brief space when Life, the mighty sculptor, has done his work, and Death, his silent servant, lifts the veil and lets us look at the marble lines he has wrought so faithfully; and lastly, while a painter who can seize all the traits of a countenance is building it up, feature after feature, from the slight outline to the finished portrait.

—— I am satisfied, that, as we grow older, we learn to look upon our bodies more and more as a temporary possession, and less and less as identified with ourselves. In early years, while the child "feels its life in every limb," it lives in the body and for the body to a very great extent. It ought to be so. There have been many very interesting children who have shown a wonderful indifference to the things of earth and an extraordinary development of the spiritual nature. There is a perfect literature of their biographies, all alike in their essentials; the same "disinclination to the usual amusements of childhood"; the same remarkable sensibility; the same docility; the same conscientiousness; in short, an almost uniform character, marked by beautiful traits, which we look at with a painful admiration. It will be found that most of these children are the subjects of some constitutional unfitness for living, the most frequent of which I need not mention. They are like the beautiful, blushing, half-grown fruit that falls before its time because its core is gnawed out. They have their meaning, — they do not live in vain, — but they are windfalls. I am convinced that many healthy children are injured morally by being forced to read too much about these little meek sufferers and their spiritual exercises. Here is a boy that loves to run, swim, kick football, turn somersets, make faces, whittle, fish, tear his clothes, coast, skate, fire crackers, blow squash "tooters," cut his name on fences, read about Robinson Crusoe and Sinbad the Sailor, eat the widest-angled slices of pie and untold cakes and candies, crack nuts with his back teeth and bite out the better part of another boy's apple with his front ones, turn up coppers, "stick" knives, call names, throw stones, knock off hats, set mousetraps, chalk doorsteps, "cut behind" anything on wheels or runners, whistle through his teeth, 'holler" Fire! on slight evidence, run after soldiers, patronize an engine-company, or, in his own words, "blow for tub No. 11," or whatever it may be; — isn't that a pretty nice sort of a boy, though he has not got anything the matter with him that takes the taste of this world out? Now, when you put into such a hot-blooded, hard-fisted, round-cheeked little rogue's hand a sad-looking volume or pamphlet, with the portrait of a thin, white-faced child, whose life is really as much a training for death as the last month of a condemned criminal's existence, what does he find in common between his own overflowing and exulting sense of vitality and the experiences of the doomed offspring of invalid parents? The time comes when we have learned to understand the music of sorrow, the beauty of resigned suffering, the holy light that plays over the pillow of those who die before their time, in humble hope and trust. But it is not until he has worked his way through the period of honest hearty animal existence, which every robust child should make the most of, — not until he has learned the use of his various faculties, which is his first duty — that a boy of courage and animal vigor is in a proper state to read these tearful records of premature decay. I have no doubt that disgust is implanted in the minds of many healthy children by early surfeits of pathological piety. I do verily believe that He who took children in His arms and blessed them loved the healthiest and most playful of them just as well as those who were richest in the tuberculous virtues. I know what I am talking about, and there are more parents in this country who will be willing to listen to what I say than there are fools to pick a quarrel with me. In the sensibility and the sanctity which often accompany premature decay I see one of the most beautiful instances of the principle of compensation which marks the Divine benevolence. But to get the spiritual hygiene of robust natures out of the exceptional regimen of invalids is just simply what we Professors call "bad practice"; and I know by experience that there are worthy people who not only try it on their own children, but actually force it on those of their neighbors.

—— Having been photographed, and stereographed, and chromatographed, or done in colors, in only remained to be phrenologized. A polite note from Messrs. Bumpus and Crane, requesting our attendance at their Physiological Emporium, was too tempting to be resisted. We repaired to that scientific Golgotha.

Messrs. Bumpus and Crane are arranged on the plan of the man and the woman in the toy called a "weather-house," both on the same wooden arm suspended on a pivot, — so that when one comes to the door, the other retires backwards, and *vice versâ.* The more particular speciality of one is to lubricate your entrance and exit, — that of the other to polish you off phrenologically in the recesses of the establishment. Suppose yourself in a room full of casts and pictures, before a counter-full of books with taking titles. I wonder if the picture of the brain is there, "approved" by a noted Phrenologist, which was copied from *my*, the Professor's, folio plate in the work of Gall and Spurzheim. An extra convolution, No. 9, *Destructiveness*, according to the list beneath, which was not to be seen in the plate, itself a copy of Nature, was very liberally supplied by the artist, to meet the wants of the catalogue of "organs." Professor Bumpus is seated in front of a row of women, — horn-combers and gold-beaders, or somewhere about that range of life, — looking so credulous, that, if any Second-Advent Miller or Joe Smith should come along, he could string the whole lot of them on his cheapest lie, as a boy strings a dozen "shiners" on a stripped twig of willow.

The Professor (meaning ourselves) is in a hurry, as usual; let the horn-combers wait, — he shall be bumped without inspecting the antechamber.

Tape round the head, — 22 inches. (Come on, old 23 inches, if you think you are the better man!)

Feels thorax and arm, and nuzzles round among muscles as those horrid old women poke their fingers into the salt-meat on the provision-stalls at the Quincy Market. Vitality, No. 5 or 6, or something or other. *Victuality*, (organ at epigastrium,) some other number equally significant.

Mild champooing of head now commences. Extraordinary revelations! Cupidiphilous, 6! Hymeniphilous, 6+! Pædiphilous, 5! Deipniphilous, 6! Gelasmiphilous, 6! Musikiphilous, 5! Uraniphilous, 5! Glossiphilous, 8!! and so on. Meant for a linguist. — Invaluable information. Will invest in grammars and dictionaries immediately. — I have nothing against the grand total of my phrenological endowments.

I never set great store by my head, and did not think Messrs. Bumpus and Crane would give me so good a lot of organs as they did, especially considering that I was a *dead*-head on that occasion. Much obliged to them for their politeness. They have been useful in their way by calling attention to important physiological facts. (This concession is due to our immense bump of Candor.)

A short Lecture on Phrenology, read to the Boarders at our Breakfast-Table.

I shall begin, my friends, with the definition of a *Pseudo-science.* A Pseudo-science consists of *a nomenclature,* with a self-adjusting arrangement, by which all positive evidence, or such as favors its doctrines, is admitted, and all negative evidence, or such as tells against it, is excluded. It is invariably connected with some lucrative practical application. Its professors and practitioners are usually shrewd people; they are very serious with the public, but wink and laugh a good deal among themselves. The believing multitude consists of women of both sexes, feeble-minded inquirers, poetical optimists, people who always get cheated in buying horses, philanthropists who insist on hurrying up the millennium, and others of this class, with here and there a clergyman, less frequently a lawyer, very rarely a physician, and almost never a horse-jockey or a member of the detective police. — I did not say that Phrenology was one of the Pseudo-sciences.

A Pseudo-science does not necessarily consist wholly of lies. It may contain many truths, and even valuable ones. The rottenest bank starts with a little specie. It puts out a thousand promises to pay on the strength of a single dollar, but the dollar is very commonly a good one. The practitioners of the Pseudo-sciences know that common minds, after they have been baited with a real fact or two, will jump at the merest rag of a lie, or even at the bare hook. When we have one fact found us, we are very apt to supply the next out of our own imagination. (How many persons can read Judges xv. 16 correctly the first time?) The Pseudo-sciences take advantage of this. — I did not say that it was so with Phrenology.

I have rarely met a sensible man who would not allow that there was *something* in Phrenology. A broad, high forehead, it is commonly agreed, promises intellect; one that is "villanous low" and has a huge hind-head back of it, is wont to mark an animal nature. I have as rarely met an unbiassed and sensible man who really believed in the bumps. It is observed, however, that persons with what the Phrenologists call "good heads" are more prone than others toward plenary belief in the doctrine.

It is so hard to prove a negative, that, if a man should assert that the moon was in truth a green cheese, formed by the coagulable substance of the Milky Way, and challenge me to prove the contrary, I might be puzzled. But if he offer to sell me a ton of this lunar cheese, I call on him to prove the truth of the caseous nature of our satellite, before I purchase.

It is not necessary to prove the falsity of the phrenological statement. It is only necessary to show that its truth is not proved, and cannot be, by the common course of argument. The walls of the head are double, with a great air-chamber between them, over the smallest and most closely crowded "organs." Can you tell how much money there is in a safe, which also has thick double walls, by kneading its knobs with your fingers? So when a man fumbles about my forehead, and talks about the organs of *Individuality*, *Size*, etc., I trust him as much as I should if he felt of the outside of my strong-box and told me that there was a five-dollar or a ten-dollar-bill under this or that particular rivet. Perhaps there is; *only he doesn't know anything about it.* But this is a point that I, the Professor, understand, my friends, or ought to, certainly, better than you do. The next argument you will all appreciate.

I proceed, therefore, to explain the self-adjusting mechanism of Phrenology, which is *very similar* to that of the Pseudo-sciences. An example will show it most conveniently.

A. is a notorious thief. Messrs. Bumpus and Crane examine him and find a good-sized organ of Acquisitiveness. Positive fact for Phrenology. Casts and drawings of A. are multiplied, and the bump *does not lose* in the act of copying. — I did not say it gained. — What do you look so for? (to the boarders.)

Presently B. turns up, a bigger thief than A. But B. has no bump at all over Acquisitiveness. Negative fact; goes against Phrenology. — Not a bit of it. Don't you see how small Conscientiousness is? *That's* the reason B. stole.

And then comes C., ten times as much a thief as either A. or B., — used to steal before he was weaned, and would pick one of his own pockets and put its contents in another, if he could find no other way of committing petty larceny. Unfortunately, C. has a *hollow*, instead of a bump, over Acquisitiveness. Ah, but just look and see what a bump of Alimentiveness! Did not C. buy nuts and gingerbread, when a boy, with the money he stole? Of course you see why he is a thief, and how his example confirms our noble science.

At last comes along a case which is apparently a *settler*, for there is a little brain with vast and varied powers, — a case like that of Byron, for instance. Then comes out the grand reserve-reason which covers everything and renders it simply impossible ever to corner a Phrenologist. "It is not the size alone, but the *quality* of an organ, which determines its degree of power."

Oh! oh! I see. — The argument may be briefly stated thus by the Phrenologist: "Heads I win, tails you lose." Well, that's convenient.

It must be confessed that Phrenology has a certain resemblance to the Pseudo-sciences. I did not say it was a Pseudo-science.

I have often met persons who have been altogether struck up and amazed at the accuracy with which some wandering Professor of Phrenology had read their characters written upon their skulls. Of course the Professor acquires his information solely through his cranial inspections and manipulations. — What are you laughing at? (to the boarders). — But let us just *suppose*, for a moment, that a tolerably cunning fellow, who did not know or care anything about Phrenology, should open a shop and undertake to read off people's characters at fifty cents or a dollar apiece. Let us see how well he could get along without the "organs."

I will suppose myself to set up such a shop. I would invest one hundred dollars, more or less, in casts of brains, skulls, charts, and other matters that would make the most show for the money. That would do to begin with. I would then advertise myself as the celebrated Professor Brainey, or whatever name I might choose, and wait for my first customer. My first customer is a middle-aged man. I look at him, — ask him a question or two, so as to hear him talk. When I have got the hang of him, I ask him to sit down, and proceed to fumble his skull, dictating as follows: —

SCALE FROM 1 TO 10.

List of Faculties for Customer.	Private Notes for my Pupil: *Each to be accompanied with a wink.*
Amativeness, 7.	Most men love the conflicting sex, and all men love to be told they do.
Alimentiveness, 8.	Don't you see that he has burst off his lowest waistcoat-button with feeding, — hey?
Acquisitiveness, 8.	Of course. A middle-aged Yankee.
Approbativeness, 7.+	Hat well brushed. Hair ditto. Mark the effect of that *plus* sign.
Self-esteem, 6.	His face shows that.
Benevolence, 9.	That'll please him.
Conscientiousness, 8½.	That fraction looks first-rate.
Mirthfulness, 7.	Has laughed twice since he came in.
Ideality, 9.	That sounds well.
Form, Size, Weight, Color, Locality, Eventuality, etc., etc.,	4 to 6. Average everything that can't be guessed.

And so of the other faculties.

Of course, you know, that isn't the way the Phrenologists do. They go only by the bumps. — What do you keep laughing so for? (to the boarders.) I only said that is the way *I* should practise "Phrenology" for a living.

End of my Lecture.

—— The Reformers have good heads, generally. Their faces are commonly serene enough, and they are lambs in private intercourse, even though their voices may be like

> The wolf's long howl from Oonalaska's shore,

when heard from the platform. Their greatest spiritual danger is from the perpetual *flattery of abuse* to which they are exposed. These lines are meant to caution them.

SAINT ANTHONY THE REFORMER.

HIS TEMPTATION.

No fear lest praise should make us proud!
  We know how cheaply that is won;
The idle homage of the crowd
  Is proof of tasks as idly done.

A surface-smile may pay the toil
  That follows still the conquering Right,
With soft, white hands to dress the spoil
  That sunbrowned valor clutched in fight.

Sing the sweet song of other days,
  Serenely placid, safely true,
And o'er the present's parching ways
  Thy verse distils like evening dew.

But speak in words of living power,—
  They fall like drops of scalding rain

That plashed before the burning shower
  Swept o'er the cities of the plain!

Then scowling Hate turns deadly pale,—
  Then Passion's half-coiled adders spring,
And, smitten through their leprous mail,
  Strike right and left in hope to sting.

If thou, unmoved by poisoning wrath,
  Thy feet on earth, thy heart above,
Canst walk in peace thy kingly path,
  Unchanged in trust, unchilled in love,—

Too kind for bitter words to grieve,
  Too firm for clamor to dismay,
When Faith forbids thee to believe,
  And Meekness calls to disobey,—

Ah, then beware of mortal pride!
  The smiling pride that calmly scorns
Those foolish fingers, crimson dyed
  In laboring on thy crown of thorns!

IX.

ONE of our boarders — perhaps more than one was concerned in it — sent in some questions to me, the other day, which, trivial as some of them are, I felt bound to answer.

1. — Whether a lady was ever known to write a letter covering only a single page?

To this I answered, that there was a case on record where a lady had but half a sheet of paper and no envelope; and being obliged to send through the post-office, she *covered* only one side of the paper (crosswise, lengthwise, and diagonally).

2.— What constitutes a man a gentleman?

To this I gave several answers, adapted to particular classes of questioners.

a. Not trying to be a gentleman.

b. Self-respect underlying courtesy.

c. Knowledge and observance of the *fitness of things* in social intercourse.

d. £. *s.* *d.* (as many suppose.)

3.— Whether face or figure is most attractive in the female sex?

Answered in the following epigram, by a young man about town:—

> Quoth Tom, "Though fair her features be,
> It is her figure pleases me."
> "What may her figure be?" I cried.
> "*One hundred thousand!*" he replied.

When this was read to the boarders, the young man John said he should like a chance to "step up" to a figger of that kind, if the girl was one of the right sort.

The landlady said them that merried for money didn't deserve the blessin' of a good wife. Money was a great thing when them that had it made a good use of it. She had seen better days herself, and knew what it was never to want for anything. One of her cousins merried a very rich old gentleman, and she had heerd that he said he lived ten year longer than if he'd staid by himself without anybody to take care of him. There was nothin' like a wife for nussin' sick folks and them that couldn't take care of themselves.

The young man John got off a little wink, and pointed slyly with his thumb in the direction of our diminutive friend, for whom he seemed to think this speech was intended.

If it was meant for him, he didn't appear to know that it was. Indeed, he seems somewhat listless of late, except when the conversation falls upon one of those larger topics that specially interest him, and then he grows excited, speaks loud and fast, sometimes almost savagely,—and, I have noticed once or twice, presses his left hand to his right side, as if there were something that ached, or weighed, or throbbed in that region.

While he speaks in this way, the general conversation is interrupted, and we all listen to him. Iris looks steadily in his face, and then he will turn as if magnetized and meet the amber eyes with his own melancholy gaze. I do believe that they have some kind of understanding together, that they meet elsewhere than at our table, and that there is a mystery, which is going to break upon us all of a sudden, involving the relations of these two persons. From the very first, they have taken to each other. The one thing they have in common is the heroic will. In him, it shows itself in thinking his way straightforward, in doing battle for "free trade and no right of search" on the high seas of religious controversy, and especially in fighting the battles of his crooked old city. In her, it is standing up for her little friend with the most queenly disregard of the code of boarding-house etiquette. People may say or look what they like, — she will have her way about this sentiment of hers.

The Poor Relation is in a dreadful fidget whenever the Little Gentleman says anything that interferes with her own infallibility. She seems to think Faith must go with her face tied up, as if she had the toothache, — and that if she opens her mouth to the quarter the wind blows from, she will catch her "death o' cold."

The landlady herself came to him one day, as I have found out, and tried to persuade him to hold his tongue. — The boarders was gettin' uneasy, — she said, — and some of 'em would go, she mistrusted, if he talked any more about things that belonged to the ministers to settle. She was a poor woman, that had known better days, but all her livin' depended on her boarders, and she was sure there wasn't any of 'em she set so much by as she did by him; but there was them that never liked to hear about sech things, except on Sundays.

The Little Gentleman looked very smiling at the landlady, who smiled even more cordially in return, and adjusted her cap-ribbon with an unconscious movement, — a reminiscence of the long-past pairing-time, when she had smoothed her locks and softened her voice, and won her mate by these and other bird-like graces. — My dear Madam, — he said, — I will remember your interests, and speak only of matters to which I am totally indifferent. — I don't doubt he meant this; but a day or two after, something stirred him up, and I heard his voice uttering itself aloud, thus: —

—— It must be done, Sir! — he was saying, — it must be done! Our religion has been Judaized, it has been Romanized, it has been Orientalized, it has been Anglicized, and the time is at hand when it must be AMERICANIZED! Now, Sir, you see what Americanizing is in politics; — it means that a man shall have a vote because he is a man, — and shall vote for whom he pleases, without his neighbor's interference. If he chooses to vote for the Devil, that is his lookout; — perhaps he thinks the Devil is better than the other candidates; and I don't doubt he's often right, Sir!

Just so a man's soul has a vote in the spiritual community; and it doesn't do, Sir, or it won't do long, to call him "schismatic" and "heretic" and those other wicked names that the old murderous Inquisitors have left us to help along "peace and good-will to men"!

As long as you could catch a man and drop him into an *oubliette*, or pull him out a few inches longer by machinery, or put a hot iron through his tongue, or make him climb up a ladder and sit on a board at the top of a stake so that he should be slowly broiled by the fire kindled round it, there was some sense in these words; they led to something. But since we have done with those tools, we had better give up those words. I should like to see a Yankee advertisement like this! — (the Little Gentleman laughed fiercely as he uttered the words,—)

—— Patent thumb-screws, — will crush the bone in three turns.

—— The cast-iron boot, with wedge and mallet, — only five dollars!

—— The celebrated extension-rack, warranted to stretch a man six inches in twenty minutes,— money returned, if it proves unsatisfactory.

I should like to see such an advertisement, I say, Sir! Now, what's the use of using the words that belonged with the thumb-screws, and the Blessed Virgin with the knives under her petticoats and sleeves and bodice, and the *dry pan and gradual fire*, if we can't have the things themselves, Sir? What's the use of *painting* the fire round a poor fellow, when you think it won't do to kindle one under him, — as they did at Valencia or Valladolid, or wherever it was?

—— What story is that?—I said.

Why, — he answered, — at the last *auto-da-fe*, in 1824 or '5, or somewhere there, — it's a traveller's story, but a mighty knowing traveller he is, — they had a "heretic" to use up according to the statutes provided for the crime of private opinion. They couldn't quite make up their minds to burn him, so they only *hung* him in a hogshead painted all over with flames!

No, Sir! when a man calls you names because you go to the ballot-box and vote for your candidate, or because you say this or that is your opinion, he forgets in which half of the world he was born, Sir! It won't be long, Sir, before we have Americanized religion as we have Americanized government; and then, Sir, every soul God sends into the world will be good in the face of all men for just so much of His "inspiration" as "giveth him understanding"!—None of my words, Sir! none of my words!

——If Iris does not love this Little Gentleman, what does love look like when one sees it? She follows him with her eyes, she leans over toward him when he speaks, her face changes with the changes of his speech, so that one might think it was with her as with Christabel, —

> That all her features were resigned
> To this sole image in her mind.

But she never looks at him with such intensity of devotion as when he says anything about the soul and the soul's atmosphere, religion.

Women are twice as religious as men; — all the world knows that. Whether they are any *better*, in the eyes of Absolute Justice, might be questioned; for the additional religious element supplied by sex hardly seems to be a matter of praise or blame. But in all common aspects they are so much above us that we get most of our religion from them, — from their teachings, from their example, — above all, from their pure affections.

Now this poor little Iris had been talked to strangely in her childhood. Especially she had been told that she hated all good things, — which every sensible parent knows well enough is not true of a great many children, to say the least. I have sometimes questioned whether many libels on human nature had not been a natural consequence of the celibacy of the clergy, which was enforced for so long a period.

The child had met this and some other equally

encouraging statements as to her spiritual conditions, early in life, and fought the battle of spiritual independence prematurely, as many children do. If all she did was hateful to God, what was the meaning of the approving or else the disapproving conscience, when she had done "right" or "wrong"? No "shoulder-striker" hits out straighter than a child with its logic. Why, I can remember lying in my bed in the nursery and settling questions which all that I have heard since and got out of books has never been able to raise again. If a child does not assert itself in this way in good season, it becomes just what its parents or teachers were, and is no better than a plaster image. — How old was I at the time? — I suppose about 5823 years old, — that is, counting from Archbishop Usher's date of the Creation, and adding the life of the race, whose accumulated intelligence is a part of my inheritance, to my own. A good deal older than Plato, you see, and much more experienced than my Lord Bacon and most of the world's teachers. — Old books, as you well know, are books of the world's youth, and new books are fruits of its age. How many of all these ancient folios round me are like so many old cupels! The gold has passed out of them long ago, but their pores are full of the dross with which it was mingled.

And so Iris — having thrown off that first lasso,

which not only fetters, but *chokes* those whom it can hold, so that they give themselves up trembling and breathless to the great soul-subduer, who has them by the windpipe — had settled a brief creed for herself, in which love of the neighbor, whom we have seen, was the first article, and love of the Creator, whom we have not seen, grew out of this as its natural development, being necessarily second in order of time to the first unselfish emotions which we feel for the fellow-creatures who surround us in our early years.

The child must have some place of worship. What would a young girl be who never mingled her voice with the songs and prayers that rose all around her with every returning day of rest? And Iris was free to choose. Sometimes one and sometimes another would offer to carry her to this or that place of worship; and when the doors were hospitably opened, she would often go meekly in by herself. It was a curious fact, that two churches as remote from each other in doctrine as could well be divided her affections.

The Church of Saint Polycarp had very much the look of a Roman Catholic chapel. I do not wish to run the risk of giving names to the ecclesiastical furniture which gave it such a Romish aspect; but there were pictures, and inscriptions in antiquated characters, and there were reading-stands, and flowers on the altar, and other elegant arrangements. Then there were boys to sing alternately in choirs responsive to each other, and there was much bowing, with very loud responding, and a long service and a short sermon, and a bag, such as Judas used to hold in the old pictures, was carried round to receive contributions Everything was done not only "decently and in order," but, perhaps one might say, with a certain air of magnifying their office on the part of the dignified clergymen, often two or three in number. The music and the free welcome were grateful to Iris, and she forgot her prejudices at the door of the chapel. For this was a church with open doors, with seats for all classes and all colors alike, — a church of zealous worshippers after their faith, of charitable and serviceable men and women, one that took care of its children and never forgot its poor, and whose people were much more occupied in looking out for their own souls than in attacking the faith of their neighbors. In its mode of worship there was a union of two qualities, — the taste and refinement, which the educated require just as much in their churches as elsewhere, and the air of stateliness, almost of pomp, which impresses the common worshipper, and is often not without its effect upon those who think they hold outward forms as of little value. Under the half-Romish aspect of the Church of Saint Polycarp, the young girl found a devout and loving and singularly cheerful religious spirit. The artistic sense, which betrayed itself in the dramatic proprieties of its ritual, harmonized with her taste. The mingled murmur of the loud responses, in those rhythmic phrases, so simple, yet so fervent, almost as if every tenth heart-beat, instead of its dull *tic-tac*, articulated itself as "Good Lord, deliver us!" — the sweet alternation of the two choirs, as their holy song floated from side to side, — the keen young voices rising like a flight of singing-birds that passes from one grove to another, carrying its music with it back and forward, — why should she not love these gracious outward signs of those inner harmonies which none could deny made beautiful the lives of many of her fellow-worshippers in the humble, yet not inelegant Chapel of Saint Polycarp?

The young Marylander, who was born and bred to that mode of worship, had introduced her to the chapel, for which he did the honors for such of our boarders as were not otherwise provided for. I saw them looking over the same prayer-book one Sunday, and I could not help thinking that two such young and handsome persons could hardly worship together in safety for a great while. But they seemed to mind nothing but their prayer-book. By-and-by the silken bag was handed round. — I don't believe she will; — so awkward, you know; — besides, she only came by invitation. There she is, with her hand in her pocket, though,—and sure enough, her little bit of silver tinkled as it struck the coin beneath. God bless her! she hasn't much to give; but her eye glistens when she gives it, and that is all Heaven asks.—That was the first time I noticed these young people together, and I am sure they behaved with the most charming propriety,—in fact, there was one of our silent lady-boarders with them, whose eyes would have kept Cupid and Psyche to their good behavior. A day or two after this I noticed that the young gentleman had left his seat, which you may remember was at the corner diagonal to that of Iris, so that they have been as far removed from each other as they could be at the table. His new seat is three or four places farther down the table. Of course I made a romance out of this, at once. So stupid not to see it! How could it be otherwise?—Did you speak, Madam? I beg your pardon. (To my lady-reader.)

I never saw anything like the tenderness with which this young girl treats her little deformed neighbor. If he were in the way of going to church, I know she would follow him. But his worship, if any, is not with the throng of men and women and staring children.

I, the Professor, on the other hand, am a regular church-goer. I should go for various reasons, if I did not love it; but I am happy enough to find great pleasure in the midst of devout multitudes, whether I can accept all their creeds or not. One place of worship comes nearer than the rest to my ideal standard, and to this it was that I carried our young girl.

The Church of the Galileans, as it is called, is even humbler in outside pretensions than the Church of Saint Polycarp. Like that, it is open to all comers. The stranger who approaches it looks down a quiet street and sees the plainest of chapels, — a kind of wooden tent, that owes whatever grace it has to its pointed windows and the high, sharp roof, — traces, both, of that upward movement of ecclesiastical architecture which soared aloft in cathedral-spires, shooting into the sky as the spike of a flowering aloe from the cluster of broad, sharp-wedged leaves below. This suggestion of mediæval symbolism, aided by a minute turret in which a hand-bell might have hung and found just room enough to turn over, was all of outward show the small edifice could boast. Within there was very little that pretended to be attractive. A small organ at one side, and a plain pulpit, showed that the building was a church; but it was a church reduced to its simplest expression.

Yet when the great and wise monarch of the East sat upon his throne, in all the golden blaze of the spoils of Ophir and the freights of the navy of Tarshish, his glory was not like that of this simple chapel in its Sunday garniture. For the lilies of the field, in their season, and the fairest flowers of the year, in due succession, were clustered every Sunday morning over the preacher's desk. Slight, thin-tissued blossoms of pink and blue and virgin white in early spring, then the full-breasted and deep-hearted roses of summer, then the velvet-robed crimson and yellow flowers of autumn, and in the winter delicate exotics that grew under skies of glass in the false summers of our crystal palaces without knowing that it was the dreadful winter of New England which was rattling the doors and frosting the panes, — in their language the whole year told its history of life and growth and beauty from that simple desk. There was always at least one good sermon, — this floral homily. There was at least one good prayer, — that brief space when all were silent, after the manner of the Friends at their devotions.

Here, too, Iris found an atmosphere of peace and love. The same gentle, thoughtful faces, the same cheerful but reverential spirit, the same quiet, the same life of active benevolence. But in all else how different from the Church of Saint Polycarp! No clerical costume, no ceremonial forms no carefully trained choirs. A liturgy they have to be sure, which does not scruple to borrow from the time-honored manuals of devotion, but also does not hesitate to change its expressions to its own liking.

Perhaps the good people seem a little easy with each other; — they are apt to nod familiarly, and have even been known to whisper before the minister came in. But it is a relief to get rid of that old Sunday — no, — *Sabbath* face, which suggests the idea that the first day of the week is commemorative of some most mournful event. The truth is, these brethren and sisters meet very much as a family does for its devotions, not putting off their humanity in the least, considering it on the whole quite a delightful matter to come together for prayer and song and good counsel from kind and wise lips. And if they are freer in their demeanor than some very precise congregations, they have not the air of a worldly set of people. Clearly they have *not* come to advertise their tailors and milliners, nor for the sake of exchanging criticisms on the literary character of the sermon they may hear. There is no restlessness and no restraint among these quiet, cheerful worshippers. One thing that keeps them calm and happy during the season so evidently trying to many congregations is, that they join very generally in the singing. In this way they get rid of that accumulated nervous force which escapes in all sorts of fidgety movements, so that a minister trying to keep his congregation still reminds one of a boy with his hand over the nose of a pump which another boy is working, — this spirting impatience of the people is so like the jets that find their way through his fingers, and the grand rush out at the final Amen! has such a wonderful likeness to the gush that takes place when the boy pulls his hand away, with immense relief, as it seems, to both the pump and the officiating youngster.

How sweet is this blending of all voices and all hearts in one common song of praise! Some will sing a little loud, perhaps, — and now and then an impatient chorister will get a syllable or two in advance, or an enchanted singer so lose all thought of time and place in the luxury of a closing cadence that he holds on to the last semibreve upon his private responsibility; but how much more of the spirit of the old Psalmist in the music of these imperfectly trained voices than in the academic niceties of the paid performers who take our musical worship out of our hands!

I am of the opinion that the creed of the Church of the Galileans is not laid down in as many details as that of the Church of Saint Polycarp. Yet I suspect, if one of the good people from each of those churches had met over the bed of a suffering fellow-creature, or for the promotion of any charitable object, they would have found they had more in common than all the special beliefs or want of beliefs that separated them would amount to. There are always many who believe that the fruits of a tree afford a better test of its condition than a statement of the composts with which it is dressed, — though the last has its meaning and importance, no doubt.

Between these two churches, then, our young Iris divides her affections. But I doubt if she listens to the preacher at either with more devotion than she does to her little neighbor when he talks of these matters.

What does he believe? In the first place, there is some deep-rooted disquiet lying at the bottom of his soul, which makes him very bitter against all kinds of usurpation over the right of private judgment. Over this seems to lie a certain tenderness for humanity in general, bred out of life-long trial, I should say, but sharply streaked with fiery lines of wrath at various individual acts of wrong, especially if they come in an ecclesiastical shape, and recall to him the days when his mother's great-grandmother was strangled on Witch Hill, with a text from the Old Testament for her halter. With all this, he has a boundless belief in the future of this experimental hemisphere, and especially in the destiny of the free thought of its northeastern metropolis.

—— A man can see further, Sir, — he said one day, — from the top of Boston State-House, and see more that is worth seeing, than from all the pyramids and turrets and steeples in all the places in the world! No smoke, Sir; no fog, Sir; and a clean sweep from the Outer Light and the sea beyond it to the New Hampshire mountains! Yes, Sir,—and there are great truths that are higher than mountains and broader than seas, that people are looking for from the tops of these hills of ours,—such as the world never saw, though it might have seen them at Jerusalem, if its eyes had been open!—Where do they have most crazy people? Tell me that, Sir!

I answered, that I had heard it said there were more in New England than in most countries, perhaps more than in any part of the world.

Very good, Sir,—he answered.—When have there been most people killed and wounded in the course of this century?

During the wars of the French Empire, no doubt,—I said.

That's it! that's it!—said the Little Gentleman;—where the battle of intelligence is fought, there are most minds bruised and broken! We're battling for a faith here, Sir.

The divinity-student remarked, that it was rather late in the world's history for men to be looking out for a new faith.

I didn't say a new faith,—said the Little Gentleman;—old or new, it can't help being different here in this American mind of ours from anything that ever was before; the *people* are new, Sir, and that makes the difference. One load of corn goes to the sty, and makes the fat of swine, — another goes to the farm-house, and becomes the muscle that clothes the right arms of heroes. It isn't where a pawn stands on the board that makes the difference, but what the game round it is when it is on this or that square.

Can any man look round and see what Christian countries are now doing, and how they are governed, and what is the general condition of society, without seeing that Christianity is the flag under which the world sails, and not the rudder that steers its course? No, Sir! There was a great raft built about two thousand years ago, — call it an ark, rather, — the world's great ark! big enough to hold all mankind, and made to be launched right out into the open waves of life, — and here it has been lying, one end on the shore and one end bobbing up and down in the water, men fighting all the time as to who should be captain and who should have the state-rooms, and throwing each other over the side because they could not agree about the points of compass, but the great vessel never getting afloat with its freight of nations and their rulers; — and now, Sir, there is and has been for this long time a fleet of "heretic" lighters sailing out of Boston Bay and they have been saying, and they say now, and they mean to keep saying, "Pump out your bilge-water, shovel over your loads of idle ballast, get out your old rotten cargo, and we will carry it out into deep waters and sink it where it will never be seen again; so shall the ark of the world's hope float on the ocean, instead of sticking in the dock-mud where it is lying!"

It's a slow business, this of getting the ark launched. The Jordan wasn't deep enough, and the Tiber wasn't deep enough, and the Rhone wasn't deep enough, and the Thames wasn't deep enough, — and perhaps the Charles isn't deep enough; but I don't feel sure of that, Sir, and I love to hear the workmen knocking at the old blocks of tradition and making the ways smooth with the oil of the Good Samaritan. I don't know, Sir, — but I do think she stirs a little, — I do believe she slides; — and when I think of what a work that is for the dear old three-breasted mother of American liberty, I would not take all the glory of all the greatest cities in the world for my birthright in the soil of little Boston!

—— Some of us could not help smiling at this burst of local patriotism, especially when it finished with the last two words.

And Iris smiled, too. But it was the radiant smile of pleasure which always lights up her face when her little neighbor gets excited on the great topics of progress in freedom and religion, and especially on the part which, as he pleases himself with believing, his own city is to take in that consummation of human development to which he looks forward.

Presently she looked into his face with a changed expression, — the anxiety of a mother that sees her child suffering.

You are not well, — she said.

I am never well, — he answered. — His eyes fell mechanically on the death's-head ring he wore on his right hand. She took his hand as if it had been a baby's, and turned the grim device so that it should be out of sight. One slight, sad, slow movement of the head seemed to say, "The death-symbol is still there!"

A very odd personage, to be sure! Seems to know what is going on, — reads books, old and new, — has many recent publications sent him, they tell me, — but, what is more curious, keeps up with the every-day affairs of the world, too. Whether he hears everything that is said with preternatural acuteness, or whether some confidential friend visits him in a quiet way, is more than I can tell. I can make nothing more of the noises I hear in his room than my old conjectures. The movements I mention are less frequent, but I often hear the plaintive cry, — I observe that it is rarely laughing of late; -

I never have detected one articulate word, but I never heard such tones from anything but a human voice.

There has been, of late, a deference approaching to tenderness, on the part of the boarders generally, so far as he is concerned. This is doubtless owing to the air of suffering which seems to have saddened his look of late. Either some passion is gnawing at him inwardly, or some hidden disease is at work upon him.

—— What's the matter with Little Boston?— said the young man John to me one day.— There a'n't much of him, anyhow; but 't seems to me he looks peakeder than ever. The old woman says he's in a bad way, 'n' wants a nuss to take care of him. Them nusses that take care of old rich folks marry 'em sometimes,—'n' they don't commonly live a great while after that. *No, Sir!* I don't see what he wants to die for, after he's taken so much trouble to live in such poor accommodations as that crooked body of his. I should like to know how his soul crawled into it, 'n' how it's goin' to get out. What business has he to die, I should like to know? Let Ma'am Allen (the gentleman with the *diamond*) die, if he likes, and be (this is a family-magazine); but we a'n't goin' to have *him* dyin'. Not by a great sight. Can't do without him anyhow. A'n't it fun to hear him blow off his steam?

I believe the young fellow would take it as a personal insult, if the Little Gentleman should show any symptoms of quitting our table for a better world.

—— In the mean time, what with going to church in company with our young lady, and taking every chance I could get to talk with her, I have found myself becoming, I will not say intimate, but well acquainted with Miss Iris. There is a certain frankness and directness about her that perhaps belong to her artist nature. For, you see, the one thing that marks the true artist is a clear perception and a firm, bold hand, in distinction from that imperfect mental vision and uncertain touch which give us the feeble pictures and the lumpy statues of the mere artisans on canvas or in stone. A true artist, therefore, can hardly fail to have a sharp, well-defined mental physiognomy. Besides this, many young girls have a strange audacity blended with their instinctive delicacy. Even in physical daring many of them are a match for boys; whereas you will find few among mature women, and especially if they are mothers, who do not confess, and not unfrequently proclaim, their timidity. One of these young girls, as many of us hereabouts remember, climbed to the top of a jagged, slippery rock lying out in the waves, — an ugly height to get up, and a worse one to get down, even for a bold young fellow of sixteen. Another was in the way of climbing tall trees for crows' nests, — and crows generally know about how far boys can "shin up," and set their household establishments above that high-water-mark. Still another of these young ladies I saw for the first time in an open boat, tossing on the ocean ground-swell, a mile or two from shore, off a lonely island. She lost all her daring, after she had some girls of her own to look out for.

Many blondes are very gentle, yielding in character, impressible, unelastic. But the *positive* blondes, with the golden tint running through them, are often full of character. They come, probably enough, from those deep-bosomed German women that Tacitus portrayed in such strong colors. The *negative* blondes, or those women whose tints have faded out as their line of descent has become impoverished, are of various blood, and in them the soul has often become pale with that blanching of the hair and loss of color in the eyes which makes them approach the character of Albinesses.

I see in this young girl that union of strength and sensibility which, when directed and impelled by the strong instinct so apt to accompany this combination of active and passive capacity, we call *genius*. She is not an accomplished artist, certainly, as yet; but there is always an air in every careless figure she draws, as it were of upward aspiration, — the *élan* of John of Bologna's

Mercury, — a lift to them, as if they had on winged sandals, like the herald of the Gods. I hear her singing sometimes; and though she evidently is not trained, yet is there a wild sweetness in her fitful and sometimes fantastic melodies, — such as can come only from the inspiration of the moment, — strangely enough, reminding me of those long passages I have heard from my little neighbor's room, yet of different tone, and by no means to be mistaken for those weird harmonies.

I cannot pretend to deny that I am interested in the girl. Alone, unprotected, as I have seen so many young girls left in boarding-houses, the centre of all the men's eyes that surround the table, watched with jealous sharpness by every woman, most of all by that poor relation of our landlady, who belongs to the class of women that like to catch others in mischief when they themselves are too mature for indiscretions, (as one sees old rogues turn to thief-catchers,) one of Nature's *gendarmerie*, clad in a complete suit of wrinkles, the cheapest coat-of-mail against the shafts of the great little enemy, — so surrounded, Iris spans this commonplace household-life of ours with her arch of beauty, as the rainbow, whose name she borrows, looks down on a dreary pasture with its feeding flocks and herds of indifferent animals.

These young girls that live in boarding-houses can do pretty much as they will. The female *gendarmes* are off guard occasionally. The sitting-room has its solitary moments, when any two boarders who wish to meet may come together accidentally, (*accidentally*, I said, Madam, and I had not the slighest intention of Italicizing the word,) and discuss the social or political questions of the day, or any other subject that may prove interesting. Many charming conversations take place at the foot of the stairs, or while one of the parties is holding the latch of a door,—in the shadow of porticos, and especially on those outside balconies which some of our Southern neighbors call "stoops," the most charming places in the world when the moon is just right and the roses and honeysuckles are in full blow,—as we used to think in eighteen hundred and never mention it.

On such a balcony or "stoop," one evening, I walked with Iris. We were on pretty good terms now, and I had coaxed her arm under mine,—my left arm, of course. That leaves one's right arm free to defend the lovely creature, if the riva.—odious wretch!—attempt to ravish her from your side. Likewise if one's heart should happen to beat a little, its mute language will not be without its meaning, as you will perceive when the arm you hold begins to tremble,—a circumstance like to occur, if you happen to be a good-looking young fellow, and you two have the "stoop" to yourselves.

We had it to ourselves that evening. The Koh-i-noor, as we called him, was in a corner with our landlady's daughter. The young fellow John was smoking out in the yard. The *gendarme* was afraid of the evening air, and kept inside. The young Marylander came to the door, looked out and saw us walking together, gave his hat a pull over his forehead and stalked off. I felt a slight spasm, as it were, in the arm I held, and saw the girl's head turn over her shoulder for a second. What a kind creature this is! She has no special interest in this youth, but she does not like to see a young fellow going off because he feels as if he were not wanted.

She had her locked drawing-book under her arm. — Let me take it, — I said.

She gave it to me to carry.

This is full of caricatures of all of us, I am sure, — said I.

She laughed, and said, — No, — not all of you.

I was there, of course?

Why, no, — she had never taken so much pains with me.

Then she would let me see the inside of it?

She would think of it.

Just as we parted, she took a little key from

her pocket and handed it to me. — This unlocks my naughty book, — she said, — you shall see it. I am not afraid of you.

I don't know whether the last words exactly pleased me. At any rate, I took the book and hurried with it to my room. I opened it, and saw, in a few glances, that I held the heart of Iris in my hand.

—— I have no verses for you this month, except these few lines suggested by the season.

MIDSUMMER.

Here! sweep these foolish leaves away, —
I will not crush my brains to-day! —
Look! are the southern curtains drawn?
Fetch me a fan, and so begone!

Not that, — the palm-tree's rustling leaf
Brought from a parching coral-reef!
Its breath is heated; — I would swing
The broad gray plumes, — the eagle's wing.

I hate these roses' feverish blood! —
Pluck me a half-blown lily-bud,
A long-stemmed lily from the lake,
Cold as a coiling water-snake.

Rain me sweet odors on the air,
And wheel me up my Indian chair,

And spread some book not overwise
Flat out before my sleepy eyes.

— Who knows it not, — this dead recoil
Of weary fibres stretched with toil, —
The pulse that flutters faint and low
When Summer's seething breezes blow?

O Nature! bare thy loving breast
And give thy child one hour of rest, —
One little hour to lie unseen
Beneath thy scarf of leafy green!

So, curtained by a singing pine,
Its murmuring voice shall blend with mine,
Till, lost in dreams, my faltering lay
In sweeter music dies away.

X.

Iris, her Book.

I PRAY thee by the soul of her that bore thee,
By thine own sister's spirit I implore thee,
Deal gently with the leaves that lie before thee!

For Iris had no mother to infold her,
Nor ever leaned upon a sister's shoulder,
Telling the twilight thoughts that Nature told her.

She had not learned the mystery of awaking
Those chorded keys that soothe a sorrow's aching,
Giving the dumb heart voice, that else were breaking.

Yet lived, wrought, suffered. Lo, the pictured token!
Why should her fleeting day-dreams fade unspoken,
Like daffodils that die with sheaths unbroken?

She knew not love, yet lived in maiden fancies,—
Walked simply clad, a queen of high romances,
And talked strange tongues with angels in her trances.

Twin-souled she seemed, a twofold nature wearing,—
Sometimes a flashing falcon in her daring,
Then a poor mateless dove that droops despairing.

Questioning all things: Why her Lord had sent her?
What were these torturing gifts, and wherefore lent her?
Scornful as spirit fallen, its own tormentor.

And then all tears and anguish: Queen of Heaven,
Sweet Saints, and Thou by mortal sorrows riven,
Save me! oh, save me! Shall I die forgiven?

And then —— Ah, God! But nay, it little matters:
Look at the wasted seeds that autumn scatters,
The myriad germs that Nature shapes and shatters!

If she had —— Well! She longed, and knew not wherefore.
Had the world nothing she might live to care for?
No second self to say her evening prayer for?

She knew the marble shapes that set men dreaming,
Yet with her shoulders bare and tresses streaming
Showed not unlovely to her simple seeming.

Vain? Let it be so! Nature was her teacher.
What if a lonely and unsistered creature
Loved her own harmless gift of pleasing feature,

Saying, unsaddened, — This shall soon be faded,
And double-hued the shining tresses braided,
And all the sunlight of the morning shaded?

—— This her poor book is full of saddest follies,
Of tearful smiles and laughing melancholies,
With summer roses twined and wintry hollies.

In the strange crossing of uncertain chances,
Somewhere, beneath some maiden's tear-dimmed glances
May fall her little book of dreams and fancies.

Sweet sister! Iris, who shall never name thee,
Trembling for fear her open heart may shame thee,
Speaks from this vision-haunted page to claim thee.

Spare her, I pray thee! If the maid is sleeping,
Peace with her! she has had her hour of weeping.
No more! She leaves her memory in thy keeping.

These verses were written in the first leaves of the locked volume. As I turned the pages, I hesitated for a moment. Is it quite fair to take advantage of a generous, trusting impulse to read the unsunned depths of a young girl's nature, which I can look through, as the balloon-voyagers tell us they see from their hanging-baskets through the translucent waters which the keenest eye of such as sail over them in ships might strive to pierce in vain? Why has the child trusted *me* with such artless confessions, — self-revelations, which might be whispered by trembling lips, under the veil of twilight, in sacred confessionals but which I cannot look at in the light of day without a feeling of wronging a sacred confidence?

To all this the answer seemed plain enough after a little thought. She did not know how fearfully she had disclosed herself; she was too profoundly innocent. Her soul was no more ashamed than the fair shapes that walked in Eden without a thought of over-liberal loveliness. Having nobody to tell her story to, — having, as she said in her verses, no musical instrument to laugh and cry with her, — nothing, in short, but the language of pen and pencil, — all the veinings of her nature were impressed on these pages, as those of a fresh leaf are transferred to the blank sheets which inclose it. It was the same thing which I remember seeing beautifully shown in a child of some four or five years we had one day at our boarding-house. This child was a deaf mute. But its soul had the inner sense that answers to hearing, and the shaping capacity which through natural organs realizes itself in words. Only it had to talk with its face alone; and such speaking eyes, such rapid alternations of feeling and shifting expressions of thought as flitted over its face, I have never seen in any other human countenance.

I wonder if something of spiritual *transparency*

is not typified in the golden-*blonde* organization. There are a great many little creatures, — many small fishes, for instance, — which are literally transparent, with the exception of some of the internal organs. The heart can be seen beating as if in a case of clouded crystal. The central nervous column with its sheath runs as a dark stripe through the whole length of the diaphanous muscles of the body. Other little creatures are so darkened with pigment that we can see only their surface. Conspirators and poisoners are painted with black, beady eyes and swarthy hue; Judas, in Leonardo's picture, is the model of them all.

However this may be, I should say there never had been a book like this of Iris, — so full of the heart's silent language, so transparent that the heart itself could be seen beating through it. I should say there never could have been such a book, but for one recollection, which is not peculiar to myself, but is shared by a certain number of my former townsmen. If you think I overcolor this matter of the young girl's book, hear this, which there are others, as I just said, besides myself, will tell you is strictly true.

The Book of the Three Maiden Sisters.

IN the town called Cantabridge, now a city, water-veined and gas windpiped, in the street running down to the Bridge, beyond which dwelt

Sally, told of in a book of a friend of mine, was of old a house inhabited by three maidens. They left no near kinsfolk, I believe; if they did, I have no ill to speak of them; for they lived and died in all good report and maidenly credit. The house they lived in was of the small, gambrel-roofed cottage pattern, after the shape of Esquires' houses, but after the size of the dwellings of handicraftsmen. The lower story was fitted up as a shop. Specially was it provided with one of those half-doors now so rarely met with, which are to whole doors as spencers worn by old folk are to coats. They speak of limited commerce united with a social or observing disposition on the part of the shopkeeper,—allowing, as they do, talk with passers-by, yet keeping off such as have not the excuse of business to cross the threshold. On the door-posts, at either side, above the half-door, hung certain perennial articles of merchandise, of which my memory still has hanging among its faded photographs a kind of netted scarf and some pairs of thick woollen stockings. More articles, but not very many, were stored inside; and there was one drawer, containing children's books, out of which I once was treated to a minute quarto ornamented with handsome cuts. This was the only purchase I ever *knew* to be made at the shop kept by the three maiden ladies, though it is probable there were others. So long as I remember the shop, the same scarf and, I should say, the same stockings hung on the door-posts. — [You think I am exaggerating again, and that shopkeepers would not keep the same article exposed for years. Come to me, the Professor, and I will take you in five minutes to a shop in this city where I will show you an article hanging now in the very place where more than *thirty years ago* I myself inquired the price of it of the present head of the establishment.]

The three maidens were of comely presence, and one of them had had claims to be considered a Beauty. When I saw them in the old meeting-house on Sundays, as they rustled in through the aisles in silks and satins, not gay, but more than decent, as I remember them, I thought of My Lady Bountiful in the history of "Little King Pippin," and of the Madam Blaize of Goldsmith (who, by the way, must have taken the hint of it from a pleasant poem, "Monsieur de la Palisse," attributed to De la Monnoye, in the collection of French songs before me).* There was some story of an old romance in which the Beauty had played her part. Perhaps they all had had lovers; for, as I said, they were shapely and seemly personages, as I remember them; but their lives were out of the flower and in the berry at the time of my first recollections.

* Vide Bartlett's "Familiar Quotations."

One after another they all three dropped away, objects of kindly attention to the good people round, leaving little or almost nothing, and nobody to inherit it. Not absolutely nothing, of course. There must have been a few old dresses, — perhaps some bits of furniture, a Bible, and the spectacles the good old souls read it through, and little keepsakes, such as make us cry to look at, when we find them in old drawers; — such relics there must have been. But there was more. There was a manuscript of some hundred pages, closely written, in which the poor things had chronicled for many years the incidents of their daily life. After their death it was passed round somewhat freely, and fell into my hands. How I have cried and laughed and colored over it! There was nothing in it to be ashamed of, perhaps there was nothing in it to laugh at, but such a picture of the mode of being of poor simple good old women I do believe was never drawn before. And there were all the smallest incidents recorded, such as do really make up humble life, but which die out of all mere literary memoirs, as the houses where the Egyptians or the Athenians lived crumble and leave only their temples standing. I know, for instance, that on a given day of a certain year, a kindly woman, herself a poor widow, now, I trust, not without special mercies in heaven for her good deeds, —

for I read her name on a proper tablet in the churchyard a week ago, — sent a fractional pudding from her own table to the Maiden Sisters, who, I fear, from the warmth and detail of their description, were fasting, or at least on short allowance, about that time. I know who sent them the segment of melon, which in her riotous fancy one of them compared to those huge barges to which we give the ungracious name of mud-scows. But why should I illustrate further what it seems almost a breach of confidence to speak of? Some kind friend, who could challenge a nearer interest than the curious strangers into whose hands the book might fall, at last claimed it, and I was glad that it should be henceforth sealed to common eyes. I learned from it that every good and, alas! every evil act we do may slumber unforgotten even in some earthly record. I got a new lesson in that humanity which our sharp race finds it so hard to learn. The poor widow, fighting hard to feed and clothe and educate her children, had not forgotten the poorer ancient maidens. I remembered it the other day, as I stood by her place of rest, and I felt sure that it was remembered elsewhere. I know there are prettier words than *pudding*, but I can't help it, — the pudding went upon the record, I feel sure, with the mite which was cast into the treasury by that other poor widow whose deed the world shall remember forever, and with the coats and garments which the good women cried over, when Tabitha, called by interpretation Dorcas, lay dead in the upper chamber, with her charitable needlework strewed around her.

—— Such was the Book of the Maiden Sisters. You will believe me more readily now when I tell you that I found the soul of Iris in the one that lay open before me. Sometimes it was a poem that held it, sometimes a drawing, — angel, arabesque, caricature, or a mere hieroglyphic symbol of which I could make nothing. A rag of cloud on one page, as I remember, with a streak of red zigzagging out of it across the paper as naturally as a crack runs through a China bowl. On the next page a dead bird, — some little favorite, I suppose; for it was worked out with a special love, and I saw on the leaf that sign with which once or twice in my life I have had a letter sealed, — a round spot where the paper is slightly corrugated, and, if there is writing there, the letters are somewhat faint and blurred. Most of the pages were surrounded with emblematic traceries. It was strange to me at first to see how often she introduced those homelier wild-flowers which we call *weeds*, — for it seemed there was none of them too humble for her to love, and none too little cared for by Nature to be without its beauty for her artist eye and pencil. By the side of the garden-flowers, — of Spring's curled darlings, the hyacinths, of rosebuds, dear to sketching maidens, of flower-de-luces and morning-glories, — nay, oftener than these, and more tenderly caressed by the colored brush that rendered them, — were those common growths which fling themselves to be crushed under our feet and our wheels, making themselves so cheap in this perpetual martyrdom that we forget each of them is a ray of the Divine beauty.

Yellow japanned buttercups and star-disked dandelions, — just as we see them lying in the grass, like sparks that have leaped from the kindling sun of summer; the profuse daisy-like flower which whitens the fields, to the great disgust of liberal shepherds, yet seems fair to loving eyes, with its button-like mound of gold set round with milk-white rays; the tall-stemmed succory, setting its pale blue flowers aflame, one after another, sparingly, as the lights are kindled in the candelabra of decaying palaces where the heirs of dethroned monarchs are dying out; the red and white clovers; the broad, flat leaves of the plantain, — "the white man's foot," as the Indians called it, — the wiry, jointed stems of that iron creeping plant which we call "knot-*grass*," and which loves its life so dearly that it is next to impossible to murder it with a hoe, as it clings to the cracks of the pavement; — all these plants, and many more, she wove into her fanciful garlands and borders. — On one of the pages were some musical notes. I touched them from curiosity on a piano belonging to one of our boarders. Strange! There are passages that I have heard before, plaintive, full of some hidden meaning, as if they were gasping for words to interpret them. She must have heard the strains that have so excited my curiosity, coming from my neighbor's chamber. The illuminated border she had traced round the page that held these notes took the place of the words they seemed to be aching for. Above, a long monotonous sweep of waves, leaden-hued, anxious and jaded and sullen, if you can imagine such an expression in water. On one side an Alpine *needle*, as it were, of black basalt, girdled with snow. On the other a threaded waterfall. The red morning-tint that shone in the drops had a strange look, — one would say the cliff was bleeding; — perhaps she did not mean it. Below, a stretch of sand, and a solitary bird of prey, with his wings spread over some unseen object. — And on the very next page a procession wound along, after the fashion of that on the title-page of Fuller's "Holy War," in which I recognized without difficulty every boarder at our table in all the glory of the most resplendent caricature, — three only excepted,—the Little Gentleman, myself, and one other.

I confess I did expect to see something that would remind me of the girl's little deformed neighbor, if not portraits of him.—There is a left arm again, though;—no,—that is from the "Fighting Gladiator,"—the "*Jeune Héros combattant*" of the Louvre;—there is the broad ring of the shield. From a cast, doubtless. [The separate casts of the "Gladiator's" arm look immense; but in its place the limb looks light, almost slender,—such is the perfection of that miraculous marble. I never felt as if I touched the life of the old Greeks until I looked on that statue.]—Here is something very odd, to be sure. An Eden of all the humped and crooked creatures! What could have been in her head when she worked out such a fantasy? She has contrived to give them all beauty or dignity or melancholy grace. A Bactrian camel lying under a palm. A dromedary flashing up the sands,—spray of the dry ocean sailed by the "ship of the desert." A herd of buffaloes, uncouth, shaggy-maned, heavy in the forehand, light in the hind-quarter. [The buffalo is the *lion* of the ruminants.] And there is a Norman horse, with his huge, rough collar, echoing, as it were, the natural form of the other beast. And here are twisted serpents; and stately swans, with answering curves in their bowed necks, as if they had snake's blood under their white feathers; and grave, high-shouldered herons, standing on one foot like cripples, and looking at life round them with the cold stare of monumental effigies. — A very odd page indeed! Not a creature in it without a curve or a twist, and not one of them a mean figure to look at. You can make your own comment; I am fanciful, you know. I believe she is trying to idealize what we vulgarly call deformity, which she strives to look at in the light of one of Nature's eccentric curves, belonging to her system of beauty, as the hyperbola and parabola belong to the conic sections, though we cannot see them as symmetrical and entire figures, like the circle and ellipse. At any rate, I cannot help referring this paradise of twisted spines to some idea floating in her head connected with her friend whom Nature has warped in the moulding. — That is nothing to another transcendental fancy of mine. I believe her soul thinks itself in his little crooked body at times, — if it does not really get freed or half freed from her own. Did you ever see a case of catalepsy? You know what I mean, — transient loss of sense, will, and motion; body and limbs taking any position in which they are put, as if they belonged to a lay-figure. She had been talking with him and listening to him one day when he boarders moved from the table nearly all at once. But she sat as before, her cheek resting on her hand, her amber eyes wide open and still. I went to her, — she was breathing as usual, and her heart was beating naturally enough, — but she did not answer. I bent her arm; it was as plastic as softened wax, and kept the place I gave it. — This will never do, though, — and I sprinkled a few drops of water on her forehead. She started and looked round. — I have been in a dream, — she said; — I feel as if all my strength were in this arm; — give me your hand! — She took my right hand in her left, which looked soft and white enough, but — Good Heaven! I believe she will crack my bones! All the nervous power in her body must have flashed through those muscles; as when a crazy lady snaps her iron window-bars, — she who could hardly glove herself when in her common health. Iris turned pale, and the tears came to her eyes; — she saw she had given pain. Then she trembled, and might have fallen but for me; — the poor little soul had been in one of those trances that belong to the spiritual pathology of higher natures, mostly those of women.

To come back to this wondrous book of Iris. Two pages faced each other which I took for symbolical expressions of two states of mind. On the left hand, a bright blue sky washed over the page, specked with a single bird. No trace of earth, but still the winged creature seemed to be soaring upward and upward. Facing it, one of those black dungeons such as Piranesi alone of all men has pictured. I am sure she must have seen those awful prisons of his, out of which the Opium-Eater got his nightmare vision, described by another as "cemeteries of departed greatness, where monstrous and forbidden things are crawling and twining their slimy convolutions among mouldering bones, broken sculpture, and mutilated inscriptions." Such a black dungeon faced the page that held the blue sky and the single bird; at the bottom of it something was coiled, — what, and whether meant for dead or alive, my eyes could not make out.

I told you the young girl's soul was in this book. As I turned over the last leaves I could not help starting. There were all sorts of faces among the arabesques which laughed and scowled in the borders that ran round the pages. They had mostly the outline of childish or womanly or manly beauty, without very distinct individuality. But at last it seemed to me that some of them were taking on a look not wholly unfamiliar to me; there were features that did not seem new. — Can it be so? Was there ever such innocence in a creature so full of life? She tells her heart's secrets as a three-years-old child betrays itself without need of being questioned! This was no common miss, such as are turned out in scores from the young-lady-factories, with parchments warranting them accomplished and virtuous, — in case anybody should question the fact. I began to understand her; — and what is so charming as to read the secret of a real *femme incomprise?* — for such there are, though they are not the ones who think themselves uncomprehended women.

Poets are never young, in one sense. Their delicate ear hears the far-off whispers of eternity, which coarser souls must travel towards for scores of years before their dull sense is touched by them. A moment's insight is sometimes worth a life's experience. I have frequently seen children, long exercised by pain and exhaustion, whose features had a strange look of advanced age. Too often one meets such in our charitable institutions. Their faces are saddened and wrinkled, as if their few summers were threescore years and ten.

And so, many youthful poets have written as if their hearts were old before their time; their pensive morning twilight has been as cool and saddening as that of evening in more common lives. The profound melancholy of those lines o Shelley,

"I could lie down like a tired child
And weep away the life of care
Which I have borne and yet must bear,"

came from a heart, as he says, "too soon grown old," — at *twenty-six years*, as dull people count time, even when they talk of poets.

I know enough to be prepared for an exceptional nature, — only this gift of the hand in rendering every thought in form and color, as well as in words, gives a richness to this young girl's alphabet of feeling and imagery that takes me by surprise. And then besides, and most of all, I am puzzled at her sudden and seemingly easy confidence in me. Perhaps I owe it to my —— Well, no matter! How one must love the editor who first calls him the *venerable* So-and-So!

—— I locked the book and sighed as I laid it down. The world is always ready to receive talent with open arms. Very often it does not know what to do with genius. Talent is a docile creature. It bows its head meekly while the world slips the collar over it. It backs into the shafts like a lamb. It draws its load cheerfully, and is patient of the bit and of the whip. But genius is always impatient of its harness; its wild blood makes it hard to train.

Talent seems, at first, in one sense, higher than genius, — namely, that it is more uniformly and absolutely submitted to the will, and therefore more distinctly human in its character. Genius, on the other hand, is much more like those instincts which govern the admirable movements of the lower creatures, and therefore seems to have something of the lower or animal character. A goose flies by a chart which the Royal Geographical Society could not mend. A poet, like the goose, sails without visible landmarks to unexplored regions of truth, which philosophy has yet to lay down on its atlas. The philosopher gets his track by observation; the poet trusts to his inner sense, and makes the straighter and swifter line.

And yet, to look at it in another light, is not even the lowest instinct more truly divine than any voluntary human act done by the suggestion of reason? What is a bee's architecture but an *un*obstructed divine thought?—what is a builder's approximative rule but an obstructed thought of the Creator, a mutilated and imperfect copy of some absolute rule Divine Wisdom has established, transmitted through a human soul as an image through clouded glass?

Talent is a very common family-trait; genius belongs rather to individuals;—just as you find one giant or one dwarf in a family, but rarely a whole brood of either. Talent is often to be envied, and genius very commonly to be pitied. It stands twice the chance of the other of dying in a hospital, in jail, in debt, in bad repute. It is a perpetual insult to mediocrity; its every word is a trespass against somebody's vested ideas,—

blasphemy against somebody's *O'm*, or intangible private truth.

——What is the use of my weighing out antitheses in this way, like a rhetorical grocer?—You know twenty men of talent, who are making their way in the world; you may, perhaps, know one man of genius, and very likely do not want to know any more. For a divine instinct, such as drives the goose southward and the poet heavenward, is a hard thing to manage, and proves too strong for many whom it possesses. It must have been a terrible thing to have a friend like Chatterton or Burns. And here is a being who certainly has more than talent, at once poet and artist in tendency, if not yet fairly developed,—a woman, too;—and genius grafted on womanhood is like to overgrow it and break its stem, as you may see a grafted fruit-tree spreading over the stock which cannot keep pace with its evolution.

I think now you know something of this young person. She wants nothing but an atmosphere to expand in. Now and then one meets with a nature for which our hard, practical New England life is obviously utterly incompetent. It comes up, as a Southern seed, dropped by accident in one of our gardens, finds itself trying to grow and blow into flower among the homely roots and the hardy shrubs that surround it. There is no question that certain persons who are born among us find themselves many degrees too far north. Tropical by organization, they cannot fight for life with our eastern and northwestern breezes without losing the color and fragrance into which their lives would have blossomed in the latitude of myrtles and oranges. Strange effects are produced by suffering any living thing to be developed under conditions such as Nature had not intended for it. A French physiologist confined some tadpoles under water in the dark. Removed from the natural stimulus of light, they did not develop legs and arms at the proper period of their growth, and so become frogs; they swelled and spread into gigantic tadpoles. I have seen a hundred colossal *human* tadpoles, — overgrown *larvæ* or embryos; nay, I am afraid we Protestants should look on a considerable proportion of the Holy Father's one hundred and thirty-nine millions as spiritual *larvæ*, sculling about in the dark by the aid of their caudal extremities, instead of standing on their legs, and breathing by gills, instead of taking the free air of heaven into the lungs made to receive it. Of course *we* never try to keep young souls in the tadpole state, for fear they should get a pair or two of legs by-and-by and jump out of the pool where they have been bred and fed! Never! Never. Never?

Now to go back to our plant. You may know, that, for the earlier stages of development of almost any vegetable, you only want air, water, light, and warmth. But by-and-by, if it is to have special complex principles as a part of its organization, they must be supplied by the soil; — your pears will crack, if the root of the tree gets no iron, — your asparagus-bed wants salt as much as you do. Just at the period of adolescence, the mind often suddenly begins to come into flower and to set its fruit. Then it is that many young natures, having exhausted the spiritual soil round them of all it contains of the elements they demand, wither away, undeveloped and uncolored, unless they are transplanted.

Pray for these dear young souls! This is the second *natural* birth; — for I do not speak of those peculiar religious experiences which form the point of transition in many lives between the consciousness of a general relation to the Divine nature and a special personal relation. The litany should count a prayer for them in the list of its supplications; masses should be said for them as for souls in purgatory; all good Christians should remember them as they remember those in peril through travel or sickness or in warfare.

I would transport this child to Rome at once, if I had my will. She should ripen under an Italian sun. She should walk under the frescoed vaults of palaces, until her colors deepened to those of Venetian beauties, and her forms were perfected into rivalry with the Greek marbles, and the east wind was out of her soul. Has she not exhausted this lean soil of the elements her growing nature requires?

I do not know. The magnolia grows and comes into full flower on Cape Ann, many degrees out of its proper region. I was riding once along that delicious road between the hills and the sea, when we passed a thicket where there seemed to be a chance of finding it. In five minutes I had fallen on the trees in full blossom, and filled my arms with the sweet, resplendent flowers. I could not believe I was in our cold, northern Essex, which, in the dreary season when I pass its slate-colored, unpainted farm-houses, and huge, square, windy, 'squire-built "mansions," looks as brown and unvegetating as an old rug with its patterns all trodden out and the colored fringe worn from all its border.

If the magnolia can bloom in northern New England, why should not a poet or a painter come to his full growth here just as well? Yes, but if the gorgeous tree-flower is rare, and only as if by a freak of Nature springs up in a single spot among the beeches and alders, is there not as much reason to think the perfumed flower of imaginative genius will find it hard to be born and harder to spread its leaves in the clear, cold atmosphere of our ultra-temperate zone of humanity?

Take the poet. On the one hand, I believe that a person with the poetical faculty finds material everywhere. The grandest objects of sense and thought are common to all climates and civilizations. The sky, the woods, the waters, the storms, life, death, love, the hope and vision of eternity, — these are images that write themselves in poetry in every soul which has anything of the divine gift.

On the other hand, there is such a thing as a lean, impoverished life, in distinction from a rich and suggestive one. Which our common New England life might be considered, I will not decide. But there are some things I think the poet misses in our western Eden. I trust it is not unpatriotic to mention them in this point of view, as they come before us in so many other aspects.

There is no sufficient flavor of humanity in the soil out of which we grow. At Cantabridge, near the sea, I have once or twice picked up an Indian arrowhead in a fresh furrow. At Canoe Meadow, in the Berkshire Mountains, I have found Indian arrowheads. So everywhere Indian arrowheads. Whether a hundred or a thousand years old, who knows? who cares? There is no history to the red race, — there is hardly an individual in it; — a few instincts on legs and holding a tomahawk — there is the Indian of all time. The story of one red ant is the story of all red ants. So, the poet, in trying to wing his way back through the life that has kindled, flitted, and faded along our watercourses and on our southern hillsides for unknown generations, finds nothing to breathe or fly in; he meets

> "A vast vacuity! all unawares,
> Fluttering his pennons vain, plumb down he drops
> Ten thousand fathom deep."

But think of the Old World, — that part of it which is the seat of ancient civilization! The stakes of the Britons' stockades are still standing in the bed of the Thames. The ploughman turns up an old Saxon's bones, and beneath them is a tessellated pavement of the time of the Cæsars. In Italy, the works of mediæval Art seem to be of yesterday, — Rome, under her kings, is but an intruding new-comer, as we contemplate her in the shadow of the Cyclopean walls of Fiesole or Volterra. It makes a man human to live on these old humanized soils. He cannot help marching in step with his kind in the rear of such a procession. They say a dead man's hand cures swellings, if laid on them. There is nothing like the dead cold hand of the Past to take down our tumid egotism and lead us into the solemn flow of the life of our race. Rousseau came out of one of his sad self-torturing fits, as he cast his eye on the arches of the old Roman aqueduct, the Pont du Gard.

I am far from denying that there is an attrac tion in a thriving railroad village. The new "dépôt," the smartly-painted pine houses, the spacious brick hotel, the white meeting-house, and the row of youthful and leggy trees before it, *are* exhilarating. They speak of progress, and the time when there shall be a city, with a His Honor the Mayor, in the place of their trim but transient architectural growths. Pardon me, if I prefer the pyramids. They seem to me crystals formed from a stronger solution of humanity than the steeple of the new meeting-house. I may be wrong, but the Tiber has a voice for me, as it whispers to the piers of the Pons Ælius, even more full of meaning than my well-beloved Charles eddying round the piles of West Boston Bridge.

Then, again, we Yankees are a kind of gypsies, — a mechanical and migratory race. A poet wants a home. He can dispense with an apple-parer and a reaping-machine. I feel this more for others than for myself, for the home of my birth and childhood has been as yet exempted from the change which has invaded almost everything around it.

—— Pardon me a short digression. To what small things our memory and our affections attach themselves! I remember, when I was a child, that one of the girls planted some Star-of-Bethlehem bulbs in the southwest corner of our front-yard. Well, I left the paternal roof and wandered in other lands, and learned to think in the words of strange people. But after many years, as I looked on the little front-yard again, it occurred to me that there used to be some Stars-of-Bethlehem in the southwest corner. The grass was tall there, and the blade of the plant is very much like grass, only thicker and glossier. Even as Tully parted the briers and brambles when he hunted for the sphere-containing cylinder that marked the grave of Archimedes, so did I comb the grass with my fingers for my monumental memorial-flower. Nature had stored my keepsake tenderly in her bosom; the glossy, faintly streaked blades were there; they are there still, though they never flower, darkened as they are by the shade of the elms and rooted in the matted turf.

Our hearts are held down to our homes by innumerable fibres, trivial as that I have just recalled; but Gulliver was fixed to the soil, you remember, by pinning his head a hair at a time. Even a stone with a whitish band crossing it, belonging to the pavement of the back-yard, insisted on becoming one of the talismans of memory. This intussusception of the ideas of inanimate objects, and their faithful storing away among the sentiments, are curiously prefigured in the material structure of the thinking centre itself. In the very core of the brain, in the part where Des Cartes placed the soul, is a small mineral deposit, consisting, as I have seen it in the microscope, of grape-like masses of crystalline matter.

But the plants that come up every year in the same place, like the Stars-of-Bethlehem, of all the lesser objects, give me the liveliest home-feeling. Close to our ancient gambrel-roofed house is the dwelling of pleasant old Neighbor Walrus. I remember the sweet honeysuckle that I saw in flower against the wall of his house a few months ago, as long as I remember the sky and stars. That clump of peonies, butting their purple heads through the soil every spring in just the same circle, and by-and-by unpacking their hard balls of buds in flowers big enough to make a double handful of leaves, has come up in just that place, Neighbor Walrus tells me, for more years than I have passed on this planet. It is a rare privilege in our nomadic state to find the home of one's childhood and its immediate neighborhood thus unchanged. Many born poets, I am afraid, flower poorly in song, or not at all, because they have been too often transplanted.

Then a good many of our race are very hard and unimaginative; — their voices have nothing caressing; their movements are as of machinery without elasticity or oil. I wish it were fair to print a letter a young girl, about the age of our

Iris, wrote a short time since. "I am *** *** ***," she says, and tells her whole name outright. Ah! — said I, when I read that first frank declaration, — you are one of the right sort! — She was. A winged creature among close-clipped barn-door fowl. How tired the poor girl was of the dull life about her, — the old woman's "skeleton hand" at the window opposite, drawing her curtains, — "Ma'am ——— *shooing* away the hens," — the vacuous country eyes staring at her as only country eyes can stare, — a routine of mechanical duties, — and the soul's half-articulated cry for sympathy, without an answer! Yes, — pray for her, and for all such! Faith often cures their longings; but it is so hard to give a soul to heaven that has not first been trained in the fullest and sweetest human affections! Too often they fling their hearts away on unworthy objects. Too often they pine in a secret discontent, which spreads its leaden cloud over the morning of their youth. The immeasurable distance between one of these delicate natures and the average youths among whom is like to be her only choice makes one's heart ache. How many women are born too finely organized in sense and soul for the highway they must walk with feet unshod! Life is adjusted to the wants of the stronger sex. There are plenty of torrents to be crossed in its journey; but their stepping-stones are measured by the stride of man, and not of woman.

Women are more subject than men to *atrophy of the heart*. So says the great medical authority, Laennec. Incurable cases of this kind used to find their hospitals in convents. We have the disease in New England, — but not the hospitals. I don't like to think of it. I will not believe our young Iris is going to die out in this way. Providence will find her some great happiness, or affliction, or duty, — and which would be best for her, I cannot tell. One thing is sure: the interest she takes in her little neighbor is getting to be more engrossing than ever. Something is the matter with him, and she knows it, and I think worries herself about it.

I wonder sometimes how so fragile and distorted a frame has kept the fiery spirit that inhabits it so long its tenant. He accounts for it in his own way.

The air of the Old World is good for nothing, — he said, one day. — Used up, Sir, — breathed over and over again. You must come to this side, Sir, for an atmosphere fit to breathe nowadays. Did not worthy Mr. Higginson say that a breath of New England's air is better than a sup of Old England's ale? I ought to have died when I was a boy, Sir; but I couldn't die in this Boston air, — and I think I shall have to go to New York one of these days, when it's time for me to drop this bundle, — or to New Orleans, where they have the yellow fever, — or to Philadelphia, where they have so many doctors.

This was some time ago; but of late he has seemed, as I have before said, to be ailing. An experienced eye, such as I think I may call mine, can tell commonly whether a man is going to die, or not, long before he or his friends are alarmed about him. I don't like it.

Iris has told me that the Scottish gift of second-sight runs in her family, and that she is afraid she has it. Those who are so endowed look upon a well man and see a shroud wrapt about him. According to the degree to which it covers him, his death will be near or more remote. It is an awful faculty; but science gives one too much like it. Luckily for our friends, most of us who have the scientific second-sight school ourselves not to betray our knowledge by word or look.

Day by day, as the Little Gentleman comes to the table, it seems to me that the shadow of some approaching change falls darker and darker over his countenance. Nature is struggling with something, and I am afraid she is under in the wrestling-match. You do not care much, perhaps, for my particular conjectures as to the nature of his difficulty. I should say, however, from the sudden flushes to which he is subject, and certain other marks which, as an expert, I know how to interpret, that his heart was in trouble; but then he presses his hand to the *right* side, as if there were the centre of his uneasiness.

When I say difficulty about the heart, I do not mean any of those sentimental maladies of that organ which figure more largely in romances than on the returns which furnish our Bills of Mortality. I mean some actual change in the organ itself, which may carry him off by slow and painful degrees, or strike him down with one huge pang and only time for a single shriek, — as when the shot broke through the brave Captain Nolan's breast, at the head of the Light Brigade at Balaklava, and with a loud cry he dropped dead from his saddle.

I thought it only fair to say something of what I apprehended to some who were entitled to be warned. The landlady's face fell when I mentioned my fears.

Poor man! — she said. — And will leave the best room empty! Hasn't he got any sisters or nieces or anybody to see to his things, if he should be took away? Such a sight of cases, full of everything! Never thought of his failin' so suddin. A complication of diseases, she expected. Liver-complaint one of 'em?

After this first involuntary expression of the too natural selfish feelings, (which we must not judge very harshly, unless we happen to be poor widows ourselves, with children to keep filled, covered, and taught, — rents high, — beef eighteen to twenty cents per pound,) — after this first squeak of selfishness, followed by a brief movement of curiosity, so invariable in mature females, as to the nature of the complaint which threatens the life of a friend or any person who may happen to be mentioned as ill, — the worthy soul's better feelings struggled up to the surface, and she grieved for the doomed invalid, until a tear or two came forth and found their way down a channel worn for them since the early days of her widowhood.

Oh, this dreadful, dreadful business of being the prophet of evil! Of all the trials which those who take charge of others' health and lives have to undergo, this is the most painful. It is all so plain to the practised eye! — and there is the poor wife, the doting mother, who has never suspected anything, or at least has clung always to the hope which you are just going to wrench away from her! — I must tell Iris that I think her poor friend is in a precarious state. She seems nearer to him than anybody.

I did tell her. Whatever emotion it produced, she kept a still face, except, perhaps, a little trembling of the lip. — Could I be certain that there was any mortal complaint? — Why, no, I could not be certain; but it looked alarming to me. — He shall have some of my life, — she said.

I suppose this to have been a fancy of hers, of

a kind of magnetic power she could give out; — at any rate, I cannot help thinking she *wills* her strength away from herself, for she has lost vigor and color from that day. I have sometimes thought he gained the force she lost; but this may have been a whim, very probably.

One day she came suddenly to me, looking deadly pale. Her lips moved, as if she were speaking; but I could not at first hear a word. Her hair looked strangely, as if lifting itself, and her eyes were full of wild light. She sunk upon a chair, and I thought was falling into one of her trances. Something had frozen her blood with fear; I thought, from what she said, half audibly, that she believed she had seen a shrouded figure.

That night, at about eleven o'clock, I was sent for to see the Little Gentleman, who was taken suddenly ill. Bridget, the servant, went before me with a light. The doors were both unfastened, and I found myself ushered, without hindrance, into the dim light of the mysterious apartment I had so longed to enter.

I found these stanzas in the young girl's book, among many others. I give them as characterizing the tone of her sadder moments.

UNDER THE VIOLETS.

HER hands are cold; her face is white;
No more her pulses come and go;
Her eyes are shut to life and light;—
Fold the white vesture, snow on snow,
And lay her where the violets blow.

But not beneath a graven stone,
To plead for tears with alien eyes;
A slender cross of wood alone
Shall say, that here a maiden lies
In peace beneath the peaceful skies.

And gray old trees of hugest limb
Shall wheel their circling shadows round
To make the scorching sunlight dim
That drinks the greenness from the ground,
And drop their dead leaves on her mound.

When o'er their boughs the squirrels run,
And through their leaves the robins call,
And, ripening in the autumn sun,
The acorns and the chestnuts fall,
Doubt not that she will heed them all.

For her the morning choir shall sing
Its matins from the branches high,
And every minstrel-voice of spring,
That trills beneath the April sky,
Shall greet her with its earliest cry

When, turning round their dial-track,
  Eastward the lengthening shadows pass,
Her little mourners, clad in black,
  The crickets, sliding through the grass,
  Shall pipe for her an evening mass.

At last the rootlets of the trees
  Shall find the prison where she lies,
And bear the buried dust they seize
  In leaves and blossoms to the skies.
  So may the soul that warmed it rise!

If any, born of kindlier blood,
  Should ask, What maiden lies below?
Say only this: A tender bud,
  That tried to blossom in the snow,
  Lies withered where the violets blow.

XI.

You will know, perhaps, in the course of half an hour's reading, what has been haunting my hours of sleep and waking for months. I cannot tell, of course, whether you are a nervous person or not. If, however, you are such a person, — if it is late at night, — if all the rest of the household have gone off to bed, — if the wind is shaking your windows as if a human hand were rattling the sashes, — if your candle or lamp is low and will soon burn out, — let me advise you to take up some good quiet sleepy volume, or attack the "Critical Notices" of the last Quarterly, and leave this to be read by daylight, with cheerful voices round, and people near by who would hear you, if you slid from your chair and came down in a lump on the floor.

I do not say that your heart will beat as mine did, I am willing to confess, when I entered the dim chamber. Did I not tell you that I was sensitive and imaginative, and that I had lain awake with thinking what were the strange movements and sounds which I heard late at night in my little neighbor's apartment? It had come to that pass that I was truly unable to separate what I had really heard from what I had dreamed in those nightmares to which I have been subject, as before mentioned. So, when I walked into the room, and Bridget, turning back, closed the door and left me alone with its tenant, I do believe you could have grated a nutmeg on my skin, such a "goose-flesh" shiver ran over it. It was not fear, but what I call nervousness, — unreasoning, but irresistible; as when, for instance, one looking at the sun going down says, "I will count fifty before it disappears"; and as he goes on and it becomes doubtful whether he will reach the number, he gets strangely flurried, and his imagination pictures life and death and heaven and hell as the issues depending on the completion or non-completion of the fifty he is counting. Extreme curiosity will excite some people as much as fear, or what resembles fear, acts on some other less impressible natures.

I may find myself in the midst of strange facts in this little conjurer's room. Or, again, there may be nothing in this poor invalid's chamber but some old furniture, such as they say came over in the Mayflower. All this is just what I mean to find out while I am looking at the Little Gentleman, who has suddenly become my patient. The simplest things turn out to be unfathomable mysteries; the most mysterious appearances prove to be the most commonplace objects in disguise.

I wonder whether the boys that live in Roxbury and Dorchester are ever moved to tears or filled with silent awe as they look upon the rocks and fragments of "puddingstone" abounding in those localities. I have my suspicions that those boys "heave a stone" or "fire a brickbat," composed of the conglomerate just mentioned, without any more tearful or philosophical contemplations than boys of less favored regions expend on the same performance. Yet a lump of puddingstone is a thing to look at, to think about, to study over, to dream upon, to go crazy with, to beat one's brains out against. Look at that pebble in it. From what cliff was it broken? On what beach rolled by the waves of what ocean? How and *when* imbedded in soft ooze, which itself became stone, and by-and-by was lifted into bald summits and steep cliffs, such as you may see on Meeting-house-Hill any day — yes, and mark the scratches on their faces left when the boulder-carrying glaciers planed the surface of the continent with such rough tools that the storms have not worn the marks out of it with all the polishing of ever so many thousand years?

Or as you pass a roadside ditch or pool in spring-time, take from it any bit of stick or straw which has lain undisturbed for a time. Some little worm-shaped masses of clear jelly containing specks are fastened to the stick: eggs of a small snail-like shell-fish. One of these specks magnified proves to be a crystalline sphere with an opaque mass in its centre. And while you are looking, the opaque mass begins to stir, and by-and-by slowly to turn upon its axis like a forming planet, — life beginning in the microcosm, as in the great worlds of the firmament, with the revolution that turns the surface in ceaseless round to the source of life and light.

A pebble and the spawn of a mollusk! Before you have solved their mysteries, this earth where you first saw them may be a vitrified slag, or a vapor diffused through the planetary spaces. Mysteries are common enough, at any rate, whatever the boys in Roxbury and Dorchester think of "brickbats" and the spawn of creatures that live in roadside puddles.

But then a great many seeming mysteries are relatively perfectly plain, when we can get at them so as to turn them over. How many ghosts that "thick men's blood with cold" prove to be shirts hung out to dry! How many mermaids have been made out of seals! How many times have horse-mackerels been taken for the sea-serpent!

—— Let me take the whole matter coolly, while I see what is the matter with the patient. That is what I say to myself, as I draw a chair to the bedside. — The bed is an old-fashioned, dark mahogany four-poster. It was never that which made the noise of something moving. It is too heavy to be pushed about the room. — The Little Gentleman was sitting, bolstered up by pillows, with his hands clasped and their united palms resting on the back of the head, — one of the three or four positions specially affected by persons whose breathing is difficult from disease of the heart or other causes.

Sit down, Sir, — he said, — sit down! I have come to the hill Difficulty, Sir, and am fighting my way up. — His speech was laborious and interrupted.

Don't talk, — I said, — except to answer my questions. — And I proceeded to "prospect" for the marks of some local mischief, which you know is at the bottom of all these attacks, though we do not always find it. I suppose I go to work pretty much like other professional folks of my temperament. Thus: —

Wrist, if you please. — I was on his right side, but he presented his left wrist, crossing it over the other. — I begin to count, holding watch in left hand. One, two, three, four, —— What a handsome hand! — wonder if that splendid stone is a carbuncle. — One, two, three, four, five, six, seven, —— Can't see much, it is so dark, except one white object. — One, two, three, four, —— Hang it! eighty or ninety in the minute, I guess. — Tongue, if you please. — Tongue is put out. Forget to look at it, or, rather, to take any particular notice of it; — but what *is* that white object, with the long arm stretching up as if pointing to the sky, just as Vesalius and Spigelius and those old fellows used to put their skeletons? I don't think anything of such objects, you know; but what should *he* have it in his chamber for? — As I had found his pulse irregular and intermittent, I took out a stethoscope, which is a pocket-spyglass for looking into people's chests with your ears, and laid it over the place where the heart beats. I missed the usual beat of the organ. — How is this? — I said, — where is your heart gone to? — He took the stethoscope and shifted it across to the right side; there was a displacement of the organ. — I am ill-packed, — he said; — there was no room for my heart in its place as it is with other men. — God help him!

It is hard to draw the line between scientific curiosity and the desire for the patient's sake to learn all the details of his condition. I must look at this patient's chest, and thump it and listen to it. For this is a case of *ectopia cordis*, my boy, — displacement of the heart; and it isn't every day you get a chance to overhaul such an interesting malformation. And so I managed to do my duty and satisfy my curiosity at the same time. The torso was slight and deformed; the right arm attenuated, — the left full, round, and of perfect symmetry. It had run away with the life of the other limbs, — a common trick enough of Nature's, as I told you before. If you see a man with legs withered from childhood, keep out of the way of his arms, if you have a quarrel with him. He has the strength of four limbs in two; and if he strikes you, it is an arm-blow *plus* a kick administered from the shoulder instead of the haunch, where it should have started from.

Still examining him as a patient, I kept my eyes about me to search all parts of the chamber, and went on with the double process, as before. — Heart hits as hard as a fist, — *bellows-sound over mitral valves* (professional terms you need not attend to). — What the deuse is that long case for? Got his witch grandmother mummied in it? And three big mahogany presses, — hey? — A diabolical suspicion came over me which I had had once before, — that he might be one of our modern *alchemists*, — you understand, — make gold, you know, or *what looks like it*, sometimes with the head of a king or queen or of Liberty to embellish one side of the piece. — Don't I remember hearing him shut a door and lock it once? What do you think was kept under that lock? Let's have another look at his hand, to see if there are any calluses. One can tell a man's business, if it is a handicraft, very often by just taking a look at his open hand. — Ah! Four calluses at the end of the fingers of the right hand. None on those of the left. Ah, ha! What do those mean?

All this seems longer in the telling, of course, than it was in fact. While I was making these observations of the objects around me, I was also forming my opinion as to the kind of case with which I had to deal.

There are three wicks, you know, to the lamp of a man's life: brain, blood, and breath. Press the brain a little, its light goes out, followed by both the others. Stop the heart a minute and out go all three of the wicks. Choke the air out of the lungs, and presently the fluid ceases to supply the other centres of flame, and all is soon stagnation, cold, and darkness. The "tripod of life" a French physiologist called these three organs. It is all clear enough which leg of the tripod is going to break down here. I could tell you exactly what the difficulty is; — which would be as intelligible and amusing as a watchmaker's description of a diseased timekeeper to a ploughman. It is enough to say, that I found just what I expected to, and that I think this attack is only the prelude of more serious consequences, — which expression means you very well know what.

And now the secrets of this life hanging on a thread must surely come out. If I have made a mystery where there was none, my suspicions will be shamed, as they have often been before. If there is anything strange, my visits will clear it up.

I sat an hour or two by the side of the Little Gentleman's bed, after giving him some henbane to quiet his brain, and some foxglove, which an imaginative French professor has called the "Opium of the Heart." Under their influence he gradually fell into an uneasy, half-waking slumber the body fighting hard for every breath, and the mind wandering off in strange fancies and old recollections, which escaped from his lips in broken sentences.

—— The last of 'em, — he said, — the last of

'em all, — thank God! And the grave he lies in will look just as well as if he had been straight. Dig it deep, old Martin, dig it deep, — and let it be as long as other folks' graves. And mind you get the sods flat, old man, — flat as ever a straight-backed young fellow was laid under. And then, with a good tall slab at the head, and a footstone six foot away from it, it'll look just as if there was a man underneath.

A man! Who said he was a man? No more men of that pattern to bear *his* name! — Used to be a good-looking set enough. — Where's all the manhood and womanhood gone to since his great-grandfather was the strongest man that sailed out of the town of Boston, and poor Leah there the handsomest woman in Essex, if she was a witch?

—— Give me some light, — he said, — more light. — I want to see the picture.

He had started either from a dream or a wandering reverie. I was not unwilling to have more light in the apartment, and presently had lighted an astral lamp that stood on a table. — He pointed to a portrait hanging against the wall. — Look at her, — he said, — look at her! Wasn't that a pretty neck to slip a hangman's noose over?

The portrait was of a young woman, something more than twenty years old, perhaps. There were few pictures of any merit painted in New England before the time of Smibert, and I am at a loss to know what artist could have taken this half-length, which was evidently from life. It was somewhat stiff and flat, but the grace of the figure and the sweetness of the expression reminded me of the angels of the early Florentine painters. She must have been of some consideration, for she was dressed in paduasoy and lace with hanging sleeves, and the old carved frame showed how the picture had been prized by its former owners. A proud eye she had, with all her sweetness. — I think it was that which hanged her, as his strong arm hanged Minister George Burroughs; — but it may have been a little mole on one cheek, which the artist had just hinted as a beauty rather than a deformity. You know, I suppose, that nursling imps addict themselves, after the fashion of young opossums, to these little excrescences. "Witch-marks" were good evidence that a young woman was one of the Devil's wet-nurses; — I should like to have seen you make fun of them in those days! — Then she had a brooch in her bodice, that might have been taken for some devilish amulet or other; and she wore a ring upon one of her fingers, with a red stone in it, that flamed as if the painter had dipped his pencil in fire; — who knows but that it was given her by a midnight suitor fresh from that fierce element, and licensed for a season to leave his couch of flame to tempt the unsanctified hearts of earthly maidens and brand their cheeks with the print of his scorching kisses?

She and I,—he said, as he looked steadfastly at the canvas,—she and I are the last of 'em.—She will stay, and I shall go. They never painted me,—except when the boys used to make pictures of me with chalk on the board-fences. They said the doctors would want my skeleton when I was dead.—You are my friend, if you are a doctor,—a'n't you?

I just gave him my hand. I had not the heart to speak.

I want to lie still,—he said,—after I am put to bed upon the hill yonder. Can't you have a great stone laid over me, as they did over the first settlers in the old burying-ground at Dorchester, so as to keep the wolves from digging them up? I never slept easy over the sod;—I should like to lie quiet under it. And besides,—he said, in a kind of scared whisper,—I don't want to have my bones stared at, as my body has been. I don't doubt I was a *remarkable case;* but, for God's sake, oh, for God's sake, don't let 'em make a show of the cage I have been shut up in and looked through the bars of for so many years!

I have heard it said that the art of healing makes men hardhearted and indifferent to human suffering. I am willing to own that there is often a professional hardness in surgeons, just as there is in theologians, — only much less in degree than in these last. It does not commonly improve the sympathies of a man to be in the habit of thrusting knives into his fellow-creatures and burning them with red-hot irons, any more than it improves them to hold the blinding-white cautery of Gehenna by its cool handle and score and crisp young souls with it until they are scorched into the belief of — Transubstantiation or the Immaculate Conception. And, to say the plain truth, I think there are a good many coarse people in both callings. A delicate nature will not commonly choose a pursuit which implies the habitual infliction of suffering, so readily as some gentler office. Yet, while I am writing this paragraph, there passes by my window, on his daily errand of duty, not seeing me, though I catch a glimpse of his manly features through the oval glass of his chaise, as he rides by, a surgeon of skill and standing, so friendly, so modest, so tender-hearted in all his ways, that, if he had not approved himself at once adroit and firm, one would have said he was of too kindly a mould to be the minister of pain, even if it were saving pain.

You may be sure that some men, even among those who have chosen the task of pruning their fellow-creatures, grow more and more thoughtful and truly compassionate in the midst of their cruel experience. They become less nervous, but more sympathetic. They have a truer sensibility for others' pain, the more they study pain and disease in the light of science. I have said this without claiming any special growth in humanity for myself, though I do hope I grow tenderer in my feelings as I grow older. At any rate, this was not a time in which professional habits could keep down certain instincts of older date than these.

This poor little man's appeal to my humanity against the supposed rapacity of Science, which he feared would have her "specimen," if his ghost should walk restlessly a thousand years, waiting for his bones to be laid in the dust, touched my heart. But I felt bound to speak cheerily.

—— We won't die yet awhile, if we can help it, — I said, — and I trust we can help it. But don't be afraid; if I live longest, I will see that your resting-place is kept sacred till the dandelions and buttercups blow over you.

He seemed to have got his wits together by this time, and to have a vague consciousness that he might have been saying more than he meant for anybody's ears. — I have been talking a little wild, Sir, eh? — he said. — There is a great buzzing in my head with those drops of yours, and I doubt if my tongue has not been a little looser than I would have it, Sir. But I don't much want to live, Sir; that's the truth of the matter;

and it does rather please me to think that fifty years from now nobody will know that the place where I lie doesn't hold as stout and straight a man as the best of 'em that stretch out as if they were proud of the room they take. You may get me well, if you can, Sir, if you think it worth while to try; but I tell you there has been no time for this many a year when the smell of fresh earth was not sweeter to me than all the flowers that grow out of it. There's no anodyne like your good clean gravel, Sir. But if you can keep me about awhile, and it amuses you to try, you may show your skill upon me, if you like. There is a pleasure or two that I love the daylight for, and I think the night is not far off, at best. — I believe I shall sleep now; you may leave me, and come, if you like, in the morning.

Before I passed out, I took one more glance round the apartment. The beautiful face of the portrait looked at me, as portraits often do, with a frightful kind of intelligence in its eyes. The drapery fluttered on the still outstretched arm of the tall object near the window; — a crack of this was open, no doubt, and some breath of wind stirred the hanging folds. In my excited state, I seemed to see something ominous in that arm pointing to the heavens. I thought of the figures in the Dance of Death at Basle, and that other on the panels of the covered Bridge at Lucerne and it seemed to me that the grim mask who mingles with every crowd and glides over every threshold was pointing the sick man to his far home, and would soon stretch out his bony hand and lead him or drag him on the unmeasured journey towards it.

The fancy had possession of me, and I shivered again as when I first entered the chamber. The picture and the shrouded shape; I saw only these two objects. They were enough. The house was deadly still, and the night-wind, blowing through an open window, struck me as from a field of ice, at the moment I passed into the creaking corridor. As I turned into the common passage, a white figure, holding a lamp, stood full before me. I thought at first it was one of those images made to stand in niches and hold a light in their hands. But the illusion was momentary, and my eyes speedily recovered from the shock of the bright flame and snowy drapery to see that the figure was a breathing one. It was Iris, in one of her statue-trances. She had come down, whether sleeping or waking, I knew not at first, led by an instinct that told her she was wanted, — or, possibly, having overheard and interpreted the sound of our movements, — or, it may be, having learned from the servant that there was trouble which might ask for a woman's hand. I sometimes think women have a sixth sense, which tells them that others, whom they cannot see or hear, are in suffering. How surely we find them at the bedside of the dying! How strongly does Nature plead for them, that we should draw our first breath in their arms, as we sigh away our last upon their faithful breasts!

With white, bare feet, her hair loosely knotted, dressed as the starlight knew her, and the morning when she rose from slumber, save that she had twisted a scarf round her long dress, she stood still as a stone before me, holding in one hand a lighted coil of wax-taper, and in the other a silver goblet. I held my own lamp close to her, as if she had been a figure of marble, and she did not stir. There was no breach of propriety then, to scare the Poor Relation with and breed scandal out of. She had been "warned in a dream," doubtless suggested by her waking knowledge and the sounds which had reached her exalted sense. There was nothing more natural than that she should have risen and girdled her waist, and lighted her taper, and found the silver goblet with "*Ex dono pupillorum*" on it, from which she had taken her milk and possets through all her childish years, and so gone blindly out to find her place at the bedside, — a Sister of Charity without the cap and rosary; nay, unknowing whither her feet were leading her, and with wide, blank eyes seeing nothing but the vision that beckoned her along.—Well, I must wake her from her slumber or trance.—I called her name, but she did not heed my voice.

The Devil put it into my head that I would kiss one handsome young girl before I died, and now was my chance. She never would know it, and I should carry the remembrance of it with me into the grave, and a rose perhaps grow out of my dust, as a brier did out of Lord Lovel's, in memory of that immortal moment! Would it wake her from her trance? and would she see me in the flush of my stolen triumph, and hate and despise me ever after? Or should I carry off my trophy undetected, and always from that time say to myself, when I looked upon her in the glory of youth and the splendor of beauty, "My lips have touched those roses and made their sweetness mine forever"? You think my cheek was flushed, perhaps, and my eyes were glittering with this midnight flash of opportunity. On the contrary, I believe I was pale, very pale, and I know that I trembled. Ah, it is the pale passions that are the fiercest,—it is the violence of the chill that gives the measure of the fever! The fighting-boy of our school always turned white when he went out to a pitched battle with the bully of some neighboring village; but we knew what his bloodless cheeks meant,—the blood was all in his stout heart,—he was a slight boy, and there was not enough to redden his face and fill his heart both at once.

Perhaps it is making a good deal of a slight matter, to tell the internal conflicts in the heart of a quiet person something more than juvenile and something less than senile, as to whether he should be guilty of an impropriety, and, if he were, whether he would get caught in his indiscretion. And yet the memory of the kiss that Margaret of Scotland gave to Alain Chartier has lasted four hundred years, and put it into the head of many an ill-favored poet, whether Victoria, or Eugénie would do as much by him, if she happened to pass him when he was asleep. And have we ever forgotten that the fresh cheek of the young John Milton tingled under the lips of some high-born Italian beauty, who, I believe, did not think to leave her card by the side of the slumbering youth, but has bequeathed the memory of her pretty deed to all coming time? The sound of a kiss is not so loud as that of a cannon, but its echo lasts a deal longer.

There is one disadvantage which the man of philosophical habits of mind suffers, as compared with the man of action. While he is taking an enlarged and rational view of the matter before him, he lets his chance slip through his fingers. Iris woke up, of her own accord, before I had made up my mind what I was going to do about it.

When I remember how charmingly she looked, I don't blame myself at all for being tempted; but if I had been fool enough to yield to the impulse, I should certainly have been ashamed to tell of it. She did not know what to make of it, finding herself there alone, in such guise, and me staring at her. She looked down at her white robe and bare feet, and colored, — then at the goblet she held in her hand, — then at the taper; and at last her thoughts seemed to clear up.

I know it all, — she said. — He is going to die, and I must go and sit by him. Nobody will care for him as I shall, and I have nobody else to care for.

I assured her that nothing was needed for him that night but rest, and persuaded her that the excitement of her presence could only do harm. Let him sleep, and he would very probably awake better in the morning. There was nothing to be said, for I spoke with authority; and the young girl glided away with noiseless step and sought her own chamber.

The tremor passed away from my limbs, and the blood began to burn in my cheeks. The beautiful image which had so bewitched me faded gradually from my imagination, and I returned to the still perplexing mysteries of my little neighbor's chamber. All was still there now. No plaintive sounds, no monotonous murmurs, no shutting of windows and doors at strange hours, as if something or somebody were coming in or going out, or there was something to be hidden in those dark mahogany presses. Is there an inner apartment that I have not seen? The way in which the house is built might admit of it. As I thought it over, I at once imagined a Bluebeard's chamber. Suppose, for instance, that the narrow bookshelves to the right are really only a masked door, such as we remember leading to the private study of one of our most distinguished townsmen, who loved to steal away from his stately library to that little silent cell. If this were lighted from above, a person or persons might pass their days there without attracting attention from the household, and wander where they pleased at night,— to Copp's-Hill burial-ground, if they liked, — I said to myself, laughing, and pulling the bedclothes over my head. There is no logic in superstitious fancies any more than in dreams. A she-ghost wouldn't want an inner chamber to herself. A live woman, with a valuable soprano voice, wouldn't start off at night to sprain her ankles over the old graves of the North-End cemetery.

It is all very easy for you, middle-aged reader sitting over this page in the broad daylight, to call me by all manner of asinine and anserine unchristian names, because I had these fancies run ning through my head. I don't care much for your abuse. The question is not, what it is reasonable for a man to think about, but what he actually does think about, in the dark, and when he is alone, and his whole body seems but one great nerve of hearing, and he sees the phosphorescent flashes of his own eyeballs as they turn suddenly in the direction of the last strange noise, — what he actually does think about, as he lies and recalls all the wild stories his head is full of, his fancy hinting the most alarming conjectures to account for the simplest facts about him, his common-sense laughing them to scorn the next minute, but his mind still returning to them, under one shape or another, until he gets very nervous and foolish, and remembers how pleasant it used to be to have his mother come and tuck him up and go and sit within call, so that she could hear him at any minute, if he got very much scared and wanted her. Old babies that we are!

Daylight will clear up all that lamp-light has left doubtful. I longed for the morning to come, for I was more curious than ever. So, between my fancies and anticipations, I had but a poor night of it, and came down tired to the breakfast-table. My visit was not to be made until after this morning hour; — there was nothing urgent, so the servant was ordered to tell me.

It was the first breakfast at which the high

chair at the side of Iris had been unoccupied. — You might jest as well take away that chair, — said our landlady, — he'll never want it again. He acts like a man that's struck with death, 'n' I don't believe he'll ever come out of his chamber till he's laid out and brought down a corpse. — These good women do put things so plainly! There were two or three words in her short remark that always sober people, and suggest silence or brief moral reflections.

—— Life is dreadful uncerting, — said the Poor Relation, — and pulled in her social tentacles to concentrate her thoughts on this fact of human history.

—— If there was anything a fellah could do, — said the young man John, so called, — a fellah 'd like the chance o' helpin' a little cripple like that. He looks as if he couldn't turn over any handier than a turtle that's laid on his back; and I guess there a'n't many people that know how to lift better than I do. Ask him if he don't want any watchers. I don't mind settin' up any more 'n' a cat-owl. I was up all night twice last month.

[My private opinion is, that there was no small amount of punch absorbed on those two occasions which I think I heard of at the time; — but the offer is a kind one, and it isn't fair to question how he would like sitting up without the punch and the company and the songs and smoking

He means what he says, and it would be a more considerable achievement for him to sit quietly all night by a sick man than for a good many other people. I tell you this odd thing: there are a good many persons, who, through the habit of making other folks uncomfortable, by finding fault with all their cheerful enjoyments, at last get up a kind of hostility to comfort in general, even in their own persons. The correlative to loving our neighbors as ourselves is hating ourselves as we hate our neighbors. Look at old misers; first they starve their dependants, and then themselves. So I think it more for a lively young fellow to be ready to play nurse than for one of those useful but forlorn martyrs who have taken a spite against themselves and love to gratify it by fasting and watching.]

—— The time came at last for me to make my visit. I found Iris sitting by the Little Gentleman's pillow. To my disappointment, the room was darkened. He did not like the light, and would have the shutters kept nearly closed. It was good enough for me; — what business had I to be indulging my curiosity, when I had nothing to do but to exercise such skill as I possessed for the benefit of my patient? There was not much to be said or done in such a case; but I spoke as encouragingly as I could, as I think we are always bound to do. He did not seem to pay any very anxious attention, but the poor girl listened as if her own life and more than her own life were depending on the words I uttered. She followed me out of the room, when I had got through my visit.

How long? — she said.

Uncertain. Any time; to-day, — next week, — next month, — I answered. — One of those cases where the issue is not doubtful, but may be sudden or slow.

The women of the house were kind, as women always are in trouble. But Iris pretended that nobody could spare the time as well as she, and kept her place, hour after hour, until the landlady insisted that she'd be killin' herself, if she begun at that rate, 'n' haf to give up, if she didn't want to be clean beat out in less 'n a week.

At the table we were graver than common. The high chair was set back against the wall, and a gap left between that of the young girl and her nearest neighbor's on the right. But the next morning, to our great surprise, that good-looking young Marylander had very quietly moved his own chair to the vacant place. I thought he was creeping down that way, but I was not prepared for a leap spanning such a tremendous parenthesis of boarders as this change of position included. There was no denying that the youth and maiden were a handsome pair, as they sat side by side.

But whatever the young girl may have thought of her new neighbor, she never seemed for a moment to forget the poor little friend who had been taken from her side. There are women, and even girls, with whom it is of no use to talk. One might as well reason with a bee as to the form of his cell, or with an oriole as to the construction of his swinging nest, as try to stir these creatures from their own way of doing their own work. It was not a question with Iris, whether she was entitled by any special relation or by the fitness of things to play the part of a nurse. She was a wilful creature that must have her way in this matter. And it so proved that it called for much patience and long endurance to carry through the duties, say rather the kind offices, the painful pleasures, that she had chosen as her share in the household where accident had thrown her. She had that genius of ministration which is the special province of certain women, marked even among their helpful sisters by a soft, low voice, a quiet footfall, a light hand, a cheering smile, and a ready self-surrender to the objects of their care, which such trifles as their own food, sleep, or habits of any kind never presume to interfere with.

Day after day, and too often through the long watches of the night, she kept her place by the pillow.—That girl will kill herself over me, Sir

— said the poor Little Gentleman to me, one day, — she will kill herself, Sir, if you don't call in all the resources of your art to get me off as soon as may be. I shall wear her out, Sir, with sitting in this close chamber and watching when she ought to be sleeping, if you leave me to the care of Nature without dosing me.

This was rather strange pleasantry, under the cir cumstances. But there are certain persons whose existence is so out of parallel with the larger laws in the midst of which it is moving, that life becomes to them as death and death as life. — How am I getting along? — he said, another morning. He lifted his shrivelled hand, with the death's-head ring on it, and looked at it with a sad sort of complacency. By this one movement, which I have seen repeatedly of late, I know that his thoughts have gone before to another condition, and that he is, as it were, looking back on the infirmities of the body as accidents of the past. For, when he was well, one might see him often looking at the handsome hand with the flaming jewel on one of its fingers. The single well-shaped limb was the source of that pleasure which in some form or other Nature almost always grants to her least richly endowed children. Handsome hair, eyes, complexion, feature, form, hand, foot, pleasant voice, strength, grace, agility, intelligence, — how few there are that have not just enough of one at least of these gifts to show them that the good Mother, busy with her millions of children, has not quite forgotten them! But now he was thinking of that other state, where, free from all mortal impediments, the memory of his sorrowful burden should be only as that of the case he has shed to the insect whose "deep-damasked wings" beat off the golden dust of the lily-anthers, as he flutters in the ecstasy of his new life over their full-blown summer glories.

No human being can rest for any time in a state of equilibrium, where the desire to live and that to depart just balance each other. If one has a house, which he has lived and always means to live in, he pleases himself with the thought of all the conveniences it offers him, and thinks little of its wants and imperfections. But once having made up his mind to move to a better, every incommodity starts out upon him, until the very ground-plan of it seems to have changed in his mind, and his thoughts and affections, each one of them packing up its little bundle of circumstances, have quitted their several chambers and nooks and migrated to the new home, long before its apartments are ready to receive their bodily tenant. It is so with the body. Most persons have died before they expire, — died to all earthly longings, so that the last breath is only, as it were, the locking of the door of the already deserted mansion. The fact of the tranquillity with which the great majority of dying persons await this locking of those gates of life through which its airy angels have been going and coming, from the moment of the first cry, is familiar to those who have been often called upon to witness the last period of life. Almost always there is a preparation made by Nature for unearthing a soul, just as on the smaller scale there is for the removal of a milk-tooth. The roots which hold human life to earth are absorbed before it is lifted from its place. Some of the dying are weary and want rest, the idea of which is almost inseparable in the universal mind from death. Some are in pain, and want to be rid of it, even though the anodyne be dropped, as in the legend, from the sword of the Death-Angel. Some are stupid, mercifully narcotized that they may go to sleep without long tossing about. And some are strong in faith and hope, so, that, as they draw near the next world, they would fain hurry toward it, as the caravan moves faster over the sands when the foremost travellers send word along the file that water is in sight. Though each little party that follows in a foot-track of its own will have it that the water to which others think they are hastening is a mirage, not the less has it been true in all ages and for human beings of every creed which recognized a future, that those who have fallen worn out by their march through the Desert have dreamed at least of a River of Life, and thought they heard its murmurs as they lay dying.

The change from the clinging to the present to the welcoming of the future comes very soon, for the most part, after all hope of life is extinguished, provided this be left in good degree to Nature, and not insolently and cruelly forced upon those who are attacked by illness, on the strength of that odious foreknowledge often imparted by science, before the white fruit whose core is ashes, and which we call *death*, has set beneath the pallid and drooping flower of sickness. There is a singular sagacity very often shown in a patient's estimate of his own vital force. His physician knows the state of his material frame well enough, perhaps, — that this or that organ is more or less impaired or disintegrated; but the patient has a sense that he can hold out so much longer, — sometimes that he must and will live for a while, though by the logic of disease he ought to die without any delay.

The Little Gentleman continued to fail, until it became plain that his remaining days were few. I told the household what to expect. There was a good deal of kind feeling expressed among the boarders, in various modes, according to their characters and style of sympathy. The landlady was urgent that he should try a certain nostrum which had saved somebody's life in jest sech a case. The Poor Relation wanted me to carry, as from her, a copy of "Allein's Alarm," etc. I objected to the title, reminding her that it offended people of old, so that more than twice as many of the book were sold when they changed the name to "A Sure Guide to Heaven." The good old gentleman whom I have mentioned before has come to the time of life when many old men cry easily, and forget their tears as children do. — He was a worthy gentleman, — he said, — a very worthy gentleman, but unfortunate, — very unfortunate. Sadly deformed about the spine and the feet. Had an impression that the late Lord Byron had some malformation of this kind. Had heerd there was something the matter with the ankle-j'ints of that nobleman, but he was a man of talents. This gentleman seemed to be a man of talents. Could not always agree with his statements, — thought he was a little over-partial to this city, and had some free opinions; but was sorry to lose him, — and if — there was anything — he — could — — — —. In the midst of these kind expressions, the gentleman with the *diamond*, the Koh-i-noor, as we called him, asked, in a very unpleasant sort of way, how the old boy was likely to cut up, — meaning what money our friend was going to leave behind.

The young fellow John spoke up, to the effect that this was a diabolish snobby question, when a man was dying and not dead. — To this the Koh-i-noor replied, by asking if the other meant to insult him. — Whereto the young man John rejoined that he had no particul'r intentions one way or t'other. — The Koh-i-noor then suggested the young man's stepping out into the yard, that he, the speaker, might "slap his chops." — Let 'em alone, — said young Maryland, — it'll soon be over, and they won't hurt each other much. — So they went out.

The Koh-i-noor entertained the very common idea, that, when one quarrels with another, the simple thing to do is to *knock the man down*, and there is the end of it. Now those who have watched such encounters are aware of two things: first, that it is not so easy to knock a man down as it is to talk about it; secondly, that, if you do happen to knock a man down, there is a very good chance that he will be angry, and get up and give you a thrashing.

So the Koh-i-noor thought he would begin, as soon as they got into the yard, by knocking his man down, and with this intention swung his arm round after the fashion of rustics and those unskilled in the noble art, expecting the young fellow John to drop when his fist, having completed a quarter of a circle, should come in contact with the side of that young man's head Unfortunately for this theory, it happens that a blow struck out straight is as much shorter, and therefore as much quicker than the rustic's swinging blow, as the radius is shorter than the quarter of a circle. The mathematical and mechanical corollary was, that the Koh-i-noor felt something hard bring up suddenly against his right eye, which something he could have sworn was a paving-stone, judging by his sensations ; and as this threw his person somewhat backwards, and the young man John jerked his own head back a little, the swinging blow had nothing to stop it; and as the Jewel staggered between the hit he got and the blow he missed, he tripped and "went to grass," so far as the back-yard of our boarding-house was provided with that vegetable. It was a signal illustration of that fatal mistake, so frequent in young and ardent natures with inconspicuous calves and negative pectorals, that they can settle most little quarrels on the spot by "knocking the man down."

We are in the habit of handling our faces so carefully, that a heavy blow, taking effect on that portion of the surface, produces a most unpleasant surprise, which is accompanied with odd sensations, as of seeing sparks, and a kind of electrical or ozone-like odor, half-sulphurous in character and which has given rise to a very vulgar and profane threat sometimes heard from the lips of bullies. A person not used to pugilistic gestures does not instantly recover from this surprise. The Koh-i-noor, exasperated by his failure, and still a little confused by the smart hit he had received, but furious, and confident of victory over a young fellow a good deal lighter than himself, made a desperate rush to bear down all before him and finish the contest at once. That is the way all angry greenhorns and incompetent persons attempt to settle matters. It doesn't do, if the other fellow is only cool, moderately quick, and has a very little science. It didn't do this time; for, as the assailant rushed in with his arms flying everywhere, like the vans of a windmill, he ran a prominent feature of his face against a fist which was travelling in the other direction, and immediately after struck the knuckles of the young man's other fist a severe blow with the part of his person known as the *epigastrium* to one branch of science and the *bread-basket* to another. This second round closed the battle. The Koh-i-noor had got enough, which in such cases is more than as good as a feast. The young fellow asked him if he was satisfied, and held out his hand. But the other sulked, and muttered something about revenge. — Jest as y' like, — said the young man John. — Clap a slice o' raw beefsteak on to that mouse o' yours 'n' 't'll take down the swellin'

(*Mouse* is a technical term for a bluish, oblong, rounded elevation occasioned by running one's forehead or eyebrow against another's knuckles.) The young fellow was particularly pleased that he had had an opportunity of trying his proficiency in the art of self-defence without the gloves. The Koh-i-noor did not favor us with his company for a day or two, being confined to his chamber, *it was said*, by a *slight feverish attack.* He was chop-fallen always after this, and got negligent in his person. The impression must have been a deep one; for it was observed, that, when he came down again, his moustache and whiskers had turned visibly white — *about the roots.* In short, it disgraced him, and rendered still more conspicuous a tendency to drinking, of which he had been for some time suspected. This, and the disgust which a young lady naturally feels at hearing that her lover has been "licked by a fellah not half his size," induced the landlady's daughter to take that decided step which produced a change in the programme of her career I may hereafter allude to.

I never thought he would come to good, when I heard him attempting to sneer at an unoffending city so respectable as Boston. After a man begins to attack the State-House, when he gets bitter about the Frog-Pond, you may be sure there is not much left of him. Poor Edgar Poe died in the hospital soon after he got into this way of talking; and so sure as you find an unfortunate fellow reduced to this pass, you had better begin praying for him, and stop lending him money, for he is on his last legs. Remember poor Edgar! He is dead and gone; but the State-House has its cupola fresh-gilded, and the Frog-Pond has got a fountain that squirts up a hundred feet into the air and glorifies that humble sheet with a fine display of provincial rainbows.

—— I cannot fulfil my promise in this number. I expected to gratify your curiosity, if you have become at all interested in these puzzles, doubts, fancies, whims, or whatever you choose to call them, of mine. Next month you shall hear all about it.

—— It was evening, and I was going to the sick-chamber. As I paused at the door before entering, I heard a sweet voice singing. It was not the wild melody I had sometimes heard at midnight: — no, this was the voice of Iris, and I could distinguish every word. I had seen the verses in her book; the melody was new to me. Let me finish my page with them.

HYMN OF TRUST.

O LOVE Divine, that stooped to share
  Our sharpest pang, our bitterest tear,
On Thee we cast each earthborn care,
  We smile at pain while Thou art near!

Though long the weary way we tread,
  And sorrow crown each lingering year,
No path we shun, no darkness dread,
  Our hearts still whispering, Thou art near.

When drooping pleasure turns to grief,
  And trembling faith is changed to fear,
The murmuring wind, the quivering leaf
  Shall softly tell us, Thou art near!

On Thee we fling our burdening woe,
  O Love Divine, forever dear,
Content to suffer, while we know,
  Living and dying, Thou art near!

XII.

A YOUNG fellow, born of good stock, in one of the more thoroughly civilized portions of these United States of America, bred in good principles, inheriting a social position which makes him at his ease everywhere, means sufficient to educate him thoroughly without taking away the stimulus to vigorous exertion, and with a good opening in some honorable path of labor, is the finest sight our private satellite has had the opportunity of inspecting on the planet to which she belongs. In some respects it was better to be a young Greek. If we may trust the old marbles, — my friend with his arm stretched over my head, above there, (in plaster of Paris,) or the discobolus, whom one may see at the principal sculpture gallery of this metropolis, — those Greek young men were of supreme beauty. Their close curls, their elegantly set heads, column-like necks, straight noses, short, curled lips, firm chins, deep chests, light flanks, large muscles, small joints, were finer than anything we ever see. It may well be questioned whether the human shape will ever present itself again in a race of such perfect symmetry. But the life of the youthful Greek was local, not planetary, like that of the young American. He had a string of legends, in place of our Gospels. He had no printed books, no newspaper, no steam caravans, no forks, no soap, none of the thousand cheap conveniences which have become matters of necessity to our modern civilization. Above all things, if he aspired to know as well as to enjoy, he found knowledge not diffused everywhere about him, so that a day's labor would buy him more wisdom than a year could master, but held in private hands, hoarded in precious manuscripts, to be sought for only as gold is sought in narrow fissures and in the beds of brawling streams. Never, since man came into this atmosphere of oxygen and azote, was there anything like the condition of the young American of the nineteenth century. Having in possession or in prospect the best part of half a world, with all its climates and soils to choose from; equipped with wings of fire and smoke that fly with him day and night, so that he counts his journey not in miles, but in degrees, and sees the seasons change as the wild fowl sees them in his annual flights; with huge leviathans always ready to take him on their broad backs and push behind them with their pectoral or caudal fins the waters that seam the continent or separate the hemispheres; heir of all old civilizations, founder of that new one which, if all the prophecies of the human heart are not lies, is to be the noblest, as it is the last; isolated in space from the races that are governed by dynasties whose divine right grows out of human wrong, yet knit into the most absolute solidarity with mankind of all times and places by the one great thought he inherits as his national birthright; free to form and express his opinions on almost every subject, and assured that he will soon acquire the last franchise which men withhold from man,—that of stating the laws of his spiritual being and the beliefs he accepts without hindrance except from clearer views of truth, — he seems to want nothing for a large, wholesome, noble, beneficent life. In fact, the chief danger is that he will think the whole planet is made for him, and forget that there are some possibilities left in the *débris* of the old-world civilization which deserve a certain respectful consideration at his hands.

The combing and clipping of this shaggy wild continent are in some measure done for him by those who have gone before. Society has subdivided itself enough to have a place for every form of talent. Thus, if a man show the least sign of ability as a sculptor or a painter, for instance, he finds the means of education and a demand for his services. Even a man who knows nothing but science will be provided for, if he does not think it necessary to hang about his birthplace all his days, — which is a most un-American weakness. The apron-strings of an American mother are made of India-rubber. Her boy belongs where he is wanted; and that young Marylander of ours spoke for all our young men, when he said that his home was wherever the stars and stripes blew over his head.

And that leads me to say a few words of this young gentleman, who made that audacious movement lately which I chronicled in my last record,

—jumping over the seats of I don't know how many boarders to put himself in the place which the Little Gentleman's absence had left vacant at the side of Iris. When a young man is found habitually at the side of any one given young lady, — when he lingers where she stays, and hastens when she leaves, — when his eyes follow her as she moves, and rest upon her when she is still, — when he begins to grow a little timid, he who was so bold, and a little pensive, he who was so gay, whenever accident finds them alone, — when he thinks very often of the given young lady, and names her very seldom, ——

What do you say about it, my charming young expert in that sweet science in which, perhaps, a long experience is not the first of qualifications?

—— But we don't know anything about this young man, except that he is good-looking, and somewhat high-spirited, and strong-limbed, and has a generous style of nature, — all very promising, but by no means proving that he is a proper lover for Iris, whose heart we turned inside out when we opened that sealed book of hers.

Ah, my dear young friend! When your mamma — then, if you will believe it, a very slight young lady, with very pretty hair and figure — came and told *her* mamma that your papa had — had — asked —— No, no, no! she couldn't say it; but her mother — oh, the depth of maternal sagacity!

— guessed it all without another word! — When your mother, I say, came and told her mother she was *engaged*, and your grandmother told your grandfather, how much did they know of the intimate nature of the young gentleman to whom she had pledged her existence? I will not be so hard as to ask how much your respected mamma knew at that time of the intimate nature of your respected papa, though, if we should compare a young girl's *man-as-she-thinks-him* with a forty-summered matron's *man-as-she-finds-him*, I have my doubts as to whether the second would be a fac-simile of the first in most cases.

The idea that in this world each young person is to wait until he or she finds that precise counterpart who alone of all creation was meant for him or her, and then fall instantly in love with it, is pretty enough, only it is not Nature's way. It is not at all essential that all pairs of human beings should be, as we sometimes say of particular couples, "born for each other." Sometimes a man or a woman is made a great deal better and happier in the end for having had to conquer the faults of the one beloved, and make the fitness not found at first, by gradual assimilation. There is a class of good women who have no right to marry perfectly good men, because they have the power of saving those who would go to ruin but for the guiding providence of a good wife. I have known many such cases. It is the most momentous question a woman is ever called upon to decide, whether the faults of the man she loves are beyond remedy and will drag her down, or whether she is competent to be his earthly redeemer and lift him to her own level.

A person of *genius* should marry a person of *character*. Genius does not herd with genius. The musk-deer and the civet-cat are never found in company. They don't care for strange scents, — they like plain animals better than perfumed ones. Nay, if you will have the kindness to notice, Nature has not gifted my lady musk-deer with the personal peculiarity by which her lord is so widely known.

Now when genius allies itself with character, the world is very apt to think character has the best of the bargain. A brilliant woman marries a plain, manly fellow, with a simple intellectual mechanism; — we have all seen such cases. The world often stares a good deal and wonders. She should have taken that other, with a far more complex mental machinery. She might have had a watch with the philosophical compensation-balance, with the metaphysical index which can split a second into tenths, with the musical chime which can turn every quarter of an hour into melody. She has chosen a plain one, that keeps good time, and that is all.

Let her alone! She knows what she is about. Genius has an infinitely deeper reverence for character than character can have for genius. To be sure, genius gets the world's praise, because its work is a tangible product, to be bought, or had for nothing. It bribes the common voice to praise it by presents of speeches, poems, statues, pictures, or whatever it can please with. Character evolves its best products for home consumption; but, mind you, it takes a deal more to feed a family for thirty years than to make a holiday feast for our neighbors once or twice in our lives. You talk of the fire of genius. Many a blessed woman, who dies unsung and unremembered, has given out more of the real vital heat that keeps the life in human souls, without a spark flitting through her humble chimney to tell the world about it, than would set a dozen theories smoking, or a hundred odes simmering, in the brains of so many men of genius. It is in *latent caloric*, if I may borrow a philosophical expression, that many of the noblest hearts give out the life that warms them. Cornelia's lips grow white, and her pulse hardly warms her thin fingers, — but she has melted all the ice out of the hearts of those young Gracchi, and her lost heat is in the blood of her youthful heroes. We are always valuing the soul's temperature by the thermometer of public deed or word. Yet the great sun himself, when he pours his noonday beams upon some vast hyaline boulder, rent from the eternal ice-quarries, and floating toward the tropics, never warms it a fraction above the thirty-two degrees of Fahrenheit that marked the moment when the first drop trickled down its side.

How we all like the spirting up of a fountain, seemingly against the law that makes water everywhere slide, roll, leap, tumble headlong, to get as low as the earth will let it! That is genius. But what is this transient upward movement, which gives us the glitter and the rainbow, to that unsleeping, all-present force of gravity, the same yesterday, to-day, and forever, (if the universe be eternal,) — the great outspread hand of God himself, forcing all things down into their places, and keeping them there? Such, in smaller proportion, is the force of character to the fitful movements of genius, as they are or have been linked to each other in many a household, where one name was historic, and the other, let me say the nobler, unknown, save by some faint reflected ray, borrowed from its lustrous companion.

Oftentimes, as I have lain swinging on the water, in the swell of the Chelsea ferry-boats, in that long, sharp-pointed, black cradle in which I love to let the great mother rock me, I have seen a tall ship glide by against the tide, as if drawn by some invisible tow-line, with a hundred strong arms pulling it. Her sails hung unfilled, her streamers were drooping, she had neither side-wheel nor stern-wheel; still she moved on, stately, in serene triumph, as if with her own life. But I knew that on the other side of the ship, hidden beneath the great hulk that swam so majestically, there was a little toiling steam-tug, with heart of fire and arms of iron, that was hugging it close and dragging it bravely on; and I knew, that, if the little steam-tug untwined her arms and left the tall ship, it would wallow and roll about, and drift hither and thither, and go off with the refluent tide, no man knows whither. And so I have known more than one *genius*, high-decked, full-freighted, wide-sailed, gay-pennoned, that, but for the bare toiling arms, and brave, warm, beating heart of the faithful little wife, that nestled close in his shadow, and clung to him, so that no wind or wave could part them, and dragged him on against all the tide of circumstance, would soon have gone down the stream and been heard of no more. — No, I am too much a lover of genius, I sometimes think, and too often get impatient with dull people, so that, in their weak talk, where nothing is taken for granted, I look forward to some future possible state of development, when a gesture passing between a beatified human soul and an archangel shall signify as much as the complete history of a planet, from the time when it curdled to the time when its sun was burned out. And yet, when a strong brain is weighed with a true heart, it seems to me like balancing a bubble against a wedge of gold.

——It takes a very *true* man to be a fitting companion for a woman of genius, but not a very great one. I am not sure that she will not embroider her ideal better on a plain ground than on one with a brilliant pattern already worked in its texture. But as the very essence of genius is truthfulness, contact with realities, (which are always ideas behind shows of form or language,) nothing is so contemptible as falsehood and pretence in its eyes. Now it is not easy to find a perfectly true woman, and it is very hard to find a perfectly true man. And a woman of genius, who has the sagacity to choose such a one as her companion, shows more of the divine gift in so doing than in her finest talk or her most brilliant work of letters or of art.

I have been a good while coming at a secret, for which I wished to prepare you before telling it. I think there is a kindly feeling growing up between Iris and our young Marylander. Not that I suppose there is any distinct understanding between them, but that the affinity which has drawn him from the remote corner where he sat to the side of the young girl is quietly bringing their two natures together. Just now she is all given up to another; but when he no longer calls upon her daily thoughts and cares, I warn you not to be surprised, if this bud of friendship open like the evening primrose, with a sound as of a sudden stolen kiss, and lo! the flower of full-blown love lies unfolded before you.

And now the days had come for our little friend, whose whims and weaknesses had interested us, perhaps, as much as his better traits, to make ready for that long journey which is easier to the cripple than to the strong man, and on which none enters so willingly as he who has borne the life-long load of infirmity during his earthly pilgrimage. At this point, under most circumstances, I would close the doors and draw the veil of privacy before the chamber where the birth which we call death, out of life into the unknown world, is working its mystery. But this friend of ours stood alone in the world, and, as the last act of his life was mainly in harmony with the rest of its drama, I do not here feel the force of the objection commonly lying against that death-bed literature which forms the staple of a certain portion of the press. Let me explain what I mean, so that my readers may think for themselves a little, before they accuse me of hasty expressions.

The Roman Catholic Church has certain formulæ

for its dying children, to which almost all of them attach the greatest importance. There is hardly a criminal so abandoned that he is not anxious to receive the "consolations of religion" in his last hours. Even if he be senseless, but still living, I think that the form is gone through with, just as baptism is administered to the unconscious new-born child. Now we do not quarrel with these forms. We look with reverence and affection upon all symbols which give peace and comfort to our fellow-creatures. But the value of the new-born child's passive consent to the ceremony is null, as testimony to the truth of a doctrine. The automatic closing of a dying man's lips on the consecrated wafer proves nothing in favor of the Real Presence, or any other dogma. And, speaking generally, the evidence of dying men in favor of any belief is to be received with great caution.

They commonly tell the truth about their present feelings, no doubt. A dying man's deposition about anything *he knows* is good evidence. But it is of much less consequence what a man thinks and says when he is changed by pain, weakness, apprehension, than what he thinks when he is truly and wholly himself. Most murderers die in a very pious frame of mind, expecting to go to glory at once; yet no man believes he shall meet a larger average of pirates and cut-throats in the streets of the New Jerusalem than of honest folks that died in their beds.

Unfortunately, there has been a very great tendency to make capital of various kinds out of dying men's speeches. The lies that have been put into their mouths for this purpose are endless. The prime minister, whose last breath was spent in scolding his nurse, dies with a magnificent apothegm on his lips, — manufactured by a reporter. Addison gets up a *tableau* and utters an admirable sentiment, — or somebody makes the posthumous dying epigram for him. The incoherent babble of green fields is translated into the language of stately sentiment. One would think, all that dying men had to do was to say the prettiest thing they could, — to make their rhetorical point, — and then bow themselves politely out of the world.

Worse than this is the torturing of dying people to get their evidence in favor of this or that favorite belief. The camp-followers of proselyting sects have come in at the close of every life where they could get in, to strip the languishing soul of its thoughts, and carry them off as spoils. The Roman Catholic or other priest who insists on the reception of his formula means kindly, we trust, and very commonly succeeds in getting the acquiescence of the subject of his spiritual surgery. But do not let us take the testimony of people who are in the worst condition to form opinions as evidence of the truth or falsehood of that which they accept. A lame man's opinion of dancing is not good for much. A poor fellow who can neither eat nor drink, who is sleepless and full of pains, whose flesh has wasted from him, whose blood is like water, who is gasping for breath, is not in a condition to judge fairly of human life, which in all its main adjustments is intended for men in a normal, healthy condition. It is a remark I have heard from the wise Patriarch of the Medical Profession among us, that the moral condition of patients with disease *above* the great breathing-muscle, the diaphragm, is much more hopeful than that of patients with disease *below* it, in the digestive organs. Many an honest ignorant man has given us pathology when he thought he was giving us psychology. With this preliminary caution I shall proceed to the story of the Little Gentleman's leaving us.

When the divinity-student found that our fellow-boarder was not likely to remain long with us, he, being a young man of tender conscience and kindly nature, was not a little exercised on his behalf. It was undeniable that on several occasions the Little Gentleman had expressed himself with a good deal of freedom on a class of subjects which, according to the divinity-student, he had no right to form an opinion upon.

He therefore considered his future welfare in jeopardy.

The Muggletonian sect have a very odd way of dealing with people. If I, the Professor, will only give in to the Muggletonian doctrine, there shall be no question through all that persuasion that I am competent to judge of that doctrine; nay, I shall be quoted as evidence of its truth, while I live, and cited, after I am dead, as testimony in its behalf; but if I utter any ever so slight Anti-Muggletonian sentiment, then I become *incompetent to form any opinion on the matter.* This, you cannot fail to observe, is exactly the way the pseudo-sciences go to work, as explained in my Lecture on Phrenology. Now I hold that he whose testimony would be accepted in behalf of the Muggletonian doctrine has a right to be heard against it. Whoso offers me any article of belief for my signature implies that I am competent to form an opinion upon it; and if my positive testimony in its favor is of any value, then my negative testimony against it is also of value.

I thought my young friend's attitude was a little too much like that of the Muggletonians. I also remarked a singular timidity on his part lest somebody should "unsettle" somebody's faith,—as if faith did not require exercise as much as any other living thing, and were not all the better for a shaking up now and then. I don't mean that it would be fair to bother Bridget, the wild Irish girl, or Joice Heth, the centenarian, or any other intellectual non-combatant; but all persons who proclaim a belief which passes judgment on their neighbors must be ready to have it "unsettled," that is, questioned, at all times and by anybody,—just as those who set up bars across a thoroughfare must expect to have them taken down by every one who wants to pass, if he is strong enough.

Besides, to think of trying to water-proof the American mind against the questions that Heaven rains down upon it shows a misapprehension of our new conditions. If to question everything be unlawful and dangerous, we had better undeclare our independence at once; for what the Declaration means is the right to question everything, even the truth of its own fundamental proposition.

The old-world order of things is an arrangement of locks and canals, where everything depends on keeping the gates shut, and so holding the upper waters at their level; but the system under which the young republican American is born trusts the whole unimpeded tide of life to the great elemental influences, as the vast rivers of the continent settle their own level in obedience to the laws that govern the planet and the spheres that surround it.

The divinity-student was not quite up to the idea of the commonwealth, as our young friend the Marylander, for instance, understood it. He could not get rid of that notion of private property in truth, with the right to fence it in, and put up a sign-board, thus: —

☞ ALL TRESPASSERS ARE WARNED OFF THESE GROUNDS!

He took the young Marylander to task for going to the Church of the Galileans, where he had several times accompanied Iris of late.

I am a Churchman, — the young man said, — by education and habit. I love my old Church for many reasons, but most of all because I think it has educated me out of its own forms into the spirit of its highest teachings. I think I belong to the "Broad Church," if any of you can tell what that means.

I had the rashness to attempt to answer the question myself. — Some say the Broad Church means the collective mass of good people of all denominations. Others say that such a definition is nonsense; that a church is an organization, and the scattered good folks are no organization at all. They think that men will eventually come together on the basis of one or two or more common articles of belief, and form a great unity. Do they see what this amounts to? It means an equal division of intellect! It is mental agrarianism! a thing that never was and never will be, until national and individual idiosyncrasies have ceased to exist. The man of thirty-nine beliefs holds the man ot one belief a pauper; he is not going to give up thirty-eight of them for the sake of fraternizing with the other in the temple which bears on its front, "*Deo erexit Voltaire.*" A church is a garden, I have heard it said, and the illustration was neatly handled. Yes, and there is no such thing as a *broad* garden. It must be fenced in, and whatever is fenced in is narrow. You cannot have arctic and tropical plants growing together in it, except by the forcing system, which is a mighty narrow piece of business. You can't make a village or a parish or a family think alike, yet you suppose that you can make a world pinch its beliefs or pad them to a single pattern! Why, the very life of an ecclesiastical organization is a life of *induction*, a state of perpetually disturbed equilibrium kept up by another charged body in the neighborhood. If the two bodies touch and share their respective charges, down goes the index of the electrometer!

Do you know that every man has a religious belief peculiar to himself? Smith is always a Smithite. He takes in exactly Smith's-worth of knowledge, Smith's-worth of truth, of beauty, of divinity. And Brown has from time immemorial been trying to burn him, to excommunicate him, to anonymous-article him, because he did not take in Brown's-worth of knowledge, truth, beauty, divinity. He cannot do it, any more than a pint-pot can hold a quart, or a quart-pot be filled by a pint. Iron is essentially the same everywhere and always; but the sulphate of iron is never the same as the carbonate of iron. Truth is invariable; but the *Smithate* of truth must always differ from the *Brownate* of truth.

The wider the intellect, the larger and simpler the expressions in which its knowledge is embodied. The inferior race, the degraded and enslaved people, the small-minded individual, live in the details which to larger minds and more advanced tribes of men reduce themselves to axioms and laws. As races and individual minds must always differ just as sulphates and carbonates do, I cannot see ground for expecting the Broad Church to be founded on any fusion of *intellectual* beliefs, which of course implies that those who hold the larger number of doctrines as essential shall come down to those who hold the smaller number. These doctrines are to the *negative* aristocracy what the quarterings of their coats are to the *positive* orders of nobility.

The Broad Church, I think, will never be based on anything that requires the use of *language*. Freemasonry gives an idea of such a church, and a brother is known and cared for in a strange land where no word of his can be understood. The apostle of this church may be a deaf mute carrying a cup of cold water to a thirsting fellow-creature. The cup of cold water does not require to be translated for a foreigner to understand it. I am afraid the only Broad Church possible is one that has its creed in the heart, and not in the head, — that we shall know its members by their fruits, and not by their words. If you say this communion of well-doers is no church, I can only answer, that all *organized* bodies have their limits of size, and that when we find a man a hundred feet high and thirty feet broad across the shoulders, we will look out for an organization that shall include all Christendom.

Some of us do practically recognize a Broad Church and a Narrow Church, however. The Narrow Church may be seen in the ship's boats of humanity, in the long boat, in the jolly boat, in the captain's gig, lying off the poor old vessel, thanking God that *they* are safe, and reckoning how soon the hulk containing the mass of their fellow-creatures will go down. The Broad Church is on board, working hard at the pumps, and very slow to believe that the ship will be swallowed up with so many poor people in it, fastened down under the hatches ever since it floated.

—— All this, of course, was nothing but my

poor notion about these matters. I am simply an "outsider," you know; only it doesn't do very well for a nest of Hingham boxes to talk too much about outsiders and insiders!

After this talk of ours, I think these two young people went pretty regularly to the Church of the Galileans. Still they could not keep away from the sweet harmonies and rhythmic litanies of Saint Polycarp on the great Church festival-days; so that, between the two, they were so much together, that the boarders began to make remarks, and our landlady said to me, one day, that, though it was noon of her business, them that had eyes couldn't help seein' that there was somethin' goin' on between them two young people; she thought the young man was a very likely young man, though jest what his prospecs was was unbeknown to her; but she thought he must be doin' well, and rather guessed he would be able to take care of a femily, if he didn't go to takin' a house; for a gentleman and his wife could board a great deal cheaper than they could keep house; — but then that girl was nothin' but a child, and wouldn't think of bein' married this five year. They was good boarders, both of 'em, paid regular, and was as pooty a couple as she ever laid eyes on.

—— To come back to what I began to speak of before, — the divinity-student was exercised in his mind about the Little Gentleman, and, in the kindness of his heart, — for he was a good young man, — and in the strength of his convictions, — for he took it for granted that he and his crowd were right, and other folks and their crowd were wrong, — he determined to bring the Little Gentleman round to his faith before he died, if he could. So he sent word to the sick man, that he should be pleased to visit him and have some conversation with him; and received for answer that he would be welcome.

The divinity-student made him a visit, therefore, and had a somewhat remarkable interview with him, which I shall briefly relate, without attempting to justify the positions taken by the Little Gentleman. He found him weak, but calm. Iris sat silent by his pillow.

After the usual preliminaries, the divinity-student said, in a kind way, that he was sorry to find him in failing health, that he felt concerned for his soul, and was anxious to assist him in making preparations for the great change awaiting him.

I thank you, Sir, — said the Little Gentleman; — permit me to ask you, what makes you think I am not ready for it, Sir, and that you can do anything to help me, Sir?

I address you only as a fellow-man, — said the divinity-student, — and therefore a fellow-sinner.

I am *not* a man, Sir! — said the Little Gentleman. — I was born into this world the wreck of a man, and I shall not be judged with a race to which I do not belong. Look at this! — he said, and held up his withered arm. — See there! — and he pointed to his misshapen extremities. — Lay your hand here! — and he laid his own on the region of his misplaced heart. — I have known nothing of the life of your race. When I first came to my consciousness, I found myself an object of pity, or a sight to show. The first strange child I ever remember hid its face and would not come near me. I was a broken-hearted as well as broken-bodied boy. I grew into the emotions of ripening youth, and all that I could have loved shrank from my presence. I became a man in years, and had nothing in common with manhood but its longings. My life is the dying pang of a worn-out race, and I shall go down alone into the dust, out of this world of men and women, without ever knowing the fellowship of the one or the love of the other. I will not die with a lie rattling in my throat. If another state of being has anything worse in store for me, I have had a long apprenticeship to give me strength that I may bear it. I don't believe it, Sir! I have too much faith for that. God has not left me wholly without comfort, even here. I love this old place where I was born; — the heart of the world beats under the three hills of Boston, Sir! I love great land, with so many tall men in it, and many good, noble women. — His eyes turned the silent figure by his pillow. — I have learned to accept meekly what has been allotted to me, but I cannot honestly say that I think my sin has been greater than my suffering. I bear the ignorance and the evil-doing of whole generations in my single person. I never drew a breath of air nor took a step that was not a punishment for another's fault. I may have had many wrong thoughts, but I cannot have done many wrong deeds, — for my cage has been a narrow one, and I have paced it alone. I have looked through the bars and seen the great world of men busy and happy, but I had no part in their doings. I have known what it was to dream of the great passions; but since my mother kissed me before she died, no woman's lips have pressed my cheek, — nor ever will.

—— The young girl's eyes glittered with a sudden film, and almost without a thought, but with a warm human instinct that rushed up into her face with her heart's blood, she bent over and kissed him. It was the sacrament that washed out the memory of long years of bitterness, and I should hold it an unworthy thought to defend her.

The Little Gentleman repaid her with the only tear any of us ever saw him shed.

The divinity-student rose from his place, and, turning away from the sick man, walked to the other side of the room, where be bowed his head and was still. All the questions he had meant to ask had faded from his memory. The tests he had prepared by which to judge of his fellow-creature's fitness for heaven seemed to have lost their virtue. He could trust the crippled child of sorrow to the Infinite Parent. The kiss of the fair-haired girl had been like a sign from heaven, that angels watched over him whom he was presuming but a moment before to summon before the tribunal of his private judgment.

Shall I pray with you?—he said, after a pause. —A little before he would have said, Shall I pray *for* you?—The Christian religion, as taught by its Founder, is full of *sentiment.* So we must not blame the divinity-student, if he was overcome by those yearnings of human sympathy which predominate so much more in the sermons of the Master than in the writings of his successors, and which have made the parable of the Prodigal Son the consolation of mankind, as it has been the stumbling-block of all exclusive doctrines.

Pray!—said the Little Gentleman.

The divinity-student prayed, in low, tender tones, that God would look on his servant lying helpless at the feet of his mercy; that he would remember his long years of bondage in the flesh; that he would deal gently with the bruised reed. Thou hast visited the sins of the fathers upon this their child. Oh, turn away from him the penalties of his own transgressions! Thou hast laid upon him, from infancy, the cross which thy stronger children are called upon to take up; and now that he is fainting under it, be Thou his stay, and do Thou succor him that is tempted! Let his manifold infirmities come between him and Thy judgment; in wrath remember mercy! If his eyes are not opened to all thy truth, let thy compassion lighten the darkness that rests upon him, even as it came through the word of thy Son to blind Bartimeus, who sat by the wayside, begging!

Many more petitions he uttered, but all in the same subdued tone of tenderness. In the presence of helpless suffering, and in the fast-darkening shadow of the Destroyer, he forgot all but his Christian humanity, and cared more about consoling his fellow-man than making a proselyte of him.

This was the last prayer to which the Little Gentleman ever listened. Some change was rapidly coming over him during this last hour of which I have been speaking. The excitement of pleading his cause before his self-elected spiritual adviser, — the emotion which overcame him, when the young girl obeyed the sudden impulse of her feelings and pressed her lips to his cheek, — the thoughts that mastered him while the divinity-student poured out his soul for him in prayer, might well hurry on the inevitable moment. When the divinity-student had uttered his last petition, commending him to the Father through his Son's intercession, he turned to look upon him before leaving his chamber. His face was changed. — There is a language of the human countenance which we all understand without an interpreter, though the lineaments belong to the rudest savage that ever stammered in an unknown barbaric dialect. By the stillness of the sharpened features, by the blankness of the tearless eyes, by the fixedness of the smileless mouth, by the deadening tints, by the contracted brow, by the dilating nostril, we know that the soul is soon to leave its mortal tenement, and is already closing up its windows and putting out its fires. — Such was the aspect of the face upon which the divinity-student looked, after the brief silence which followed his prayer. The change had been rapid, though not that abrupt one which is liable to happen at any moment in these cases. — The sick man looked towards him. — Farewell, — he said — I thank you. Leave me alone with her.

When the divinity-student had gone, and the Little Gentleman found himself alone with Iris, he lifted his hand to his neck, and took from it, suspended by a slender chain, a quaint, antique-looking key, — the same key I had once seen him holding. He gave this to her, and pointed to a carved cabinet opposite his bed, one of those that had so attracted my curious eyes and set me wondering as to what it might contain.

Open it, — he said, — and light the lamp. — The young girl walked to the cabinet and unlocked the door. A deep recess appeared, lined with black velvet, against which stood in white relief an ivory crucifix. A silver lamp hung over it. She lighted the lamp and came back to the bed-side. The dying man fixed his eyes upon the figure of the dying Saviour. — Give me your hand, — he said; and Iris placed her right hand in his left. So they remained, untii presently his eyes lost their meaning, though they still remained vacantly fixed upon the white image. Yet he held the young girl's hand firmly, as if it were leading him through some deep-shadowed valley and it was all he could cling to. But presently an involuntary muscular contraction stole over him, and his terrible dying grasp held the poor girl as if she were wedged in an engine of torture. She pressed her lips together and sat still. The in-exorable hand held her tighter and tighter, until she felt as if her own slender fingers would be crushed in its gripe. It was one of the tortures of the Inquisition she was suffering, and she could not stir from her place. Then, in her great anguish, she, too, cast her eyes upon that dying figure, and, looking upon its pierced hands and feet and side and lacerated forehead, she felt that she also must suffer uncomplaining. In the moment of her sharpest pain she did not forget the duties of her tender office, but dried the dying man's moist forehead with her handkerchief, even while the dews of agony were glistening on her own. How long this lasted she never could tell. *Time* and *thirst* are two things you and I talk about; but the victims whom holy men and righteous judges used to stretch on their engines knew better what they meant than you or I! — What is that great bucket of water for? said the Marchioness de Brinvilliers, before she was placed on the rack. — *For you to drink*, — said the torturer to the little woman. — She could not think that it would take such a flood to quench the fire in her and so keep her alive for her confession. The torturer knew better than she.

After a time not to be counted in minutes, as the clock measures, — without any warning, — there came a swift change of his features; his face turned white, as the waters whiten when a sudden breath passes over their still surface; the muscles instantly relaxed, and Iris, released at once from her care for the sufferer and from his unconscious grasp, fell senseless, with a feeble cry, — the only utterance of her long agony.

Perhaps you sometimes wander in through the iron gates of the Copp's Hill burial-ground. You love to stroll round among the graves that crowd each other in the thickly peopled soil of that breezy summit. You love to lean on the freestone slab which lies over the bones of the Mathers, — to read the epitaph of stout William Clark, "Despiser of Sorry Persons and little Actions," — to stand by the stone grave of sturdy Daniel Malcolm and look upon the splintered slab that tells the old rebel's story, — to kneel by the triple stone that says how the three Worthylakes, father, mother, and young daughter, died on the same day and lie buried there; a mystery; the subject of a moving ballad, by the late Benjamin Franklin, — as may be seen in his autobiography, which will explain the secret of the triple gravestone; though the old philosopher has made a mistake, unless the stone is wrong.

Not very far from that you will find a fair mound, of dimensions fit to hold a well-grown man. I will not tell you the inscription upon the stone which stands at its head; for I do not wish you to be *sure* of the resting-place of one who could not bear to think that he should be known as a cripple among the dead, after being pointed at so long among the living. There is one sign it is true, by which, if you have been a sagacious reader of these papers, you will at once know it; but I fear you read carelessly, and must study them more diligently before you will detect the hint to which I allude.

The Little Gentleman lies where he longed to lie, among the old names and the old bones of the old Boston people. At the foot of his resting-place is the river, alive with the wings and antennæ of its colossal water-insects; over opposite are the great war-ships, and the heavy guns, which, when they roar, shake the soil in which he lies; and in the steeple of Christ Church, hard by, are the sweet chimes which are the Boston boy's *Ranz des Vaches*, whose echoes follow him all the world over.

In Pace!

I told you a good while ago that the Little Gentleman could not do a better thing than to eave all his money, whatever it might be, to the young girl who has since that established such a claim upon him. He did not, however. A considerable bequest to one of our public institutions keeps his name in grateful remembrance. The telescope through which he was fond of watching the heavenly bodies, and the movements of which had been the source of such odd fancies on my part, is now the property of a Western College. You smile as you think of my taking it for a fleshless human figure, when I saw its tube pointing to the sky, and thought it was an arm, under the white drapery thrown over it for protection. So do I smile *now;* I belong to the numerous class who are prophets after the fact, and hold my nightmares very cheap by daylight.

I have received many letters of inquiry as to the sound *resembling a woman's voice*, which occasioned me so many perplexities. Some thought there was no question that he had a second apartment, in which he had made an asylum for a deranged female relative. Others were of opinion that he was, as I once suggested, a "Bluebeard" with patriarchal tendencies, and I have even been censured for introducing so Oriental an element into my record of boarding-house experience.

Come in and see me, the Professor, some evening when I have nothing else to do, and ask me to play you *Tartini's Devil's Sonata* on that extraordinary instrument in my possession, well known to amateurs as one of the master-pieces of *Joseph Guarnerius.* The *vox humana* of the great Haerlem organ is very lifelike, and the same stop in the organ of the Cambridge chapel might be mistaken in some of its tones for a human voice; but I think you never heard anything come so near the cry of a *prima donna* as the A string and the E string of this instrument. A single fact will illustrate the resemblance. I was executing some *tours de force* upon it one evening, when the policeman of our district rang the bell sharply, and asked what was the matter in the house. He had heard a woman's screams, — he was sure of it. I had to make the instrument *sing* before his eyes before he could be satisfied that he had not heard the cries of a woman. This instrument was bequeathed to me by the Little Gentleman. Whether it had anything to do with the sounds I heard coming from his chamber, you can form your own opinion; — I have no other conjecture to offer. It is *not true* that a second apartment with a secret entrance was found; and the story of the veiled lady is the invention of one of the Reporters.

Bridget, the housemaid, always insisted that he died a Catholic. She had seen the crucifix, and believed that he prayed on his knees before it. The last circumstance is very probably true; indeed, there was a spot worn on the carpet just before this cabinet which might be thus accounted for. Why he, whose whole life was a crucifixion, should not love to look on that divine image of blameless suffering, I cannot see; on the contrary, it seems to me the most natural thing in the world that he should. But there are those who want to make private property of everything, and can't make up their minds that people who don't think as they do should claim any interest in that infinite compassion expressed in the central figure of the Christendom which includes us all.

The divinity-student expressed a hope before the boarders that he should meet him in heaven. — The question is, whether he'll meet *you*, — said the young fellow John, rather smartly. The divinity-student hadn't thought of *that*.

However, he is a worthy young man, and I trust I have shown him in a kindly and respectful light. He will get a parish by-and-by; and, as he is about to marry the sister of an old friend, — the Schoolmistress, whom some of us remember, — and as all sorts of expensive accidents happen to young married ministers, he will be under bonds to the amount of his salary, which means starvation, if they are forfeited, to think all his days as he thought when he was settled, — unless the majority of his people change with him or in advance of him. A hard case, to which nothing could reconcile a man, except that the faithful discharge of daily duties in his personal relations with his parishioners will make him useful enough in his way, though as a thinker he may cease to exist before he has reached middle age.

—— Iris went into mourning for the Little Gentleman. Although, as I have said, he left the bulk of his property, by will, to a public institution, he added a codicil, by which he disposed of various pieces of property as tokens of kind remembrance. It was in this way I became the possessor of the wonderful instrument I have spoken of, which had been purchased for him out of an Italian convent. The landlady was comforted with a small legacy. The following extract relates to Iris: "—— in consideration of her manifold acts of kindness, but only in token of grateful remembrance, and by no means as a reward for services which cannot be compensated, a certain messuage, with all the land thereto appertaining, situate in —— Street, at the North End, so called, of Boston, aforesaid, the same being the house in which I was born, but now inhabited by several families, and known as 'the Rookery.'" Iris had also the crucifix, the portrait, and the red-jewelled ring. The funeral or death's-head ring was buried with him.

It was a good while, after the Little Gentleman was gone, before our boarding-house recovered its wonted cheerfulness. There was a flavor in his whims and local prejudices that we liked, even while we smiled at them. It was hard to see the tall chair thrust away among useless lumber, to dismantle his room, to take down the picture of Leah, the handsome Witch of Essex, to move away the massive shelves that held the books he loved, to pack up the tube through which he used to study the silent stars, looking down at him like the eyes of dumb creatures, with a kind of stupid half-consciousness that did not worry him as did the eyes of men and women,—and hardest of all to displace that sacred figure to which his heart had always turned and found refuge, in the feelings it inspired, from all the perplexities of his busy brain. It was hard, but it had to be done.

And by-and-by we grew cheerful again, and the breakfast-table wore something of its old look. The Koh-i-noor, as we named the gentleman with the *diamond*, left us, however, soon after that "little mill," as the young fellow John called it, where he came off second best. His departure was no doubt hastened by a note from the landlady's daughter, inclosing a lock of purple hair which she "had valued as a pledge of affection, ere she knew the hollowness of the vows he had breathed," speedily followed by another, inclosing the landlady's bill. The next morning he was missing, as were his limited wardrobe and the trunk that held it. Three empty bottles of Mrs. Allen's celebrated preparation, each of them asserting, on its word of honor as a bottle, that its former contents were "not a dye," were all that was left to us of the Koh-i-noor.

From this time forward, the landlady's daughter manifested a decided improvement in her style of carrying herself before the boarders. She abolished the odious little flat, gummy side-curl. She left off various articles of "jewelry." She began to help her mother in some of her household duties. She became a regular attendant on the ministrations of a very worthy clergyman, having been attracted to his meetin' by witnessing a marriage ceremony in which he called a man and a woman a "gentleman" and a "lady," — a stroke of gentility which quite overcame her. She even took a part in what she called a *Sahbath* school, though it was held on Sunday, and by no means on Saturday, as the name she intended to utter implied. All this, which was very sincere, as I believe, on her part, and attended with a great improvement in her character, ended in her bringing home a young man, with straight, sandy hair, brushed so as to stand up steeply above his forehead, wearing a pair of green spectacles, and dressed in black broadcloth. His personal aspect, and a certain solemnity of countenance, led me to think he must be a clergyman; and as Master Benjamin Franklin blurted out before several of us boarders, one day, that "Sis had got a beau," I was pleased at the prospect of her becoming a minister's wife. On inquiry, however, I found that the somewhat solemn look which I had noticed was indeed a professional one, but not clerical. He was a young undertaker, who had just succeeded to a thriving business. Things, I believe, are going on well at this time of writing, and I am glad for the landlady's daughter and her mother. Sextons and undertakers are the cheerfullest people in the world at home, as comedians and circus-clowns are the most melancholy in their domestic circle.

As our old boarding-house is still in existence, I do not feel at liberty to give too minute a statement of the present condition of each and all of its inmates. I am happy to say, however, that they are all alive and well, up to this time. That kind old gentleman who sat opposite to me is growing older, as old men will, but still smiles benignantly on all the boarders, and has come to be a kind of father to all of them, — so that on his birthday there is always something like a family festival. The Poor Relation, even, has warmed into a filial feeling towards him, and on his last birthday made him a beautiful present, namely, a very handsomely bound copy of Blair's celebrated poem, "The Grave."

The young man John is still, as he says, "in fust-rate fettle." I saw him spar, not long since, at a private exhibition, and do himself great credit in a set-to with Henry Finnegass, Esq., a professional gentleman of celebrity. I am pleased to say that he has been promoted to an upper clerkship, and, in consequence of his rise in office, has taken an apartment somewhat lower down than number "forty-'leven," as he facetiously called his attic. Whether there is any truth, or not, in the story of his attachment to, and favorable reception by, the daughter of the head of an extensive wholesale grocer's establishment, I will not venture an opinion; I may say, however, that I have met him repeatedly in company with a very well-nourished and high-colored young lady, who, I understand, is the daughter of the house in question.

Some of the boarders were of opinion that Iris did not return the undisguised attentions of the handsome young Marylander. Instead of fixing her eyes steadily on him, as she used to look upon the Little Gentleman, she would turn them away, as if to avoid his own. They often went to church together, it is true; but nobody, of course, supposes there is any relation between religious sympathy and those wretched "sentimental" movements of the human heart upon which it is commonly agreed that nothing better is based than society, civilization, friendship, the relation of husband and wife, and of parent and child, and which many people must think were singularly overrated by the Teacher of Nazareth, whose whole life, as I said before, was full of sentiment, loving this or that young man, pardoning this or that sinner, weeping over the dead, mourning for the doomed city, blessing, and perhaps kissing, the little children, — so that the Gospels are still cried over almost as often as the last work of fiction!

But one fine June morning there rumbled up to the door of our boarding-house a hack containing a lady inside and a trunk on the outside. It was our friend the lady-patroness of Miss Iris, the same who had been called by her admiring pastor "The Model of all the Virtues." Once a week she had written a letter, in a rather formal hand, but full of good advice, to her young charge. And now she had come to carry her away, thinking that she had learned all she was likely to learn under her present course of teaching. The Model, however, was to stay awhile, — a week, or more, — before they should leave together.

Iris was obedient, as she was bound to be. She was respectful, grateful, as a child is with a just, but not tender parent. Yet something was wrong. She had one of her trances, and became statue-like, as before, only the day after the Model's arrival. She was wan and silent, tasted nothing at table, smiled as if by a forced effort, and often looked vaguely away from those who were looking at her, her eyes just glazed with the shining moisture of a tear that must not be allowed to gather and fall. Was it grief at parting from the place where her strange friendship had grown up with the Little Gentleman? Yet she seemed to have become reconciled to his loss, and rather to have a deep feeling of gratitude that she had been permitted to care for him in his last weary days.

The Sunday after the Model's arrival, that lady had an attack of headache, and was obliged to shut herself up in a darkened room alone. Our two young friends took the opportunity to go together to the Church of the Galileans. They said but little going, — "collecting their thoughts" for the service, I devoutly hope. My kind good friend the pastor preached that day one of his sermons that make us all feel like brothers and sisters, and his text was that affectionate one from John, "My little children, let us not love in word, neither in tongue, but in deed and in truth." When Iris and her friend came out of church, they were both pale, and walked a space without speaking.

At last the young man said, — You and I are not little children, Iris!

She looked in his face an instant, as if startled, for there was something strange in the tone of his voice. She smiled faintly, but spoke never a word.

In deed and in truth, Iris, ———

What shall a poor girl say or do, when a strong man falters in his speech before her, and can do nothing better than hold out his hand to finish his broken sentence?

The poor girl said nothing, but quietly laid her

ungloved hand in his, — the little soft white hand which had ministered so tenderly and suffered so patiently.

The blood came back to the young man's cheeks, as he lifted it to his lips, even as they walked there in the street, touched it gently with them, and said, — "It is mine!"

Iris did not contradict him.

The seasons pass by so rapidly, that I am startled to think how much has happened since these events I was describing. Those two young people would insist on having their own way about their own affairs, notwithstanding the good lady, so justly called the Model, insisted that the age of twenty-five years was as early as any discreet young lady should think of incurring the responsibilities, etc., etc. Long before Iris had reached that age, she was the wife of a young Maryland engineer, directing some of the vast constructions of his native State, — where he was growing rich fast enough to be able to decline that famous Russian offer which would have made him a kind of nabob in a few years. Iris does not write verse often, nowadays, but she sometimes draws. The last sketch of hers I have seen in my Southern visits was of two children, a boy and girl, the youngest holding a silver goblet, like the one she held that evening when I — I was so struck with her statue-like beauty. If in the later summer months you find the grass marked with footsteps around that grave on Copp's Hill I told you of, and flowers scattered over it, you may be sure that Iris is here on her annual visit to the home of her childhood and that excellent lady whose only fault was, that Nature had written out her list of virtues on ruled paper, and forgotten to rub out the lines.

One thing more I must mention. Being on the Common, last Sunday, I was attracted by the cheerful spectacle of a well-dressed and somewhat youthful papa wheeling a very elegant little carriage containing a stout baby. A buxom young lady watched them from one of the stone seats, with an interest which could be nothing less than maternal. I at once recognized my old friend, the young fellow whom we called John. He was delighted to see me, introduced me to "Madam," and would have the lusty infant out of the carriage, and hold him up for me to look at.

Now, then, — he said to the two-year-old, — show the gentleman how you hit from the shoulder. — Whereupon the little imp pushed his fat fist straight into my eye, to his father's intense satisfaction.

Fust-rate little chap, — said the papa. — Chip

of the old block. Regl'r little Johnny, you know.

I was so much pleased to find the young fellow settled in life, and pushing about one of "them little articles" he had seemed to want so much, that I took my "punishment" at the hands of the infant pugilist with great equanimity.—And how is the old boarding-house?—I asked.

A 1,—he answered.—Painted and papered as good as new. Gahs in all the rooms up to the sky-parlors. Old woman's layin' up money, they say. Means to send Ben Franklin to college.—Just then the first bell rang for church, and my friend, who, I understand, has become a most exemplary member of society, said he must be off to get ready for meetin', and told the young one to "shake dada," which he did with his closed fist, in a somewhat menacing manner. And so the young man John, as we used to call him, took the pole of the miniature carriage, and pushed the small pugilist before him homewards, followed, in a somewhat leisurely way, by his pleasant-looking lady-companion, and I sent a sigh and a smile after him.

That evening, as soon as it was dark, I could not help going round by the old boarding-house. The "gahs" was lighted, but the curtains, or, more properly, the painted shades, were not down. And so I stood there and looked in along the table where the boarders sat at the evening meal, — our old breakfast-table, which some of us feel as if we knew so well. There were new faces at it, but also old and familiar ones. — The landlady, in a wonderfully smart cap, looking young, comparatively speaking, and as if half the wrinkles had been ironed out of her forehead. — Her daughter, in rather dressy half-mourning, with a vast brooch of jet, got up, apparently, to match the gentleman next her, who was in black costume and sandy hair, — the last rising straight from his forehead, like the marble flame one sometimes sees at the top of a funeral urn. — The Poor Relation, not in absolute black, but in a stuff with specks of white; as much as to say, that, if there were any more Hirams left to sigh for her, there were pin-holes in the night of her despair, through which a ray of hope might find its way to an adorer. — Master Benjamin Franklin, grown taller of late, was in the act of splitting his face open with a wedge of pie, so that his features were seen to disadvantage for the moment. — The good old gentleman was sitting still and thoughtful. All at once he turned his face toward the window where I stood, and, just as if he had seen me, smiled his benignant smile. It was a recollection of some past pleasant moment; but it fell upon me like the blessing of a father.

I kissed my hand to them all, unseen as I

stood in the outer darkness; and as I turned and went my way, the table and all around it faded into the realm of twilight shadows and of midnight dreams.

And so my year's record is finished. The Professor has talked less than his predecessor, but he has heard and seen more. Thanks to all those friends who from time to time have sent their messages of kindly recognition and fellow-feeling! Peace to all such as may have been vexed in spirit by any utterance these pages have repeated! They will, doubtless, forget for the moment the difference in the hues of truth we look at through our human prisms, and join in singing (inwardly) this hymn to the Source of the light we all need to lead us, and the warmth which alone can make us all brothers.

A SUN-DAY HYMN.

LORD of all being! throned afar,
Thy glory flames from sun and star;
Centre and soul of every sphere,
Yet to each loving heart how near!

Sun of our life, thy quickening ray
Sheds on our path the glow of day;

Star of our hope, thy softened light
Cheers the long watches of the night.

Our midnight is thy smile withdrawn;
Our noontide is thy gracious dawn;
Our rainbow arch thy mercy's sign;
All, save the clouds of sin, are thine!

Lord of all life, below, above,
Whose light is truth, whose warmth is love,
Before thy ever-blazing throne
We ask no lustre of our own.

Grant us thy truth to make us free,
And kindling hearts that burn for thee,
Till all thy living altars claim
One holy light, one heavenly flame

THE END

INDEX.

www.ingramcontent.com/pod-product-compliance
Lightning Source LLC
LaVergne TN
LVHW020100110826
845151LV00001B/38

* 9 7 8 1 4 2 5 5 4 5 1 9 2 *